THE KING'S CHRONICLES

*how to escape the
wrath of American women
and live like a king*

Mark Blackard

The King's Chronicles:
how to escape the wrath of American women and live like a king

Copyright ©2014 by Mark Blackard
First published in 2014

Edited by a team of volunteers

All rights reserved. No part of this book may be reproduced in any form by any electronic or mechanical means including photocopying, recording, or information storage and retrieval without permission in writing from the author. Brief quotations may be used in literary reviews.

WARNING: This book contains graphic and profane language, detailed references to sex, pornography, fornication, drunkenness, adultery, and what most conservatives consider overall bad behavior. Reader discretion is strongly advised. The content of this book is the express opinion of the author. Any scientific data cited is derived from open-source reporting on the opinions of scholars. The author is admittedly, not a scholar. Many concepts will offend the cultural norm within Western society and could be viewed as being degrading toward women. Political correctness and sensitivity are both absent from the text. The intent of the book is to invoke thought about serious issues in a comical fashion while entertaining the reader. The content is meant for the open-minded.

Library of Congress Control Number: 2014903168

ISBN: 978-1-936956-04-3

Printed in the U.S.A. by:
CreateSpace - An Amazon Company
4900 LaCross Road
North Charleston, SC 29406

Also by Mark Blackard -
Killing Sheep: The Righteous Insurgent
ISBN: 978-1-936956-00-5

www.markblackard.com

*For the men of the world
who live in agony and oppression
at the hands of ungrateful women.*

ACKNOWLEDGMENTS
AND SPECIAL THANKS

I would like to thank my friend Ed, who is the godfather of *Living the Dream*. You opened my eyes to a world surreal to most. May you continue the path and live long.

Many thanks to my fellow kings, converts, and subscribers who are also living the dream. Keep spreading the word and assist your friends with their pursuit of happiness.

I want to give a big shout out to the Hoy Dog and Pablo Escobar. The adventures we have undertaken together cannot be outdone. There is nothing like traveling the globe with two of your best friends while staying drunk, chasing women, and dancing until the wee hours of the morning. Our escapades were and are a major inspiration for this manuscript. I hope we continue down the path of living life to its fullest.

I would like to thank my friend Doctor Wayne for his meticulous efforts on the final editing of the book. While no book is error-free, I think he has come close to making this a reputable document without altering the colloquial tone.

Special recognition goes out to all the trashy American women whom I have dated, lived with, or merely engaged in meaningless sex. Without your shitty attitude, sense of entitlement, and general gold-digging mentality, this book would not have been possible.

Last, but not least, let me thank the numerous bitches out there who gave me the clap. That shit wasn't funny. However, you provided motivation for this manuscript as well and deserve to be recognized accordingly. Relax, I'm not going to put you in the spotlight. I would, but I just can't remember any of your names.

Contents

Acknowledgments v

Preface ix

Introduction 1

The Declarations of Independence 11

Honey, I'm Home! 19

Financial Pimp-Hand 31

Niches in Misery 45

Chicken Buses and Cheeseburgers 61

Riding Bareback 85

The Trip of Three Divorces 103

Getting Pearl Harbor'd 119

The Art of Divorce 141

Kung Fu Freedom 167

The Secret to One-Night Stands 179

Love for the Ladies 205

I Believe in Booty 217

Player Security 229

Chok Dee Kop! 249

Preface
AND WORDS OF CAUTION

Most of this book was written while I was under the influence of rum—plain and simple. Realize that up front. If it wasn't rum, it was beer or occasionally Jack Daniel's whiskey. The majority of the words were typed out on my laptop as I sat in some sleazy bar in the back alleys of Southeast Asia or the Philippines. With less than reputable women simultaneously rubbing my back and feeding me mangoes, it's the perfect environment to be creative, I can assure you.

Therefore, some of the grammar and sentence structure might not be in line with what you would consider good literary prose. The tone is colloquial because that's the only way I know how to write and talk. If you're searching for pure literary genius, you've definitely purchased the wrong book. I suggest Hemingway, instead.

For my female friends in America: I realize you may disown me after reading this text. I am prepared for that. However, the culture has to be challenged. *If the shoe fits, wear it.* If it doesn't, just enjoy the stories.

With those disclaimers out of the way, let me get to some more important information about this work of art. This book contains graphic and profane language, detailed references to sex, pornography, fornication, drunkenness, adultery, and what most conservatives consider overall bad behavior. Reader discretion is strongly advised. In other words, you don't want your daughter reading this book. If you have a son, buy two copies and have him memorize the words.

INTRODUCTION
THE ORIGINS OF KINGDOM RULE

What the hell is Kingdom Rule? Does that have anything to do with kings and castles during the Middle Ages? Well, yes, and no, but I have applied some of the principles of ruling a kingdom to modern-day life. *Kingdom Rule* is my own personal philosophy about how to live your life as a man. It's my philosophy on how to live your life, period. It's about how to govern your family. It's about how to manage your finances. It's about being a gentleman. It's about taking care of your wife and kids. It's a reset of certain values and procedures which bond a family together and keep it from falling apart. It's a philosophy about making changes when your home life has spun out of control and become unbearable. It has nothing to do with religion as I am not a religious person. It is a shocking concept outside the norm, admittedly Napoleonic, and is certainly considered chauvinistic and biased against some American women.

Many will accuse me of spending too much time with my Muslim friends and that Islamic culture is rubbing off on me. A small part of that accusation has some merit to it but it has nothing to do with Islam or the Middle East. It has everything to do with the fact that families outside of Western societies tend to stay together as the norm. The father is still the head of the household. In the West, divorce is the norm. Fathers are marginalized by volumes of laws which prevent them from properly governing their dependents.

During my travels around the world, I observed the way families interacted in places such as Central America, the Middle East, Afghanistan, and Southeast Asia, and took note. Elements of what I observed only added to my already-formulated philosophy of *Kingdom Rule*. While I will predominately focus on the happiness and welfare of my fellow man, don't think that he is my only concern. Only if you are a chess player will you understand the big picture and the positive, second and third-order effects the philosophy of *Kingdom Rule* can have on a family.

● ● ●

(The following paragraph was written circa 2010.) I have never written a book before. As a matter of fact, if this book makes it to print I will personally be amazed. Not because the content isn't good—it's already changed several lives for the better. I am certain it will change many more. It's just that I've been told by more than a few friends I have attention deficit disorder. This opinion was formulated years ago because of my dealings with women. When we would hit the clubs I could not stay focused on one woman. Even if I was talking to a beautiful girl I would easily be distracted once an ugly one with a nice ass walked by. Thus, they began to accuse me of suffering from ADD. Maybe I am suffering from it. I don't know. I sometimes start projects and leave them unfinished. Even with that in mind, I found myself bound and determined to put my thoughts about American women into a manuscript and share them with my fellow man.

● ● ●

(Back to 2014...) Actually, I have written a book before. This is the second book I have finished, although I started it a year before writing the first words of *Killing Sheep - The Righteous Insurgent*. I decided to let that first paragraph stand since it was historical and accurate at the time.

Ernest Hemingway was known for using Key West and the Caribbean as a haven in which to write. While I do love the Florida Keys, I found myself spending most of my time on the other side of the world. I fell in love with Southeast Asia and eventually settled down in the Kingdom of Thailand. Personally, I believe that Thailand is the closest thing to paradise on earth. The environment, the climate, and the culture inspires me to write. For what reason might you ask? I don't know. It's because I feel free here—yes, even during a military coup and martial law.

I love America but it has become over-policed, over-regulated, over-taxed, and over-governed. Americans are afraid of the government and are reluctant to speak out against any topic which goes against political correctness or the principles of the Bible, i.e., *God and Country*. It is difficult for me to be creative when I feel as if I'm expected to adhere to a certain philosophy dictated by the church and those sitting in cubicles in Washington. In Thailand, I don't feel as if I have to portray myself as someone I'm not.

Who is Mark Blackard? Certainly no one special, intelligent, nor even respectable. I'm a middle-aged, middle-class white guy from nowhere in particular. I admit that claiming middle-class status might be stretching it just a bit, but hey, a guy can dream. When I say nowhere, I mean the middle of nowhere. I'm originally from the backwoods of Mississippi (the poorest state in the nation). I was born in Tupelo, not far from where Elvis Presley came into this world. I lived in the Atlanta, Georgia area for twenty years and often refer to that as home (in the United States). A sampling of my professional life is detailed in the book *Killing Sheep: The Righteous Insurgent*, although my career in law enforcement has nothing to do with the reason for this manuscript.

What credentials do I possess to be able to call myself a writer? Absolutely none. To tell you the truth, I really don't consider myself to be a writer. I often tell people I'm just a dumb redneck who knows how to type. That's my only real qualification for this business.

● ● ●

Like any man in America, I've had my share of problems with women. After three divorces, dozens of failed relationships, and after two decades of chasing *pussy*, I do consider myself a subject-matter expert on dealing with disreputable bitches. Did I mention that this book is not written with political correctness in mind? It is my intent to publish the book myself to prevent any corporate attorneys from chopping precious words. If you are offended by profanity, stop reading right now and close the book. You are either a woman with class, who understandably doesn't want to be subjected to brash material, or you're a man with no balls. For the men: get over it, quit being such a sensitive weakling, and keep reading. You might just learn a thing or two.

One of the problems with women in America is that they're more organized than men these days. However, I'm not saying they're organized as in they have their act together. When I say organized, I mean they have a bigger union. The union I'm referring to is comprised of Oprah, that nutcase Dr. Phil., Sally Jesse Raphael, Ellen DeGeneres, the ladies of *The View*, and all of the other talk show powerhouses (past and present) who instill shit in the brains of poor, uneducated, unemployed women.

As a side note, I don't consider being a housewife a profession nor as being employed. *Oh, come on*, that's not just me being an asshole. It's reality. If you list *homemaker* as your profession on a loan application, a damn banker will look at you like you're high. Only, he can't tell you that *homemaker* means the same as *unemployed* like I just did. Still not convinced? It doesn't matter because a *homemaker* ain't getting a loan no matter how long she's been on the job. Ponder that philosophy for just a few minutes.

The problem with these daytime talk shows is that they appeal to one demographic—the women of America who have the golden opportunity to stay at home with their children while their man slaves away at his profession trying to make ends meet. During the day while the kids are in school, millions of these women are doing absolutely nothing other than watching talk shows and inhaling chocolate ice cream. They are brainwashed by hosts and hostesses who have millions of U.S. dollars in their personal bank accounts. The personalities doing the talking are not in touch with the reality of the poor or middle-class family. Dr. Phil wants to talk and preach about compromise. Women eat that shit up— we all know they do. The problem is that none of his principles work. It's because of these principles that men cheat on women and leave their wives. I hope to explain and support this theory so that you can at least see the reasoning.

Freedom of speech in America is biased—we all know this as well. The First Amendment is supposed to apply equally to all persons and all subjects. The government is supposedly prohibited from suppressing the opinions of the citizens. However, I do expect some type of litigation by a useless women's support group (probably funded by taxpayer money) out there. All I can say to anyone in that category is, *Good Luck*. Good luck getting half of nothing. If you want, you can have all of my bills right now without a court hearing. But first, consider a tidbit of information: Most artists and authors have one thing in common and that is the fact we're all broke! Very few artists and authors actually make any money so don't waste your time calling the lawyers. Where do you think the term *starving artist* comes from? It's because we're broke and hungry.

● ● ●

I would like to detail some of the facts which qualify me to write this book. First of all, I was married to a redneck girl from Texas for seven years. She wasn't too crazy when we were married, but like most

American women she turned evil after the divorce. I endured almost ten years of torture from that bitch over child support and child custody. She put me through the same hell that many American men have been through—the hell of not being able to be a father to your child. The hell of having to pay your ex-wife damn near every dime you make. Now, the reason for our divorce was because she grew tired of me sleeping with every girl I could get my hands on.

Oh, I am a terrible person and will certainly go straight to hell for that, according to the Baptists. Maybe so, but that's history and you can't change it. It still didn't give her the authority to deny me the basic human right of seeing my child grow up. Detecting some anger in my tone? You should be. If you've already been down this road before, you know exactly where I'm coming from.

After enduring the hell of divorce in America, I immediately found myself in another seven-year relationship. This relationship isn't worth discussing but basically I served as a cabin boy for a rich girl (did what I was told) during this time period. After those self-esteem-killing years of riding the gravy train like a welfare recipient, I began to go through blood-sucking whore after blood-sucking whore. I found myself being taken for money before, during, and after every single relationship.

There were a couple of incidents which made me wake up and realize I did not want to live life the way I was living. One was a piece of advice given to me by a close friend named Dave. He's dead now and I miss him dearly. At the time, I was a basket case. My life was tumultuous and I was being self-destructive. I was sleeping with anything that moved. Whether they were beautiful, ugly, skinny, fat, physically challenged, disabled, a drug addict, an alcoholic, or if they qualified for the senior-citizens discount at Denny's, it didn't matter. I ended up in the bed with many women from each of these categories. I was drinking a lot. I caught the clap three times within three months. I was out of control. One night on the way to the bar, Dave had listened to enough of my whining, crying, feeling sorry for myself, and the bitching.

He abruptly cut me off and yelled, "The first thing you need to do is get your *fucking* dignity back!"

Silence followed as I was stunned. I just stared at him while the wheels in my drunken mind began to turn. It was a shockingly true assessment of my particular situation. He had single-handedly identified the root of all my problems and even provided me with the solution to fix everything. I had simply lost my dignity and needed to get it back.

That statement stuck with me for some reason. I considered myself a gentleman but was far from acting like one. I was allowing my life to be dictated by women who were bleeding me dry. I took his one sentence of advice to heart. At that particular moment, a king was born.

A few days later, I looked at a stack of credit-card statements and receipts for the past year. I realized that I had rented a moving truck six times within twelve months. *Six fucking times* in one year to move a bitch into my house and move a bitch out. Now, I didn't make a lot of money back then (coincidentally, I don't make a lot of money now, either). When I started adding up all the costs associated with moving, I was sick to my stomach over the issue. Overall, I was broke because I was not acting like a man. It was time for a change in the way I conducted business in general. It was the beginning stages of formulating my philosophy known as *Kingdom Rule*.

● ● ●

Within this book, I will share with you how I, and a few followers live our lives. You may not agree with the philosophy but I hope you are at least entertained. You probably won't even believe the stories but I assure you most have videos and pictures to back them up.

I will explain my theory and principles of *Kingdom Rule*. Obviously, it will not work for every marriage. It's not designed to because it goes against the grain of traditional American culture. However, it will work for every **man** to improve **his** life. Remember that this book is written for my fellow man. Maybe the next book will be for the ladies, but not this one. Gentlemen, we only have a limited number of years before it's time to hit the grave. You have to live life to its fullest and never trade happiness for convenience. Every second that you are unhappy is time stolen from you. Do not live under the illusion that you will live forever or that you will even live for one more day. Life is preciously short and can end abruptly. Never lose sight of that fact. It's no secret that I live life by three principles:

#1 **Life is short.**
#2 **Life is about a series of adventures.**
#3 **Never turn down an adventure.**

You may not choose to live your life to this extreme, but keep these points in mind: Throughout my career, which has included time in the medical field, law enforcement, and war zones, I learned something that I think about every day. *No one plans on dying.* You may be ready and willing to die for a cause but you don't wake up and say, *I'm going to die today.* Obviously, that's unless you're terminally ill or you're about to commit suicide. As a paramedic, I pulled many dead people out of cars after they had crashed and burned. On several occasions, the trunk was full of just-purchased groceries. Now, if that person had planned on dying, why in the hell would they have just spent a hundred dollars at the grocery store? The answer is that they didn't plan on dying. Even if a police officer or a soldier is killed in battle, it's not because they woke up that morning and planned it that way.

I bring this up because we, especially as Americans, have this delusion that we're going to live forever. You're programmed by our society to think like that. You're taught to think about your retirement, plan for your retirement, will you have enough money for your retirement, etc. No one really stops to think about the possibility of dying in their twenties, thirties, or forties. Once you're dead, that's it. Life is a ride where you only get one go-round. You don't get a second turn. Therefore, why would you not live life to its fullest? Why would you venture through life while being unhappy? It makes absolutely no sense to me.

If you're a man who is miserable at home with an ungrateful wife, why haven't you made any changes? You're wasting your precious days on this earth. You will not live forever. I can safely give you a guarantee on that statement without any legal ramifications.

● ● ●

My friends and I decided to publish this book so that others may learn from our mistakes and possibly benefit from them. There is no shame in our stories because we have learned from them as well. We've lived pretty-damn-exciting lives in the midst of the turmoil as a side effect. This book doesn't have all the answers but it is designed to invoke thought. Please utilize it as a starting point to living a better life as a man.

If you are a woman reading this book, make sure you take it personal. It is just as good advice for you as it is for a man. If you really want to make your marriage work and keep your husband happy, maybe you should implement some of these principles. You will at first find my writings morally repulsive, obnoxious, archaic, barbaric, and out of touch with today's *strong woman*. However, if you stop and take a look at your situation, you may come to realize that you would have little to nothing without that bastard you constantly complain about. The grocery store tabloids and the women's magazines cannot give you the education you're about to receive from this book. *Cosmo* just can't compete.

This book is dedicated to the average Joe out there who is trying to make a living and is married to an ungrateful, fat, nasty bitch. Yes, I'm going to call out the fat women. Why? Because to me, fat equates to laziness and a lack of physical activity. It equates to not giving a shit about yourself, much less taking proper care of your husband. It tells me you just don't give a shit about life in general. If you're a fat, married woman, I guarantee you that your husband is not physically attracted to you. If he says he is, he's lying. And you know what the kicker is? You have the ability, power, and opportunity to change this. You can lose weight and make yourself presentable if you really want to. Losing weight is free. You don't have to undergo surgery, join a gym, or eat expensive food. I don't care what anybody says. I lost thirty pounds in three months because I got tired of looking at my nasty self in the mirror. It only takes dedication, a little bit of exercise, and the willingness to stop stuffing food in your mouth. Simple. But, the first step is for someone to bring the problem to your attention. Ladies, I just did that for you because your husband is too afraid to say anything. If no one tells you that you're fat, you won't do anything about it. My weight gain was abruptly brought to my attention by my Aunt Donna at a family reunion when she said, "Damn son! You've gained some weight. You're getting fat, boy." That was my motivation to stop with the hamburgers, the fries, and the pizza. I will forever be in debt to her for that wake-up call.

This book is for all the men who are oppressed by their wives. This book is for the men who fear their wives. This is for the men who are only staying with their wives for the sake of the children. If you do not have a strong pimp-hand you need to continue reading, especially if you don't even know what a strong pimp-hand is. I hope that after reading this book you wake up and realize you may need to make some changes around your home. But first, I must warn you. The concept of *Kingdom Rule* has already resulted in several divorces and many newly crowned kings. Read on at your own risk. Or, as my close friend Pablo would say in Spanish, *PONTE TRUCHA!*

CHAPTER 1

THE DECLARATIONS OF INDEPENDENCE

To simplify the basic philosophy of *Kingdom Rule*, I have created the *Kingdom Rule Declarations of Independence*. Yes, the word *Declarations* is plural and not a typo. Every man should study this section, memorize *The Declarations*, and adhere to them. Once understood, they should be promptly explained to the woman in the house and implemented. None of *The Declarations* are negotiable, by the way. If you bend on even one, you will fail in your pursuit of happiness.

● ● ●

For you men with a weak pimp-hand, this part is a bit shocking. So, here's what you need to do before you read any further: Go on and head over to Walmart and buy yourself a backbone, see if you can locate your dignity you lost several years back, grab what's left of your *fucking* balls, and come to realize that I'm not joking. The reason you're living a shitty life is because no one has taken the time to teach you what I'm about to.

Here's some useful trivia for you: The word *insurgent* basically means *one who rebels against authority*. Since your wife has probably been the authority in your home for years, you *should* feel like an insurgent while reading this. It's ok to feel that way. You're going to get to experience how our forefathers felt in 1776, just on a lower level. Yes, our country, the United States of America, was founded by insurgents. In the eyes of King George, they were all traitors. Now, you have the opportunity to create something to better your own life through a rebellion of sorts. Your wife has probably been taking too much without giving anything in return—taxation without representation. It does require some courage to make a change. In the spirit of Thomas Jefferson's penmanship, here we go...

Declaration 1
The Man is the King

Why does the man of the house get to be the king? Because that's the way it was for thousands of years and families did a hell of a lot better back then than they're doing today. I'll elaborate further on Declaration 1, only if Oprah asks me to. For now, it stands by itself. The woman of the house is the queen and should be treated as such. Pretty simple concept so far, huh?

Declaration 2
The King is in Charge and Shall Establish All of the Rules of the Kingdom

There has to be a clear chain of command within the marriage. Marriage is not a democracy as purported by Dr. Phil and for good reason. Why? Because there is no one to break a tie. There are two people, thus an even number of delegates. Therefore, disputes never really get resolved. Disputes are only delayed and continued. Grudges are held. No effective government or company rules with a two-person democracy. So, why do you think you can govern a household in that manner? In the United States, we have a president and a vice president. They are both important members of the government but the president makes the final decisions on all matters.

Let me break it down into a few common scenarios so that it makes sense. If the decisions in your marriage are split fifty percent down the middle, who determines the winner if you cannot agree? If you decide to buy a new car, who gets to pick out what kind of car it is? What if the woman wants a mini-van and you want a truck? How do you arrive at the final decision? There will be a debate with both sides presenting their arguments. The problem is that there is no judge to decide after you both rest your case. The man wants his way, as does the woman. The argument will continue until one person gets pissed off to the point that they say, *Fuck it, I'm tired of arguing with this motherfucker / bitch.* Therefore, one person will prevail and the other will be pissed off indefinitely. Resentment will set in because his / her opinion wasn't respected and honored. Small issues like this will create ongoing power struggles.

Women who call themselves Christians are predominately full of shit. When they get married, an element of their wedding vows is to *obey their husband.* Not to get too far into the hypocrisy of religion, but this is a perfect example. The woman recites an oath and swears to God in front of the preacher and the guests to obey her husband. She looks into the man's eyes during the exchange of vows with tears beginning to puddle and says, *I do.* Moments after that theatrical performance she forgets all about what she just promised. *Fuck that, I'm in charge now, motherfucker. Your check belongs to me. As soon as I can pop out a kid, I've got your ass and your money for eighteen solid years, regardless.*

How do you think your children feel when they're not exactly sure who is in charge? This is a very confusing concept to young children when they are unsure about the chain of command. If a child goes to his / her father and asks for permission to do something, imagine the uncertainty in the child's mind when the answer is, "Go ask your mother." *What? What the hell do you mean, go ask my mother?* The child is left with an insecurity because the father is deferring a decision to the mother. It's as if he is too impotent to decide on his own. Stop and think about that for a minute from a child's perspective. It is quite acceptable for the mother to defer a tough decision to the father but not the other way around. A child needs to have the security that the father is the supreme being in the household—the person who has all the answers whether the answers are liked or not. No uncertainty can manifest itself because father always has a solution and knows best. Mom should have the *luxury* of deferring difficult situations to the father. That's her right. She is the queen and should not have to endure undue stress and hardship when it comes to issuing unpopular directives. That is why the man is there. Yes, my brothers, that is your job. Often, you will have to *man the fuck up* and make an unpopular decision. Quit being a *pussy* and putting the stress on your wife. She doesn't deserve to suffer because of your laziness, uncertainty, and inaction. Plus, it makes it hard for her to respect you as a man. Make *fucking* decisions like a man and she and the children will recognize you as such.

• • •

As the king, you are the policy maker. While you should certainly take into consideration the opinion of your wife and your children, the ultimate responsibility of the Rule of Law belongs to you. If there are any laws that need to be established for the good order and discipline of the kingdom, you need to implement them immediately. Call a family meeting and issue the directives. Obviously, there will be resistance to certain policies you establish. Be prepared for that and stand your ground. Unless you are truly an asshole the policies should be for the betterment of all and are warranted. Don't feel bad if you have to assign additional chores or duties or have to take away certain privileges. If you are the bastard who is paying the mortgage and the light bill, grab a set of balls and lay down the law. The king is never to be questioned. After you consider everyone's opinion and input, issue your directives. Once they are issued, they become the law. Do not allow anyone to question what you have decided. It breeds discontent and should not be tolerated. You need to have a behind-the-scenes talk with your wife so her role is clear. Her role is to support what you lay down, whether she likes it or not. In front of the children especially, she must be supportive. Any dissent on her part openly in front of the children should lead you to dismiss her immediately. If this happens, turn to the chapter entitled *The Art of Divorce* and begin the process.

The king should not be afraid to make changes, however minimal or drastic in order to provide for the kingdom. This will be difficult for the average man who has allowed his wife to rule over him for so many years. It will be difficult for the wife to accept it as well, as she will most decidedly accuse the man of losing his damn mind.

Declaration 3
The King Shall Govern the Finances of the Kingdom and Ensure the Kingdom is Living Within its Means

The king must take full responsibility for the overall financial success or failure of the kingdom. The king should be prepared to work two or three jobs, seven days a week if necessary, in order to provide for the kingdom. If additional income is needed, the king needs to dispatch the woman to go to work. The king should study the chapter entitled *Financial Pimp-Hand* thoroughly. Under no circumstances should the king defer the financial decisions or even the bill-paying to the queen. To do so indicates impotence and weakness in the man as the provider.

Declaration 4
The King Shall be Fair & Just and Treat his Woman as a Queen

A good king sacrifices for the good of the people in the kingdom. Don't be a dictator or you will fail. A king doesn't have to raise his voice or issue threats. Merely rule with confidence and compassion. Treat your woman like she is the most important person in your life, but well within your financial means. If she does not value what you provide, get rid of her. Do not be afraid of the queen nor allow her to threaten you. If the queen speaks any threats toward the king, replace her immediately. Insist on loyalty. Insist that the queen is on your team one hundred percent and nothing less. Negativity and being unappreciative on the part of the woman should result in immediate dismissal from the kingdom. However, her opinion should always be heard and considered. Constantly surprise her with random acts to show your appreciation. Never allow the queen's life to become mundane or boring. It breeds laziness.

Declaration 5
The King Shall Not be Afraid of Being the Only Member of his Kingdom

Perhaps the hardest concept for the average man to embrace is what I'm about to describe. It goes against all thought processes other than my own. It is the concept that you cannot be afraid to be the only member of your kingdom. In other words, you have to accept the fact that you may find yourself alone, living in a one-room apartment, and broke because you're still having to make a mortgage payment. If you accept this up front as a possible scenario you have taken the most crucial step toward happiness. Let me reiterate, you must be prepared to be the only member of your kingdom. Once you do that, you have suddenly put yourself back into the driver's seat and regained control of your life.

Why do you have to prepare yourself for this? Well, if women do not like the rules, they are more than welcome to rule their own kingdom. That's the freedom of the philosophy. As a king, you are not forcing your wife to do anything she doesn't want to do. But, if she is not on board with the kingdom concept, then make a change. If a woman does not like your decisions, feel free to show her the door. Make sure that she knows she is free to rule her own kingdom, but not yours. If she won't leave, pack your clothes and your laptop and relocate to a new palace.

Speaking of showing a woman the door, that's exactly the first thing I do at the start of a relationship. Ask any of them from my past. Once they walk into my house, I ask them politely to turn around and take note of the door. I advise them that if at any time they feel as if I'm not meeting their expectations or if they're unhappy with me, please go ahead and walk through it. I believe in freedom and I want them to believe in it, too. I would never advocate for a woman to stay with me if she is unhappy. I've said many times that life is short. That applies to women as well. *Therefore, take a good look at the front door, bitch.* If you are not happy with me in any way, walk your ass through the magical passage to your freedom and happiness. Don't ever be afraid to be the only member of your kingdom. Even in you live in a one-room shack in the shitty part of town, you can still live like a king.

Summary

These declarations will not be understood nor condoned by most Americans. *You're nothing but a chauvinistic pig* will be the average woman's perspective. *You are degrading women, you asshole.* Roger, I copy all that traffic. I'm all broken up inside but sorry bitches, I'm still writing. Besides, this book ain't for you. Go get a nice magazine at the grocery store if you want someone to kiss your fat ass and give you the magic secret to weight loss without exercise. This book is dedicated to my fellow man. I'm representing him. You've been represented by Dr. Phil and all of the other feminists for too long while we men have been representing ourselves. It's about damn time someone starts speaking up for the man's right to the pursuit of happiness.

● ● ●

Personally, it took me many years of adhering to the *Declarations of Independence* to finally find that one girl who I get along with. Ok, who am I kidding? I actually have found several girls who love the king.

My girls are stars as far as girlfriends go. They're not American if you hadn't already guessed. When they're with me, they live happily and content under the principles of *Kingdom Rule*. For the most part, I don't have the first problem with any of these beautiful hotties. They might not always like my decisions but they support them because they know I take care of the kingdom. The concept works well at my castle. I have very few disagreements with any of my girls. We live life to its fullest. The reason is because I have an established Rule of Law within my kingdom that cannot be circumvented. There are no fights over all of the typical issues most couples fight over. All of that has already been decided so we focus on positive things. We focus on spending time with one another, socializing, cooking, and nights out on the town. We do not argue over finances or every day operations. The hierarchy has already been settled. I will admit that a big part of this success is that these ladies are not American, nor have they been Americanized.

Either way, I'm a happy *motherfucker* on a daily basis and I can pretty much guarantee that I have a better home life than most of you reading this text. Unless you got laid more than four times yesterday like I did, allow me to be the teacher for a while. Allow me to introduce you to a different mindset and way of living. You just might like the concept and decide to make some changes.

CHAPTER 2

HONEY, I'M HOME!

While American women sit on their fat asses watching television, their husbands are out in the world struggling through the grind. At the end of the day, the man walks in the front door exhausted from a twelve-hour shift. Instead of a cold beer and a warm dinner waiting on him in front of his easy chair, he is met by a whining wife who tells him it's his turn to deal with the kids. She's had a hard day dealing with them and needs a break. *Now, let's wait just a fucking minute here.* Her lazy ass has watched television all day, which has given her the courage to complain in the first place, and now she thinks she deserves a medal? I will concede that maybe she did a load of clothes and made the bed. *Congratulations girl for doing your part. Here's your medal. You think you deserve something but in actuality you're merely doing your duty within the kingdom. You don't get special recognition for earning your keep. Work a little bit to pay for that bucket of ice cream you tore up while watching your soap operas.* Now back to the poor man who just dragged himself into the house. If he has a weak pimp-hand and has never read this book, he will obey what his wife tells him to do and deal with the kids. The reason is that *The Union* (Oprah and Dr. Phil) has changed the way American women perceive how a marriage should function.

• • •

Under *Kingdom Rule* the man is the king. There is nothing more important than the king because the king makes everything in the kingdom happen. In today's world, the king works and brings home a paycheck. With this paycheck from the king, the kingdom has a castle (house), the electricity and water is on, the cable TV is hooked up, the

Internet is on, the car payment is paid, and food is purchased to feed the people. Without the king, there would be no castle, no electricity, no water, no food, no television, no Internet, no vehicle, and no money to spend at the mall. Men and women alike have lost sight of this concept. As long as the king is happy, he will continue to provide for the people. If he is not happy, the king will become distracted with a girlfriend or some other outside influence which is not productive for the kingdom. He will spend money on things just to stay away from the misery. Then, the entire kingdom suffers.

So, why don't American women recognize this? They need to recognize the fact that their number-one priority is to serve the king and make sure he is happy. I am referring to everything from daily life to sex. When a man comes home from a grueling twelve-hour shift at the factory, he should be met in the driveway by his wife. Why the driveway? Because the wife has nothing more important in her life at that particular moment than to greet the king as soon as he steps out of his vehicle. This lets the king know he is appreciated and that he is the center of attention. It also stimulates the marriage by displaying closeness toward one another. When the king steps out of his car the wife should take his briefcase off his hands and give him a big hug and kiss. If there are any other items to be brought into the home, the wife should dispatch the kids to accomplish this task. If the kids aren't old enough, the wife can take care of it herself in a few minutes.

The king should be escorted to his throne (easy chair) where an ice-cold beer awaits. The preferred beer of kings (at least this king) is Singha. Ok, if you live in America, the preferred beer of kings is Bud Light. After the king is settled in front of his big-screen to catch the news, the wife should be putting the final touches on dinner. Within thirty minutes, the wife should announce to the king that dinner is ready. After making the announcement, the wife should not disturb the king any further. If after five minutes the king does not arrive at the table, the wife should fix the king a tray and serve him dinner in his easy chair. The wife and children may then enjoy their meal.

Now, some people would disagree with that last part. Yes, the king should eat with the family and sit at the head of the table. That should be the typical procedure as it is important for family unity. However, if the king decides that the current news program is pertinent to him and that he needs to view the information, then he should not be questioned. I bring this up because in the past, I, like every other man in the world, have been trying to watch the news at times when dinner is ready. Yes, I am thankful that dinner has been prepared. But if I am trying to watch the weather to determine what type of work I do the next day, I do not need to hear a woman yelling at me a hundred times to come to dinner. It does not work that way unless you have been brainwashed by Dr. Phil. It works just as I have described it in the above paragraph. It is in the woman's best interest to bring the king a plate of that good food she has prepared and then *shut the fuck up*. That's being a bit harsh but it's to the point. What in the hell does a woman think she is going to accomplish by yelling and screaming that dinner is ready, that she has slaved in the kitchen, and that the king doesn't even have the courtesy to come to dinner? That's not allowed under *Kingdom Rule*. As a matter of fact, no one is ever allowed to yell at the king. The woman needs to just bring the king some dinner and not forget who the hell paid for the food in the first place. Remember, the king pays the bills. He can eat the food at any time he likes and in whatever room of the house he chooses. He doesn't need to explain to anyone why he needs to watch the news.

After the king is done eating dinner, he should never be asked to help with the dishes. His shift ended at the twelve-hour mark when his supervisor told him he could go home. If there are children in the family, they are exactly who should be doing the dishes.

This is another problem in Western society today. Children are not being made to work. Therefore, they do not learn the basic concept of work and then play. They think that everything should be handed to them. Children in developing nations know the value of hard work because they have no choice. By all means, give your children the most out of life but make them work for it. The kitchen-cleaning duties are their domain. The wife should not even have to be a part of kitchen cleanup. If you are the king, remember that you have to be fair and just. You need to make it clear to your family that the wife cooks and the kids clean the kitchen.

Now, inevitably the kids will get lazy and try to take shortcuts. Then, the wife will step in and give them a hand. It is in her nature to be motherly. However, in this situation, you have to intervene as the king and put an end to this. The children have their assignment. It will teach them a valuable life lesson in responsibility. If the wife is in the kitchen scrubbing dishes, it is taking time away from the king who is her main focus. Issue the directive clear and concise and make sure everyone understands his / her role. Enforce the directive as though everyone's life depends on the adherence to it. Initially, there may be a few problems to deal with. But, in a couple of weeks the king will be happier, the wife will be happier, and the children will feel a sense of responsibility for being assigned a mission within the kingdom.

That is a scenario of how meals should work within the kingdom. If things operate like this every time, imagine the headache and confusion that is eliminated from your life already. There is no uncertainty about who is going to cook that night, about when dinner is going to be ready, or about who is going to do the dishes. There's no argument about whether or not the man appreciates dinner because he won't come to the table when called. Since there are potentially three meals a day, that's three different daily events now under solid control of the king.

● ● ●

After dinner, the king may want to take a nice shower or bath before settling down in front of his big-screen for some rest and relaxation. If the king chooses to take a shower, the wife should hop in there quick and get the water to that ideal temperature. Why? Because it is another efficient way of telling the king his wife is appreciative of him. Now, this is where the queen can make some money with the king. After the king has had a few minutes to relax under that nice refreshing water, the wife should join him in the shower. She should have with her an ice-cold beer. It is important that the beer be at the appropriate temperature. If it is just cool, it will not properly serve its purpose in a hot shower. That beer has to be ice cold. The wife can either set the beer in the freezer for about twenty minutes prior or just keep a six-pack iced down in a cooler.

Once she enters the shower, she should hand that ice-cold beer to the king and tell him thanks for working his ass off that day. Then, the wife should begin to bathe the king. *Oh yes, ladies.* That is part of your duty as a wife. While bathing the king, the woman should pay particular attention to the family jewels. If she bathes this region properly, it's on to the next step. The wife should bend her ass over as sexy and nasty as can be and take it from behind like a porn star. After a nice ten-minute session of being banged out from behind, the wife should get the hell out of the shower and let the king finish his beer.

This will allow her enough time to dry off, get dressed, and be waiting with a towel when she hears the king turn off the water. Once she dries off the king and helps him don his robe, she needs to give him some space to unwind. At this point the king may want to spend some time with the children or possibly report directly to his throne (the easy chair). If the king is merely watching television, he should insist that the wife sit in the chair with him and hold her closely. It is equally important for the king to let the wife know she is special and is appreciated as well. As bedtime approaches, the king and the wife together should make sure the children are in their beds. This will display unity for the children and demonstrate stability.

When it is bedtime, the king should have some nice massage oil on hand in order to rub down the queen. This is his way of showing how much he cares about her. It will also be the prelude to bedtime sex. *That's right. Can you believe that? The wife has to give it up again? Two times in one evening?* For some of us, this is exactly how we live our daily lives. For others, it is unheard of. I would say that the majority of married men never get it twice in one evening. Hell, most American men don't get it twice in an entire month. Two times a day was something couples did back when they were dating. So why, once you get married, is the woman entitled to claim she has a headache every night? She never had any *fucking* headaches when she was dating you. Was she just trying to kiss your ass until you said *I do*? After most American women get that marriage license hung up on the wall, the sex starts to dwindle. It is because men have allowed this to happen by not realizing they have the power to change things in their life. Personally, I would drop a woman immediately if I thought our sex life was degrading or even slowing down ever so slightly. *Immediately.* Life is too short to live it miserably and without a robust sex life.

The thing about bedtime sex is that it helps both the king and the queen sleep much more soundly. You are both tired from the physical activity and have a fresh dump of endorphins flowing through your body. What a better way to end the day and then fall into a deep sleep? If the woman doesn't get off during sex, the king should ensure she gets off via other means. In other words, the king needs to get his ass down there and handle business. Remember, as a king you have to be fair and just with your actions. If you get off, make sure your wife gets off as well—a one-to-one orgasm ratio. Don't forget that.

● ● ●

If the man has to routinely wake up at six in the morning, the wife needs to start setting the alarm clock for 5:30 a.m. The reason for this may be obvious at this point. Yes, it is to allow enough time for morning sex. *Holy shit!* That means the wife is expected to have sex with the king three times in one day? You're thinking at this point I've lost my damn mind. Maybe in your world, but not here.

Let me explain something that is so obvious I hate to waste ink on paper. However, I have to because the average American woman cannot seem to figure this shit out. Girls, want to know why your beloved husband or boyfriend cheated on you? Here's the golden answer that your grocery store magazines won't tell you. It's because you were not giving him enough *pussy*! There you have it—blatant and to the point. Yes, I am blaming you, the woman. The responsibility rests solely with you. By you not providing your man with enough sex or by purposely withholding sex from your man, you are screwing with nature. You've upset the natural balance within the man's body.

Let's talk about nature for a minute. Take a herd of horses or cattle for example. You have a dozen females and only one male. Why? Because one male can inseminate multiple females. That's why a man's sex drive is so high. It's the way his body is programmed. He's programmed to impregnate as many females as possible to ensure the continuity of the species. You can't argue with nature. That's why his dick is hard for twenty-three hours out of the day. Quit bitching to him about it.

What do herds of horses have to do with your marriage? Well, realize that your man, naturally, should always be on the hunt for something new to screw. Once you realize this fact, you can take steps to thwart him from fucking your sister or your cousin. You need to take proactive steps and take this natural fight out of your man. These steps include keeping the testosterone levels in his body at a minimum. It means having sex or giving him blow jobs at frequent intervals. Frequent intervals means every few hours and not every few months. Once your man blows a nut, realize that the clock starts ticking again. It's like a ticking time-bomb about to go off. You can't tell exactly when it's going to explode, but at some point it will—possibly in your cousin's ass. But, if you take care of business with him you keep resetting this dangerous timer.

The best practice is to give up the *pussy* each and every time your man wants it, and then add some to that whether he likes it or not. If you can keep his testosterone levels drained to damn near zero, he won't even have the urge to ask his secretary to dinner. He'll look at it as a chore and a waste of his money trying to seduce the stuck-up bitch. Especially if he knows he's getting sexually assaulted by his wife the minute he rolls through the front door.

Is this one hundred percent fool proof? No, it's not. Some of us are just genetically engineered to chase *pussy* even though we're getting laid three times a day at home. But, for the average American man, if you satisfy his ass at home like a porn star, he ain't going nowhere.

Why did I detail exactly how the day should go? Because if you combine a happy home life, good food, respect, and a lot of sex, the man will race home from work. If these elements are not in order, he will be tempted to hang out with his friends after work, maybe stop by a bar, and end up screwing the nasty waitress he met there.

● ● ●

Also, you could be giving your husband cancer by not giving him enough *pussy*. You heard me right. You could be killing your husband by not taking care of him sexually. This is not something I've made up. Feel free to do your own research on the subject. Some scientists believe that if a man doesn't have a regular ejaculation, a hormone begins to build up in the prostate gland. This particular hormone is carcinogenic. *Ladies, that means it can cause cancer, just like that cigarette dangling from your mouth right now.* Their theory is that regular ejaculations keep this hormone flushed out of the man's prostate and prevents it from becoming too concentrated and therefore, dangerous.

I want to expand on their scientific theory with my personal theory. The purpose of life is to perpetuate life. Once you come into this world, your primary objective is to reproduce to ensure the continuity of the human race. As long as your body believes it's still in the fight to reproduce, your organs will strive to continue to function normally. Once you stop having sex, your body believes that you are not serving its primary duty and therefore, it's ok to begin shutting down. My belief is that sex keeps you young. A lack of sex accelerates the aging and the dying process. Simple logic.

Personally, I can assure you that I'm not going down because of prostate cancer caused by a lack of sex. A heart attack brought on by exhaustion from sexual intercourse with a twenty-one-year-old bitch I pulled out of the bar? Now that's more probable.

Whether the scientists' theory and / or my personal theory is accurate or not, why take the chance? In my mind, there is absolutely no excuse for a man and a woman who live together to not be screwing like rabbits every day. It's free, people! You don't have to join a gym and pay a membership fee to workout. You don't have to waste fuel or put a bunch of miles on your car by having to drive to a gym. The gym is your bedroom, kitchen, garage, or anyplace else you can find to go at it. Frequent sex is a win-win for both the king and the queen and makes for a better, happier marriage. A lack of sex for the man will almost always result in extra-marital excursions. Think about how much physical exercise you are afforded by screwing three times a day. You're going to start shedding pounds without even realizing it. You'll look and feel better as each day passes.

Ladies, now that I've explained this to you, take some action and govern yourselves accordingly. Are you beginning to see how much Dr. Phil and *The Union* have deceived you for all of these years? You might actually think I'm onto something by now. *Damn, this asshole is starting to make sense.*

● ● ●

I always have a small talk with any woman who comes to live with me. I don't say this to be mean or insensitive but rather to be honest and up front about how I live my life. I want them to know what I expect out of a live-in girlfriend. I've told every girl I've ever lived with the following: *I'm going to have sex every day. That's a fact. Whether it's with you or not, now that's debatable. Govern yourself accordingly.*

Does that make me a terrible person? I don't think it does. I think it just conveys my expectations and tolerances. If they're not into it, then they don't need to move in with me. I can remain by myself and run different women every night. Having sex is not a bad thing, people. It's merely nature—all natural. Contrary to what you were taught in church, fucking like a porn star does not make you a bad person. It makes you a healthy, happy person.

● ● ●

I'm going to expand on this even more. You want to know why France is such a passive country? Most Americans think the French are a bunch of spineless pussies who are afraid to fight. That's the farthest thing from the truth. The real reason the French are happy, content, and not concerned with fighting unnecessary wars is because they're too busy getting laid! There is no overload of testosterone in the average male there. A Frenchman focuses on women. The typical American male focuses on football, going to the gym, and collecting guns and ammunition.

A huge problem lies with the cultural norms of the U.S. government and the geniuses in and around Washington D.C. They have created a sub-culture that has demonized the act of sex itself. You are considered immoral, unethical, and in violation of some useless policy if it's public knowledge you fucked someone. There are policies preventing government employees from fucking their co-workers, fucking their peers, fucking their boss, fucking their subordinates, fucking someone who is not their wife, fucking someone who is a contractor to the U.S. government, etc. There's a slim list of people who a government employee *is* allowed to fuck. This useless mentality spills over into any corporation or entity that tries to do business with the U.S. government and their sex police. Matter of fact, I think a new amendment to the U.S. Constitution should be introduced. If I'm ever elected to office, I will personally present it. It's called Freedom of Sex. With this amendment, adult Americans are guaranteed the right to fuck any consenting adult in any manner they see fit. Oh yeah, it's coming.

The demonization of sex is the underlying cause of aggression and one of the catalysts for the unnecessary wars which have taken place over the past sixty years. How can I argue that? Well, if you're a man, think about this for a minute: Have you ever busted a nut and the first thing you thought about was going and fighting someone? Hell no. All you think about when you bust a nut is how at peace you are with the world, how relaxed you are, and how nice the birds sound as they chirp outside your window. All of a sudden, the moments-before urge and drive you had to pound the poor girl from behind like a jackhammer until you're physically exhausted, is gone.

What's the old saying? Make love, not war? I ask any man this question: Would you rather go get into a fight or go get some *pussy*? If you say you would rather go fight someone, you're either lying, or something is seriously wrong with you either emotionally or physically, or you might be homosexual. Now, everyone calm down before you or any rights groups get offended—I'll explain.

If a man is impotent or has erectile dysfunction to where he can't get his dick hard, he has no choice other than to say he'd rather go get into a fight. He already has an overabundance of testosterone anyway, which naturally makes him *want* to fight. Starting to see the logic in the theory? This subliminally explains why the U.S. is constantly at war. What's the underlying cause? It is a lack of *pussy* for the politicians, those inhabiting the Pentagon, and those in the defense industry. They're only focused on fighting (if they're impotent and have a buildup of testosterone) or they're focused on making a lot of money (to pay for high-priced hookers if they can't get laid at home). Thus, the underlying cause of aggression and the threat to world peace is a lack of sex.

The only other reason a male would voluntarily choose to fight another man versus having sex with a woman is because he is gay. It's only logical. I formed this opinion several years ago when a friend of mine invited me to go to a UFC fight. I really had no interest in going but my buddy was a huge fan and had bought the tickets. After getting to the event, he ended up introducing me to some guy named Forrest Griffin—never heard of him. Anyway, the first fight kicked off and after only a few punches, the two grown men went to the mat. One guy had his legs wrapped around the other guy's head. It looked like he was smearing his sweaty ass and balls all over the poor guy's face. I felt sorry for the dude. I wondered if the aggressor was whispering to him, *How's these nuts taste, motherfucker? Want some more of this ass cheese?* I watched the action for a couple of minutes and turned to my buddy.

"This is gay porn except they're wearing trunks."

He wasn't amused at my assessment. However, if I were attracted to men, I would love to fight other men. I would love to be a UFC fighter. I'll illustrate this scenario in your mind using a beautiful woman. If Pamela Anderson challenged me to a UFC fight with no holds barred, I would be on my way to the ring right now. Imagine stepping into the ring with Pamela, who's only wearing a bikini and some boxing gloves, sweating, with lust in her eyes that says, *I'm going to kick your ass.*

Now, me personally, I'd be thinking, *Oh yeah, I'm going to enjoy the hell out of this shit. No matter win or lose, I'm going to get some good licks in on the girl, then wrestle the hell out of her sweaty ass, twist her up like a yummy, buttery pretzel, and possibly make her tap out while saying, OK, OK, enough King Marcos!* At the end of that bout, my dick would be so damn hard a cat couldn't scratch it... You could cut diamonds on the head of the thing... You know the sayings.

Oh yeah, if I were attracted to men, I'd rather fight you than make love to a woman. I'm not saying that professional fighters are straight, gay, or bisexual and don't really give a damn about anyone's sexual preference. I'm just using that analogy to support my argument. Listen, I've endured a lot of torture from making love to some rough and wild bitches. I actually enjoyed that pain. I've never enjoyed the pain inflicted on me during a street fight with another man.

The moral? Make love people, not war. Women of America, especially those of you married to U.S. government employees, make love to your husbands three times a day and the military-industrial-congressional complex will crumble. Thus, world peace will ensue because you decided to take some action. Think about it for a minute. I read a poll not too long ago that said most people in the world believe the United States is the biggest threat to world peace. You could change the world's perception of our country by just doing your duty as a wife. Theoretically, you could all be collectively nominated for the Nobel Peace Prize for affecting the decisions of those within the United States government—just by giving up some ass like you should already be doing now.

CHAPTER 3

FINANCIAL PIMP-HAND

The quickest way to destroy a marriage is to start having problems with your finances. It doesn't take a rocket scientist to come to this conclusion. Only if you get caught naked with your wife's eighteen-year-old sister could you possibly have a more severe marital problem than when you can't pay your bills on time. If two people spend more than they earn they will constantly be under stress. This stress leads to arguments and fights over who's at fault. What has always amazed me is that no one seems to know how to correct such a simple problem. Admittedly, I learned the hard way. I can speak on this topic because I've made many poor financial decisions which were usually, in some way, influenced by a woman.

I was never good at math in school. I could write, but I failed math every time. I never did pass algebra and can't even begin to explain what it's about. But, there is a simple solution to ensuring financial success pertaining to your marriage:

DON'T FUCKING SPEND MORE THAN YOU EARN

There you have it. That one sentence is worth a million dollars to the married man. Let me say it again. Don't spend more than you earn. How do you accomplish this one simple task? You have to immediately take control of your finances like a king should. If you are about to get married or you're already married and are having financial problems, you need to follow these steps.

First, LOCK DOWN all bank accounts and credit cards. *Sounds like a prison term.* What do I mean by this? I mean lock down every means in which your wife has the ability to spend your hard-earned money. Remember, it is *your* money that *you* earned. Do not feel any sense of guilt by taking this first step. You're not doing it to be mean or to deprive anyone of basic necessities. You're doing this for the good of the kingdom—for the good of your family.

Close the joint checking account and open an account in your name only. A joint checking account is the worst thing banks have ever offered. No man has ever benefited from having a joint checking account with a woman—not never, since the beginning of time. Joint checking accounts allow a woman to free-spend as she pleases and there is nothing you can do about it. If she overdraws the account, your ass is still responsible for covering the overage and all the fees associated with it. You had better listen to this because your credit and your freedom is on the line if you refuse to make good on her mistakes. If she decides to break bad and leave your ass, she can legally withdraw every fucking cent you have in that joint account. There's not a damn thing you can do about it. You'll have to cover the funds somehow or else your credit will tank and you could find your name on an arrest warrant for deposit account fraud. You might as well put your money in her purse instead of in a joint account. It will be just as secure and will save her from having to make a trip to the bank. Once you get this gaping security breach closed, you've built the foundation for financial success.

What? Take my wife off the account? But how will she be able to get money out of the bank? Exactly. She won't. She doesn't need to. If she thinks that she needs money, she comes to you, the king. You will determine whether or not it is a valid request for funds. If you determine that it is, you issue her the money in cash. You become the bank. You become the comptroller of the kingdom's funds. After she spends the money, she should bring you back two things: a receipt and change. If the two don't add up to what you dispersed, do not give her any more until she accounts for the missing funds.

The next step is to remove her name from all of your credit cards. Then, seize the credit cards in question from her wallet and drop them into the shredder. Once that's done, physically secure all of the credit cards bearing your name to where she can't get her grubby little hands on them. Cashiers will seldom question a woman who presents a credit card bearing the same last name as her. In other words, if she can find your cards she can go shopping. Leave the damn things at your mother's house or find a good hiding spot for them in the attic. Or, you could just tuck them somewhere between the pages of the *Help Wanted* section of the newspaper and leave it lying on the kitchen table. She'll never look there.

What? Take away her credit cards, too? Listen, there's no logical reason for a housewife to have a credit card in the first place. She's not going anywhere other than the grocery store, Walmart, and the mall. She's not going to have to suddenly fly to New York to close a big real estate deal. *Damn, that last sentence made me laugh!* A credit card is just another way for her to get you and the kingdom into a mess of debt.

Once you get these two control measures in place you have solved most of your money problems already. Now your wife can't go on credit card spending sprees which you are responsible for. If she already has a credit card or obtains one on her own, you obviously can't stop her from running up the balance. You can refuse to pay the bill when it comes in and soon her card will be cut off. Problem solved. However, if she does this in defiance of your financial plan, you need to show her the door. That's grounds for immediate dismissal from the kingdom. You have to set the conditions for the kingdom's financial success. That's exactly what you've done once the accounts are locked down.

• • •

A man's lack of financial control is the cause of the majority of America's credit problems today. Women want a bigger house, a newer vehicle, more jewelry, expensive clothes, etc. Women often pressure the man into becoming overextended and living beyond his means. I do not fault the woman for this. Remember that under *The Declarations of Independence*, the king is ultimately responsible for everything that happens in his kingdom. So, if money problems arise it is the man's fault for failure to control and supervise his kingdom. I blame the last U.S. credit crunch, global recession, and the rash of foreclosures on the weakness of today's American male and his failure to govern his finances. Specifically, his inability to say *no*. If the man would have said *no* more often to what women and children *wanted* but did not *need*, there wouldn't have been such a crisis in the United States.

But Mark, you've already said that you don't know shit about math. What the hell do you know about economics? That's a good question and you are correct to challenge my credibility on the subject. So, let me share with you some real-world experience that backs up the previous paragraph. Back in 2006, I started working at a mortgage company part time as a loan officer. What did I know about the mortgage business? Initially, absolutely nothing. I was drawn in because of the potential to make some real bank without having to do anything illegal. Back then, the housing market in Atlanta was booming and there were new homes going up everywhere. Through some contacts, I got an interview with two cats who ran a local mortgage company. They were both fairly young guys, successful, and knew their shit when it came to numbers, the stock market, the bond market, etc. I was in awe of the extent of their knowledge. They were focused on making money as if it was their favorite sport. I was up front with them about who I was, who I wasn't, and what I didn't know. They were understanding and told me not to worry. They would send me to the training classes and be there to help me learn the business. As long as I could get a customer to walk through the front door, they would assist me through the process.

I dug in and started to learn everything I could about how the game worked. I soon was amazed at how lax and irresponsible the guidelines were. The way debt-to-income ratios (DTI) were used and figured, it just didn't make any sense to me. It seemed to me that the system was allowing people to borrow twice what they could actually afford.

After getting the basics down, I started a marketing blitz which began to bring in some clients. After the first few couples walked through the door I observed a somewhat predictable trend. A young couple would sit down at my desk and I would begin to run the numbers. The wife would be staring at me, beaming, just waiting for me to tell them how much money they qualified for. The man would always be uneasy and nervous about what I was going to say. When I calculated the number, I gave it to them with an immediate caveat and some free advice.

I would tell them, "Look, I'm going to tell you what you qualify for according to the guidelines. However, I'm also going to tell you what I personally think you can afford. You don't have to listen to me but I've got to sleep at night and I want to do so with a clear conscience. You qualify for a $200,000 dollar loan."

When I would reveal this, the woman would be so giddy she couldn't sit still. The man would be anxiously waiting for what else I was about to say.

"However, what you can afford is about a $110,000 dollar loan."

The woman would look at me as if I had insulted her mother and ask me what the hell I meant by that. I would show them their net salary and subtract their potential mortgage payment, student loans, and car payments. I would add up what they *had been* spending on groceries, utilities, fuel for their vehicles, eating out, entertainment, vehicle maintenance, and a few other basic necessities and subtract that number as well. Often, there would be absolutely no money left over or even a negative balance. Real numbers don't lie. They can't. Real life doesn't lie, either. Wall Street's method of figuring out how much a couple could afford utilized complex ratios, percentages, rules, guidelines, and smoke and mirrors. My method was to add up what the couple *had been* spending and subtract that from what they *had been* putting into their bank account. It was a more accurate method of determining how much they could actually afford to pay. Simple math—addition and subtraction.

I would continue by saying to them, "Listen, the more money you borrow, the more money I put in my pocket. Think about that while you're out looking at houses. If I'm giving you advice that, if taken, could cost me a thousand bucks or so out of my paycheck, don't you think it might be valid advice?"

You could tell that the wheels were beginning to turn in the man's head. He was thinking hard about what I had just told him. He would look me straight in the eye and convey to me that he knew I was right. He knew he had to grab a set of balls and have a hard talk with his bitch about which neighborhood they would be shopping in. His eyes were thanking me for reminding him that he was a man. Meanwhile, the woman didn't have a care in the world. All she could think about was looking for that $200,000 dollar house in the neighborhood with the pool and the tennis courts. All her friends would be so impressed and even jealous of her *success*.

As they were departing my office to hunt down their dream home, I would shake hands with the man and give him one last look that said, *Lay the strong pimp-hand down on this bitch and find something you can afford.* Do I even need to elaborate on what happened at the next meeting? When they arrived back at my office after a successful house-hunting trip, I already knew what was about to transpire. It happened every time. The woman would lead the way up the steps, bouncing with joy and clutching a folder containing an accepted contract. The man would be lugging behind a bit, looking down at the ground. I would shake hands with the woman and then find myself face to face with her husband. He couldn't even look at me. I had no problem looking at him because I no longer had any respect for him. He was nothing but a spineless chump in my book.

Once they were sitting down, I would ask the question with a one hundred percent certainty of predicting the answer.

"So, what did we end up going with?" I would ask.

The man wouldn't dare speak. The woman would smile, giggle, and talk to me as if I were her new best friend.

"We found one for $219,900 and offered them $204,900. And guess what? They accepted! My parents are going to give us some money later on to help out."

I would respond by saying, "Congratulations!"

It was indeed a sincere *congratulations* at that point because I knew I was about to get paid. I was getting paid and with a clear conscience due to this *weak-ass motherfucker* slouching in the chair across from me. His inability to manage his finances was benefitting me over in my kingdom.

What's the real impact of this situation? It's the fact that I guarantee you in the majority of these cases, within six months the house was getting foreclosed on and the couple was headed for divorce court. I had shown them on paper that they would have no money left over at the end of the month if they bought a big-ass house but they still didn't listen. Due to the man's inability to say no and act like a man, his marriage failed due to becoming overextended with his finances. They became another statistic in America. Now, what would have happened in this situation if the man had thrown down the financial pimp-hand and said, *Fuck no we're not buying a $200,000 dollar house. We're buying what we can afford and doing exactly what that short little motherfucker said.* They would probably be happily married right now in their smaller house, current on their bills, and saving for their one-week yearly vacation in Panama City, Florida. You see how that works?

The men in these particular cases failed themselves and their wives by being *pussies*. Shame on all of you. You're the reason the housing market crashed in 2008 and the entire country was sent into foreclosure. Sure, I could blame the greedy bankers who created those lax and irresponsible guidelines which allowed you to qualify for that big loan in the first place. But, it's not their fault. They only gave you enough rope to hang yourself. No one forced you to put it around your neck and jump off a damn chair. You allowed your woman to make a man's decision. Therefore, you being a *pussy* was the root cause of the foreclosure mess.

...Jackass of the Moment. Let's talk about the fool who proudly announces, "I never see my check, I give it straight to my wife," during a conversation about salaries. While saying this, he chuckles as if he supports and actually approves of the situation. In reality, he has absolutely no command and control over his household and he knows it. A large percentage of American men fall into this category. Don't feel like you're alone if you

qualify for the club. You're still a jackass but you're a jackass with plenty of company. This type of jackass is the worst offender of them all when it comes to being a pussy. What always amazes me is that men actually admit to this in front of other men. I personally think this particular revelation should rank right up there in secrecy next to the time you got drunk and let your dog lick peanut butter off your balls.

•••

Let's talk about basic budgets. Most women do not understand budgeting. Now, if you are one of those girls who has an MBA and makes six figures a year, I'm not talking to you. I am speaking to the married men of America who are the primary wage earners—men who are married to uneducated women with bad credit—men who are married to women from the trailer park. You know who you are, so pay attention. Here's the way a redneck girl's mind operates. I can attest to this because I was married to one for seven years and have lived with several others.

You can try to explain the concept of a budget to a redneck bitch and show her how much money you will have left over at the end of the month. You can explain that the amount left over is dependent upon there being no emergencies which might arise and consume this often small, residual pot of money. So, let's say that if after paying all of your bills for the month, you only have $100 dollars left over. Many of the households in America find themselves in this category. If you're the man, you're breathing a sigh of relief that you have $100 dollars of rescue money in case something happens. You are content with staying home on the weekend and relaxing.

A redneck woman is going to ask you on Friday night, "You going to take me to dinner?"

As a man, you try to explain to her that you don't have the money to eat a sixty-dollar meal at Red Lobster. The woman responds by saying that you do have the money because there is $100 dollars left over. If the man refuses, the woman will get pissed off and tell all of her friends what a cheap bastard her husband is and how he doesn't take care of her. They don't see it from the perspective that by saying no to her, you are actually taking *good* care of her.

Uneducated women and redneck girls don't understand money and they never will. It is not their responsibility to understand money. It is the king's responsibility. You can take the girl out of the trailer park but you can't take the trailer park out of the girl. That's reality. Most women who come from this type of background do not have a planning horizon longer than today. They only understand the concept of, *What can I get for myself right now?* They can't plan a week out, much less an entire month. It's the way they were raised. If you're married to a woman like this she will never change. This is especially true if she is a smoker. There is a direct correlation.

• • •

Women who smoke are the worst kind of drain on your finances. Why do I single them out? Because no matter how broke you are, they will always have two packs of cigarettes in their purse. It doesn't matter if you're sitting in your house in the dark because your electricity has been cut off for not paying the bill. Out of the quiet of the darkness, you will hear the flick of a cheap lighter—*Whiccckk!* Old girl's face will temporarily be illuminated as you watch her, without any guilt, light that menthol. It will be the only light in your house. Now, let's analyze this. Let's say cigarettes cost about $5 dollars a pack. Most redneck women who smoke need at least a pack a day to support this nasty habit. That's $5 dollars a day times thirty days out of the month. That equals $150 dollars which is about how much the electric bill could run if you are conservative. See how that works?

Now, I didn't factor in the custom of how redneck women only buy two packs at a time. Therefore, you are looking at an average of fifteen trips to the convenience store per month to buy cigarettes. With gas at an average of $3 dollars per gallon, you can bet that you are also out around $50 dollars per month just on the money it takes for them to go back and forth to the store. That's a grand total of $200 dollars per month because of this shit. If you are struggling with paying your light bill, maybe as a king you need to end your wife's drain on the kingdom by terminating the financial support for this addiction. You may need to establish a directive that says no one is allowed to smoke.

Remember to never issue ultimatums. Only issue directives that are for the good of the kingdom. In this particular case, it is very good for the kingdom and is reasonable by anyone's standards. Well, maybe not by the chain-smoking redneck women of the world. Here's what it boils down to: As a king, it is your responsibility to take care of your kingdom. Within that kingdom is your wife and your children. If the basic needs of your children cannot be met because of expensive and unnecessary activity like smoking cigarettes, then you need to grab a set of balls and make a change. Do not allow your children to suffer because you are weak. Now, I know that scares the hell out of most of you. It's because right now you are a *pussy*. You are not acting as a man within your relationship and therefore haven't achieved the status of a king. Take some damn responsibility and set this shit straight. It makes me mad as hell to know that people can't feed their kids but they always have enough money for cigarettes.

Ever wonder why your kids are always at the emergency room with a cough? If you're a redneck, you will tend to believe that it's bronchitis, the whooping cough, the flu, double pneumonia, triple pneumonia, walking pneumonia, cat-scratch fever, or little Johnny's danged-old allergies kicking up again. That's all bullshit. It's because you have a woman in the house who is chain-smoking around your young children which is causing them health problems. Guess who's on the hook for the emergency room bill? Yep, that would be you, the weak *motherfucker* giving your wife money for cigarettes. *Hmmmm... Did I just connect your weakness as a man to your kids' health problems?* I most certainly did.

• • •

Do not be afraid to spend your own money. You earned it. Especially in a household where the man is the only wage earner. As a king, you do not answer to anyone. No one questions the king. Therefore, if you're responsibly managing your kingdom and are taking good care of everyone in it, do not feel guilty about spending money as you see fit. I am saying this with a caveat: A good king puts his own interests after the welfare of his people. However, if everyone is doing well, then spend your money. If you feel the need to buy a Harley-Davidson because you want one, then buy it. But, only if it is well within your means and only after you have made sure your kingdom is safe and secure. If buying a Harley is within your reach and what you want to spend your money on, do your research and make the purchase.

Do not feel that you have to seek approval from your wife. That's not how it works. Grab a set of balls, go to the Harley store, and ride one of those *motherfuckers* home. Pull up in the yard and rev the engine so loud your wife comes out to see what's going on. When she walks out, put a helmet on her head and take her for a ride through the mountains. If she bitches or hesitates one bit, ride through the mountains by yourself or with your buddies. Then, she can be pissed off and gripe at the walls.

If you return from your ride and she still has something negative to say, feel free to show her the door. Remember, you are the king and the king cannot be questioned. I will offer this observation as well: If you pull up on a new Harley and your wife refuses to go on a ride with you, it should tell you something about your marriage. It should tell you that she is an angry bitch who doesn't appreciate you. It should tell you that she does not trust your judgment with the finances nor your ability to pilot a motorcycle. Take that seriously because it is only the tip of bigger issues. Now, if you pull up and your wife gets so excited that all she does is throw that helmet on and jump on the back, then she loves you. She is still in love with you. If she does that, she is not questioning your decision and is willing to make the best of a situation. That indicates she is happy to be a part of your kingdom. Keep that bitch around. Additionally, she will probably get off a dozen times during the ride because of the vibration. She will always want to go riding with you after that side effect. What kind of a woman turns down an adventure on a Harley, anyway? No woman in her right mind would ever turn down a motorcycle ride, especially on a Harley-Davidson.

 Let's talk about this issue further. How many times have you heard a man say, *I've got to sell my wife on it first,* or, *If my wife will let me buy it,* when he wants to purchase a big-ticket item? It makes me sick just thinking about these statements. *What the hell do you mean you have to ask your wife if you can buy something? I don't get it.* If you stay at home and are unemployed then you may have to seek approval from your wife if she is the bread winner. If you are the only person in your kingdom bringing home the bacon, why the *fuck* would you have to ask your wife for approval to spend your own money? Somebody needs to explain to me how our culture evolved into this. Let me get this straight: I have to ask my wife, who sits at home all day, if I can spend money that I went out into the world and made? Men who act like this are in a special category of weakness in my opinion.

● ● ●

 On one occasion about four years ago, I was on a trip with the Hoy Dog and Pablo Escobar down south of the border. During this trip, I spent all of my cash on hand and hit an ATM in town to recharge my pocket change. In order to avoid having to try and find an ATM while traveling through no-man's land, I took out $500 dollars one day and $500 dollars the next. Problem solved.

My two compadres had laundered some of their own money from their wives and were flying under the radar. Hey, that was the way they chose to live back then. Not me. It was my money. I have absolutely no guilt in taking my money out of my account and putting it into my pocket. During the trip, the Hoy Dog put in a call to his old lady to check in. She questioned him as to why I had taken out $1,000 dollars from an ATM. *What the fuck?* How in the hell did the Hoy Dog's wife know I had taken out a cool grand and why was she questioning *him* about *my* finances.

Listen, I'm not stupid. I already knew the answer to both of those questions. My wife was obviously the culprit trying to snoop around in our business. Apparently while the two were talking, she casually inquired as to why I had to take out $1,000 dollars in such a short period of time. I was furious. First of all, why is my wife discussing my finances with my buddy's wife? Why is my wife discussing my finances with anyone? Why is she questioning me about what I do with the kingdom's money? *I'm the fucking king.* I'm the one who made the damn money in the first place.

After I got her on the telephone, I reiterated to her that she would never again discuss my financial transactions with anyone. Once she acknowledged the re-education campaign, I issued her a directive.

"Immediately, without delay, go to the bank, withdraw $3,000 dollars and send it to me via Western Union," I told her.

She complied and the next day I had to scramble to locate a damn Western Union to pick up the money. The rest of that trip, I was as nervous as a whore in church sitting on the front row. I had four grand in my front pocket during some adventuring where I didn't need to have four grand in my front pocket. I ended up only spending about five hundred of the original money I took out of the ATM. As soon as I got back to the States, it was a race to the bank to get that money secured. I breathed a sigh of relief when the teller handed me the receipt for the deposit. It was money I didn't need and never intended on spending in the first place. I wanted to prove a point to my old lady who had suffered a temporary lapse in judgment and lost sight of a critical fact.

It was my money to allocate as I saw fit. She was very well taken care of at the time and wanted for nothing. For her to question me was a violation of *The Declarations of Independence*. Therefore, if you question me about where I spend $20 dollars, I'll go out and spend a thousand. If you don't like it, then think back to when I showed you that rectangular portal to freedom that's commonly referred to as the front door. Then, walk through it. The moral of this story is that it's your money. Do not allow anyone to question you about where and how you spend it, especially your unemployed wife. Just remember that the principles say you have to take care of your wife and the kingdom first. If your kids need new shoes or the vacuum cleaner is broke, don't take your ass out and buy a new motorcycle. You're not being a king. You're being an irresponsible asshole.

●●●

Lock down the finances. Once you do, you may find that you are suddenly able to work only fifty hours per week versus the seventy you're working now. You'll be able to spend more time with your children. Life will go on and you'll become a better parent and husband as a result of it. You'll be able to spend more quality time with your wife and potentially reignite your sex life. People only need basic items to survive. Excess spending is not necessary to achieve happiness. Eating out, shopping, vacation, cigarettes, etc., are extreme luxuries and not rights. If a woman expects something or believes it to be a right, let her run her own kingdom with the fifty percent of your salary the court will inevitably award her. Be happy and rule your kingdom alone in your studio apartment. Remember, in the end it always works out better for the man. The man will get richer and better looking as time goes by. The woman will end up poor, wrinkled, fat, and working for minimum wage. Don't believe me? Look up my first wife and see how she's doing these days. Is that cruel? Absolutely. But, what goes around, comes around. You reap what you sow. *Karma.*

CHAPTER 4

NICHES IN MISERY

I want to share a few case studies with you and talk about some learning points which may apply to your current situation. The backgrounds and situations are real and often all too typical. I may or may not provide you with any useful solutions but hopefully, I'll at least invoke thought. Why would I tell everyone about how much of a *pussy* I used to be? To begin with, I'm on the downhill slope of life and to be honest, I really don't give a shit about much these days. I'm a self-employed writer so it's not like I'm concerned about the company's ethics policy. Besides, I'm not embarrassed by my past. It's something that cannot be changed no matter how hard you try. So, why deny it? You think I'm worried about damaging my reputation or my ego? Ha! Now that's funny. You'd have to actually have a reputation first. The only thing I'm known for is being absolutely crazy. The good thing about it is that it allows me to pretty much act like an idiot all the time and not raise any alarms. Don't try this at home, though. There is a downside.

● ● ●

I'm sharing this so that the younger generation of men in America might learn a damn thing or two. All of my friends and I have sons, so we have a vested interest in allowing others to learn from our mistakes. Let's evaluate some of the problems my fellow players and I have endured while dealing with American women. I've also included a case study pertaining to an Asian girl as an added bonus. I'm going to throw out some quick snapshots of specific problems you may be able to relate to. If these situations sound foreign to you, it is possible that you're married to a good lady or you may just need to wait a little bit longer.

Doggone John

Let me tell you a quick story about a friend of mine who we'll call Doggone John. John's story is sad, but not out of the ordinary. At the time of this incident I am going to speak of, John had been faithfully married to his wife for about thirteen years. They had two wonderful children together. John worked full time throughout the week, usually putting in over fifty-plus hours. On the weekends, John would lay tile for extra money. This often put him working seven days a week from sun up to sun down. He and his wife lived in an average home. His wife had a brand new vehicle while John's old truck frequently broke down. He loved his children dearly and spent all of his free time with them. He was not the type to hit the bars after work and did not drink at all. He was a good man and a good father. However, he led an extremely miserable existence by my assessment.

First of all, John's wife had sex with him once a year on his birthday. I'm not exaggerating one bit. This is an accurate statement. Sex was his fucking birthday present from that useless bitch. This had been going on since the birth of their second child. I could not even imagine living like that. We all knew about the arrangement and frequently tried to give him advice about it. John wouldn't listen because he loved his children and was afraid of his wife. I don't know why. His wife was not a good-looking woman and that's putting it politely in case she gets a copy of this book. Wait a minute, let me be honest with you. She was one dog-ugly bitch. She didn't work. She was not educated. She had nothing to her name. If something had happened to John, her ass would have been down at the Waffle House waiting tables.

But, here is the point of the story and the lesson learned. John's wife had a small dog and she insisted on allowing it to sleep in the bed with them. The dog's place was right in the middle of the two. He had trouble sleeping because of the dog and constantly complained among his friends about it. We finally ganged up on old John and told him that he needed to grab a set of balls and do something about the situation. I told him to go home and tell his wife that under no circumstances was the damn dog sleeping in the bed with them anymore. It should have been an open and shut case. However, that fool went home and issued an ultimatum. *Dumb-ass.* You just can't do that.

As a king, NEVER issue an ultimatum. Your word is binding without any conditions or concessions. John went home and told his wife, *Either the dog goes or I go.* He lost the battle from the start because he issued an ultimatum to a woman. Do not issue *if thens* or the old *or else this*. Since that night, John has been sleeping on the couch in his own house. His wife told him that he would have to go because the dog wasn't leaving. He allowed his wife to banish him from his own bedroom to the living room. If he is still with her today, I would imagine he is sleeping on the couch as I type these words.

What kind of message does this send to his children? Think about it for a minute from a child's perspective. It sends a very damaging and confusing message to his children in my opinion. They see their father work two jobs to ensure they are provided for. However, they see him go to sleep on the couch every night because he is afraid of their unemployed, uneducated mother. They see that their mother values a damn dog more than she does their father. They see their father as weak and impotent. How can the children respect their father as they should?

• • •

When we heard the news we obviously ridiculed him for not following our directions. Had he gone home and merely told his wife that the dog was no longer going to sleep in the bed, everything would have been fine. Had she not complied with the directive, I would have assisted John with dropping the dog off at animal control. Problem solved. Not the way that it had to be handled, but his wife would have forced John to take that type of action. If the wife ultimately decided to change her attitude about the situation, John could have rescued the dog from the pound. Remember, be fair and just, but be firm. We would not have been taking the dog to the pound out of meanness or spite. It would have been only out of necessity. Sometimes, ruling a kingdom is not always pretty. Hard decisions have to be made in order to preserve discipline for the good of the people.

If I had to guess, John probably didn't leave his wife until the children were grown and might still be with her. Life is short my friends. Do not live miserable for eighteen years of your life because of your children. Children know exactly what is going on whether you want to believe they do or not. It is not healthy for them to grow up in a household that is not happy. If you are staying with your wife only because you cite the children as justification, you're making the wrong call. You are really just using your kids as an excuse because you fear your wife and are afraid to make a change. The last time I spoke with John was around a decade ago. When I last saw him, he had been working out and had lost a ton of weight. He had gone from the Pillsbury Doughboy to a rather fit, attractive, middle-aged guy. He was hitting the gym and running cross-country races. As a by-product of this, the young ladies had started to take an interest in him. Why would he not take on a girlfriend or two considering the circumstances in his home? You can't blame him if he did. I tell this short story to illustrate how a small issue such as a damn dog can affect your kingdom if you allow it. John certainly was not conducting himself as a king or even as a man. His children witnessed this carnage because he allowed his lazy wife to rule over him.

● ● ●

While I love old John like a brother, I have to say, *Shame on you for being a pussy*. I hope that since we last spoke you have kicked that bitch to the curb and are running ho's in and out like cattle. Or, you are currently married to a twenty-five-year-old aerobics instructor who fucks like a porn star. I could go on about his story but I believe the lesson on this one is short and to the point. Many of you may find yourself in a similar situation. If so, take some action. If you need help, I will be glad to haul your wife's dog to the pound for you. Just give me a call. If it's your mother-in-law who is coming between you and your wife rather than a dog, the situation is a bit more complicated but just as easy to resolve. No, I can't haul the old bitch to the pound for you. You have to remove her from the equation by whatever fits your situation. Ban her from your house. If she still shows up in defiance of your directives, pack your shit and relocate to a new palace. Simple. Let your wife, her mother, and the dog rule their own kingdom.

Pablo the Workaholic

My good friend, who we'll call Pablo Escobar, has been married to his wife for about twenty years. They have two children together. Pablo has a successful career and makes decent money. His wife is the typical stay-at-home housewife who does nothing all day but watch Dr. Phil. Pablo's daily life had become as mundane as most married men in America. He would typically work sixty hours per week to make ends meet. However, he made the fatal flaw of allowing his wife to control his finances. He once made the statement to me that no matter how many extra hours he worked, he was still broke. That's because he had no control over his uneducated, lazy-ass wife who was handling the money.

Remember, these types of women do not understand budgets and finances. All they know is that if there is money in the account they can spend it. That's exactly what was happening in his case. Pablo thought he was getting ahead by working more hours. *Wrong, motherfucker.* The more hours you worked, the more money your woman spent at the mall. What really pissed me off was that his wife bitched whenever he drank. Now, Pablo wasn't the type to go hang out at bars and get drunk (at least initially). He worked too much to even think about that. Pablo was the type who came home from a twelve-hour shift, grabbed a beer, and tried to unwind in his easy chair. The minute he did, that lazy-ass wife of his would start complaining. She would rant and rave and accuse him of being an alcoholic. Pablo told me that he had to hide his liquor because if she found it she would pour it out. Now, let me get this straight. Pablo is the only wage earner in his household. What gives this free-loading vixen the right to pour out his booze? While that is only one example of his overall problems, it is indicative of the environment he allowed to exist. Why had he allowed his household to fall into this turmoil? The reason is that he wasn't being a man and therefore could not live like a king. Those were his own words to me.

*...**An early point to take from Pablo's situation.** The point to take from Pablo's situation is that you have to get control of your finances. In Pablo's mind, he thought that if he worked more he would be getting out of debt. In Pablo's mind, his wife thought the same thing. She was not thinking the same thing and just kept free-spending. I told Pablo that he needed to stop working sixty hours a week and only work forty. I told him to lock down the finances and take control. Once he did that, he would be able to spend more time with his children and less time at work. Unfortunately, he didn't listen to my advice and had to learn the hard way.*

Pablo was unhappy at home and was only staying with his wife for the sake of his children. In his mind and possibly yours, that was the noble thing to do. I strongly disagree with this. I personally think that it is more damaging to children to see their parents in a constant state of tension and unhappiness. I believe that it is much better to go ahead and make the tough decision to separate. That way, both you and your wife can resume the pursuit of happiness. To jump ahead in history, Pablo and his wife are separated and their divorce is pending. Once you read the chapter on *The Trip of Three Divorces* you will understand the circumstances why.

Hoy's Red Bull and Cigarette Shop

A close friend of mine who we'll call Hoy, or the Hoy Dog, endured ten years of misery with his second marriage. However, everything that made him miserable was his own fault. Remember that under *Kingdom Rule*, the king is ultimately responsible for everything that goes on in the kingdom. A king has to take responsibility for his actions or inactions. Now that Hoy lives as a king, he understands that everything was his own doing. Prior to accepting this ideology, he blamed his wife like most men. I'll give you a synopsis of his background. He has a successful career, makes decent money, is a tall, good-looking man, and has no problems meeting women. He met his wife and their marriage began like many others. They were in love and decided to tie the knot. About seven months later, they had a child together. Yes, do the math. A lot of marriages start that way. No one gives a shit about that part. Within the first year, I began to see marked changes in his personality. While Hoy used to meet the boys out for a drink once a week, he suddenly started making up excuses as to why he had to get home. It is hard to fool your friends, especially your fellow players. He was becoming *pussy-whipped* in a quick sort of way. He was constantly having to call his wife and explain to her what he was doing, who he was with, where he was at, etc. When I tried to hang out with him, he spent most of his time on the phone kissing his wife's ass. It was downright shameful. As the years progressed, her hold over him kept getting tighter. It got to the point that he would have to lie and say he was at work just to have a quick burger out with friends. Does all of this sound familiar? It should, because I am probably describing your life right now. The thought of Hoy spending a night out drinking with the boys, going on an overnight hunting trip, or rolling to a concert with me was out of the question.

● ● ●

Prior to getting married, Hoy had plenty of money in the bank with no bills. I remember a time when he would have three paychecks lying on his kitchen table because he had forgotten to go put them in the bank. After a year of marriage, he was broker than General Motors in 2009. How did this happen? It happened because he relinquished control over his finances to his wife. His first mistake was to open a joint account with her. His wife was the typical uneducated and unemployed American housewife. She knew absolutely nothing about finances, budgets, and the importance of spending less than you earn. After a year, the way business was handled at his house was typical of most American households. He deposited his salary into the bank and his wife started writing checks and going shopping unsupervised. When money was tight, instead of ruling like a king and locking down the finances, Hoy just started working more hours. The problem was that no matter how many hours he worked (just like Pablo), he was always broke at the end of the week. He would always end up with $20 dollars in the bank. This never fluctuated no matter how much his income increased or decreased. Gentlemen, a woman does not understand how to survive. If you deposit $1,000 dollars into your account and allow your wife to control your finances, she will spend $1,000 dollars. If you deposit $2,000 dollars, she will spend $2,000 dollars. Especially if you are one of the many who are married to a redneck or a hood rat. Don't forget what they do all day. They watch television shows which empower them to make these decisions because they are told to be a strong woman. *Shame on you, Oprah!* Most of them do not have your business sense and have no idea how to interpret what you or Dr. Phil advocate. They can only play checkers—not chess.

As Hoy's career progressed, he began to make more and more money. However, he was still not saving. It was not because of *his* spending habits. When we took a trip down to Guatemala, Hoy haggled with the cab driver for fifteen minutes over one dollar. The entire trip he probably only saved ten dollars but put hours of effort into doing so. He would not allow himself to enjoy an expensive meal or even have a mixed drink with dinner. It was too pricey for him. It made me sick and I'll tell you why. Here was a man working sixty hours a week to provide for his family. Here was a man who would only drink water when eating out at a restaurant to save two dollars. But, here was a man who allowed his wife to go to Walmart and spend $30 dollars a week on Red Bull energy drinks when she was the only one in the house who drank them. Here was a man who allowed his wife to spend $200 dollars a month on cigarettes without any objections. Here was a man who had absolutely no control over his finances or his kingdom. How could this have happened? The same way it happens to most American men. They forget they are men. As Pablo brought up after I initially explained *Kingdom Rule* to him, You *have to be a man first and then you can be a king.* If this particular scenario sounds like you, then it is time to stand up and make some changes. But before you take any action, make sure you have thoroughly studied the chapter *Financial Pimp-Hand* so you know how to proceed.

Mark's Moving Business

This niche in misery is the easiest to explain because it is a sampling of my story. I want to share some of my experiences so that you may learn from my mistakes. It is not a very pretty picture that I'm about to paint. However, there is no shame in my game. History is history. If history is skewed or sugar-coated then nobody learns a thing. I got married young. My son was born about six months later. Yeah, do the math and get over it. I found myself living the domestic life from the start. I really didn't have any problem with being married. I was a pretty good husband and father for the most part. I just had one fatal flaw—I loved chasing women. If you take the cheating out of the equation, I wasn't too bad. I used to tell people jokingly that if my wife would get along with all of my girlfriends we'd be much better off. Regardless, that was our primary problem and it ended up costing me a divorce.

The true learning lessons from my story came later, when I found myself single and the only member of my kingdom. For some reason, I didn't appreciate the fact that living alone is a good thing. If you live by yourself, you can run bitches in and out as you please with no one to answer to. I routinely kept screwing up this arrangement because I insisted on having a girl move in with me. It would end up lasting maybe a month or two and then I had to rent a moving truck to get her shit out of my crib. It was absolute silliness. Why? Because back then, I hadn't adopted Declaration 5 yet. I was afraid of being alone. That fear routinely influenced my decisions when it came to women. I would very quickly let one move into my house with me. What did it accomplish? It meant that instead of having dinner with the girl once a week, I suddenly had to feed her breakfast, lunch, and dinner every day. That's an abrupt drain on your finances. My utility bill immediately increased due to her running a fucking hair dryer for an hour every day—not to mention a woman's love for taking hot baths. Any initial agreement that was made for a girl to assist with the household bills was never adhered to. I got taken time after time like this.

The worst girls I dealt with were the ones who had kids. Now, don't get me wrong. I love kids. I've got nothing against them. But, I don't want to have to support another man's child. That's his fucking job, not mine. My job is to support my own kid. Unfortunately, my dumb-ass on several occasions let bitches move into my home with their snot-nosed, cereal eliminators. I never stopped to ask myself, *How does this benefit me?* If I had, I would have arrived at the conclusion that it didn't. All it did was tax the hell out of me. I didn't need any of those women to move in with me. They could have kept on living right where they were when I met them and I could have still tagged that ass several times a week for free. So what if I had to wash my own dishes and sweep the floor?

The main lesson you should learn from this is that there are multiple reasons for Declaration 5. You have to program yourself to accept that being alone is often the better choice than living with someone. I know that the single mothers of America will raise hell at me for what I'm about to say, but I'm not representing them so it doesn't matter. Do not, under any circumstances, allow a woman with a kid to move in with you. *Oh, I already know I'm going to hell for saying that.* It certainly will benefit her and the child and will be looked upon as a noble gesture on your part. You'll be considered a good man because you're taking on the responsibility of helping her with the kid. Listen, I'm all about doing charity work. I've personally spent thousands of dollars of my own money toward the cause and have risked my ass in several corners of the globe to distribute food and basic needs to homeless children. I'm not telling you to not be a charitable person. What I'm telling you is that you need to take care of yourself, first. You need to make decisions that benefit you and shy away from ones that do not. Letting a woman who has kids move in with you is a huge tax on your finances. You will lose money because of the arrangement. I assure you of this. If you end up having to kick the bitch out, it will affect the child as well. Therefore, you will hesitate to make hard decisions which are in *your* best interests. You will let the welfare of her kid delay or dissuade you from doing what has to be done. It's not fair to you or the child. I don't really give a shit about how it affects the woman. Oprah and *The Union* can deal with her.

...*If you want a bitch to move in with you, get one with no kids. If you want to be a father figure or big brother to a disadvantaged youth, then go volunteer at the YMCA. Just don't mix the two together because very rarely does anything good come of it. Ask yourself if the living arrangement benefits you, the man. If it doesn't, don't do it.*

With some of the women who lived with me, I ended up liking their kids better than I liked them. You see how that can mess with your head and your decision-making process? I was ready to deep-six their mother but I kept feeling sorry for the children. I kept justifying in my mind that they're kids—they shouldn't be punished for having a fucked up mother and therefore, I can't just kick her out. I realize now that I was more involved with charity work than I was with a relationship or doing what was best for me. The problem was that I had no control over my life nor the kids' for that matter. The crazy bitch was in control. I recommend you consider these situations and steer clear of living with the single moms of America. Sorry, bitches. I'm not saying you can't come over and hang out, just plan on having breakfast the next morning at your own crib. Don't worry too much, though. There are plenty of suckers out there you can run to and live off of. You just can't freeload off this guy or my fellow kings. And by the way, stop using your kids as pawns while playing your fucked up games.

Doc Wayne and Jackass Disease

There is an old saying about the four animals a woman loves to have. Now, I didn't make this up. Some other scholar came up with this but I'm not even sure who to credit for its creation. I've heard the saying my entire life and it's pure genius.

> **There are four animals a woman wants:**
> 1. A **mink** in the closet (fur coat).
> 2. A **jaguar** in the garage (new car).
> 3. A **tiger** in bed (young buck who'll fuck like a porn star).
> 4. And... A **JACKASS** to pay for it all (self-explanatory).

Now, if you qualify as a jackass, *wouldn't you rather be the fucking tiger?* I start off with this philosophy because it directly pertains to my good friend, who we'll call Doctor Wayne. Doc Wayne is about sixty years old and is one good-hearted *motherfucker*. He's a retired dentist from the U.S. and the type of guy you would introduce to your sister. He's a kind and gentle man and is well respected. However, that kindness and gentle way is his weakness and ultimately, his demise when it comes to dealing with ruthless women.

Now, don't get me wrong. Doc Wayne is smart. That's why he gets to be called Doctor Wayne instead of *ol' Wayne* or by some other title. Because he is smart, he never married an American girl. If he had, he would now be a broke, smart guy. Instead, he chose wisely to go international from the beginning. However, he had never read the *Financial Pimp-Hand* chapter in this book. So, let me tell you about how he got taken by an Asian chick. He got clipped, but on a much lower level than if he had been dealing with a girl from the West.

Doc Wayne, like a lot of us Western guys, fell for a bar girl. What's a bar girl? It would take me an entire book to properly explain what a bar girl is and the way things are in some parts of Asia. I'll summarize instead. A bar girl in Thailand is a poor girl from the country who goes to work in a bar as a waitress / hooker in order to support her lazy-ass family back in the village. Originally good country girls, they have been brainwashed since birth into thinking they have to support their family by any means necessary. They're motivated by one thing and that's money. The good side to this is that they are predictable. If you hook up with one, realize up front they love your wallet and not your heart.

Doc Wayne got attached to a bar girl who had one kid. He basically supported the lazy bitch for five years, sent her ass to beauty school, and even set her up with a small salon of her own. Oh yeah, he shuttled a few bucks to her family in the village as well. The problem with this particular girl was that she was so damn lazy, she wouldn't even get up in the morning and open the shop! It just sat there with the *CLOSED* sign hanging on the front door. Made no damn sense whatsoever. The girl was just a dud. Most girls would cut her throat to be set up in that situation and have Doc Wayne as a boyfriend.

Every day, Doc Wayne would meet up with me at a bar for a couple of hours and vent his frustrations about the situation. I would listen as he constantly explained about how miserable his life had become. He was supposed to be enjoying his retirement but instead, he was raising an eight-year-old girl who wasn't his. He couldn't chat with me for more than two hours a day. He was too scared of that lazy bitch sitting on her ass watching Thai soap operas instead of cutting hair.

"Man, let me get this straight. This bitch was a hooker before she met you. She had absolutely nothing. You pay all the fucking bills, so why do you allow her to tell you what to do?"

Doc Wayne responded by saying, "I want to leave but I just feel sorry for her."

"Listen, I know you don't want to see her have to go back to dancing on a pole and sucking cock. It's not the way we were raised. We were raised to take care of women and nurture them. But this bitch is just using you for your money. She's making your life hell instead of treating you like a king. If she was taking good care of you, we wouldn't be having this conversation."

After weeks of this routine, Doc Wayne finally decided he had put up with enough of the free-loader. We packed our bags and rolled to the Philippines to get a change of scenery. After a couple of weeks of chasing the ladies and partying, I flew back to Thailand. Doc Wayne stayed strong and remained in place.

Ten days later, Doc Wayne called me from his Thai cell phone, unannounced. He was obviously in Thailand.

"What the hell are you doing back here? And I heard a rumor that there was something about a car? What's going on?" I asked.

"I'll explain when I get there," Doc Wayne advised.

This shit ought to be entertaining, I thought. Within a few minutes, Doc Wayne, his old lady, and the kid drove up in a brand new Nissan four-door. It still had the red drive-out tag on it. Doc Wayne got out of the driver's seat with his head down and a look of shame on his face.

"I know... I know," is all he could say.

His girl got out with an air of pride and arrogance emanating from her person. She was beaming in front of the new ride. She had that look of mission accomplishment about her and promptly gave me a tour of the forty-thousand-dollar heap of debt. She showed me each and every option and insisted I sit in the driver's seat.

"Wow, that's real nice," I said convincingly to her, yet with a sarcastic tone directed at the newly crowned jackass.

Doc Wayne and I excused ourselves and walked down to the corner bar. I had a huge smile on my face during the short jaunt while Doc Wayne just kept shaking his head. Why was I happy? Because for once, it wasn't me stuck in a shitty predicament. All of a sudden, my problems seemed miniscule compared to the story I was about to listen to. When we got to the bar and ordered a couple of Singha's, Doc Wayne began to explain the situation.

"I still cannot believe she did this," said the Doc.

"Start from the beginning and tell me the whole story. How in the hell can a broke-ass bitch like her go out and drive off the lot with a new car? We're in Thailand for Christ's sake. That's a $40,000 dollar ride. Hell, neither one of us could go buy a new car right now. What the fuck?"

"This is what happened. When I left, I took all of my things. I didn't have any intentions on coming back here. To clear my conscience, I left her enough money to live off of for six months. I figured that would give her enough time to get her business up and running and be self-sufficient," explained the Doc.

"How much did you leave the bitch?" I asked.

"Around thirty-four hundred bucks."

"Damn, man! Don't you know you can't give a dumb-ass redneck bitch a huge chunk of money? It has nothing to do with her being Thai. Hell, if you gave any one of my relatives three grand they'd be broke by tomorrow," I elaborated.

"I told her that she would have five hundred dollars a month which was more than enough to pay all of the bills. Apparently, she took some of the money and used it as a down payment on the damn car. I'm still not quite clear as to how much she spent or how much is left in her account. She hasn't shown me the books yet."

● ● ●

It was just an unbelievable, shitty situation. However, let's apply the philosophy of *Kingdom Rule*. It wasn't his girl's fault. She's just an uneducated redneck bitch from the country who has never had a dime to her name. It was Doc Wayne's fault. He set her up for failure. The responsibility rests squarely on his shoulders. There was no one to blame except for himself. There is a term used when dealing with drug addicts which applies here. The term is called an *enabler*. An enabler is someone who intentionally or unintentionally assists an addict to remain an addict. For example, a mother gives a kid money to buy drugs because she doesn't want him to have to steal the money. She is the enabler. She thinks she is doing good, but in reality she is digging a deeper hole for her child, the addict. Doc Wayne had suddenly become the enabler of this situation. He enabled a girl, who couldn't even pay her own rent, to get locked into a $40,000 dollar car loan for the next eight years. He might as well have shot her in both feet with his own gun. You don't need a crystal ball to see what's coming down the pipe. She won't be able to make even the first payment, the car will be repossessed, her credit will tank, and she'll be twice as broke as she was before receiving that huge chunk of money.

Even though Doc Wayne was trying to do the right thing and depart with a clear conscience, his kindness fucked the girl over in the worst way. She, like most poor American girls, had no training or education on how to handle money. Why do you think all of the poor people who win the lottery in America are broke after a year? They're not prepared for the sudden change in their lives. Poor people have a planning horizon of less than one day. They only think about what they can get for themselves, right now. Tomorrow is not factored into their planning. It's just the way it is. I grew up poor. I can attest to this mentality.

What's the lesson of this scenario? First of all, don't be the jackass. Being the tiger is much more fun. Second, as a king, you are responsible for all financial decisions. Don't blame your girl when she makes illogical decisions with your money. If you gave her access to the money in the first place, it's your damn fault. Be a king, maintain control of the finances, and take care of your woman. Or, be a *pussy*, let her control the money, and sit back and wait to go broke. *Jackass disease* is perhaps the second worst condition an American man can suffer from. However, it can be easily and immediately cured as it is self-inflicted. I should know because I too, used to suffer from *jackass disease.*

CHAPTER 5

CHICKEN BUSES AND CHEESEBURGERS

The Hoy Dog and I had grown so tired of dealing with American women that we decided there was only one course of action to take. It was time to go international. *Forget all these lazy American bitches with their sense of entitlement,* we thought. We would hunt girls in places where we were sure they would be appreciative of our status as gentlemen. We began a discussion on where we should go. The conversation quickly focused in on the City of Prague, in the Czech Republic. We always talked about Prague and had heard the women there were absolutely beautiful.

As we started planning and laying the ground work with our American wives at the time, the Hoy Dog unexpectedly came through with transportation arrangements. You see, he had started courting a young Chinese chick who worked for U.S. Airways. During his efforts at wooing this little cutie he had discovered that she received several free travel vouchers per year. It was a mistake on her part to let a couple of pimps like us find out about that benefit. We both decided he had to immediately step up his game of seduction for the sole purpose of acquiring a couple of those free flight vouchers. Did I mention he and I are a couple of cheap *motherfuckers*? Hey, times are hard. Anyway, it was his turn to take one for the team. He stepped up his game and even ventured into the romantic realm by assuring her that he really did love her. We both almost got sick over some of the actions he had to take, but soon he possessed two round-trip flight vouchers to anywhere U.S. Airways flew. Mission accomplished.

Munich was one of the destinations so we quickly made travel arrangements to fly into Germany and then make our way to Prague via ground transport. However, a few weeks before our scheduled departure, I found out that I was going to Iraq on some business. It screwed up the entire master plan. We had to quickly re-evaluate what we had time for. We got on the U.S. Airways website and looked at all of their destinations a bit closer to the States. We looked for the poorest place we could roll to. Hoy did some research and realized that Guatemala had one of the lowest GDP (gross domestic product) numbers per capita out of all the destinations U.S. Airways flew. Neither one of us knew what the hell GDP meant (and still don't), but Guatemala was ranked near the bottom of the list. Therefore, a quick trip down south would be in order. We would check out the scene and hunt for some nice Guatemalan girls to potentially replace our ungrateful American wives.

● ● ●

Our first trip was quite an experience. We made no travel arrangements other than our flights. When we got off the plane in Guatemala City, we just walked out of the airport with nothing but our backpacks. Actually, I had a backpack and Hoy had brought a small, shitty, roll-aboard bag. I'll never figure that one out but he learned his lesson later on while trying to drag that thing down cobblestone streets. The lesson is that when you're adventure traveling, carry one small backpack. Not a damn suitcase or the gigantic mountain-climbing pack you paid $500 dollars for.

We bypassed the row of taxis and just kept walking. We were in paradise. Guatemala turned out to be a beautiful country with beautiful weather. We both felt right at home there and soon found ourselves in the middle of Guatemala City. After a bit of scouting around we stopped in at a local hotel and secured a room. We freshened up and rolled out into our unknown and unexplored environment.

Guatemala City can be a bit shocking to the novice traveler. When you pass by an ATM machine at a bank and there's a security guard there holding a Mossberg 500 twelve-gauge shotgun, it's a bit intimidating. I will say that throughout all of our travel and adventure in the country, we never had any problems. However, we later learned that Guatemala City is the murder capital of the world. Who knew?

We acquired some street food from a vendor selling steaks. It cost next to nothing and was better than anything you can get in a steak house in America. After wandering around for about an hour just checking out the scene, we stumbled onto a nightclub that was kicking. As we approached the security guards at the front they gave us a puzzled look. To me, that's exactly what I'm looking for—the look which indicates they're not used to seeing gringos come to the club. After some quick greetings and a brief exchange in Spanish, they knew we were there to party. They laughed and patted us down for weapons. After a final *bienvenidos,* we strolled right into the middle of that disco like we owned the place. Everyone inside turned to see who the two gringos were. Fortunately for us, the music kept playing and soon we were drinking a couple of Gallo beers mingling with the crowd. Gallo (pronounced *guy-o*) is the best beer in Guatemala if you're wondering.

One phenomenon I've discovered is that my language skills increase the drunker I get. I do believe there is scientific data to back this up. The reason is that when you're sober you have many inhibitions. When you try to speak in a foreign language you hesitate because you're scared that you're not saying the right words. You end up thinking too much. But, when you're drunk you just don't give a shit. Whatever is in your head flows out of your mouth like water, whether it is correct or not.

After several Gallos I was ready to hablo some Español to the beautiful girls in the club. I wasn't worried about any turf battles from the local men because there was such a plethora of single ladies there. In addition, no one else seemed to be making any moves. Therefore, the Hoy Dog and I would lead the way.

Now, my pickup line has been the same for over twenty-five years. When I was young and just starting to hunt women, I put a lot of thought into what my initial volley with the ladies would be. As they say, you only get one chance to make a first impression. That first impression can mean the difference of whether or not you get a piece of ass that night. I did some research and evaluated all the joking, catchy, quirky, and romantic pickup lines. After an exhausting process, I settled on the perfect icebreaker which has allowed me to pull hundreds of bitches out of bars for one-night stands. I do take credit for its invention as it is a stroke of pure literary and spoken genius. I am its creator. I use the same line in any country and in any language and it always works. Pay close attention.

"Hey, how you doing? My name's Mark," I said in English to a group of six lovely ladies sitting at a table.

I had caught them off guard because once I locked onto them as potentials, I grabbed my Gallo and made a direct line for their table. I assumed they didn't speak English but I wanted them to know up front I was American from my accent. You see, too many European men travel in Central America and many of them are just pure assholes to women. I didn't want these hotties getting the wrong first impression. I wanted them to know up front that the Hoy Dog and I were from Hollywood and not Paris. As puzzled and surprised looks went around the table, one of the girls advised me that they *No hablo Ingles*. Those were the words I was waiting for. It was the green light to proceed with phase two of my sinister master plan.

"No problema. Hola chicas y como estan. Me llamo es Marcos. Mucho gusto," I said, basically repeating my pickup line in Spanish.

At that point they realized several things which I knew would be intriguing to them. Number one: I was a gringo and not Latino. Number two: I was an American gringo and not European. Number three: I was an American gringo who spoke Spanish. Number four: I wasn't scared to roll in on them strong even though it was six to one.

"Yo soy un gringo, pero tengo mucho amigos y amigas de Mexico. Estudio Español con mi libros y mi disco compactos para mi computadora," I said.

I told them I was a gringo but that I had many friends in Mexico. I said that I studied Spanish with my books and listened to CDs for my computer. That was all it took. We were in like Flynn. It went from being just the Hoy Dog and I to having an entourage of beautiful girls around us. I quickly hooked onto a blond-haired, blue-eyed girl with a nice, thick booty, who ended up being from Nicaragua. She was damn near a perfect ten. I was immediately in love with the girl. Her name was Jesse.

We ended up dancing the night away with this crew. The Hoy Dog kept grumbling about the language barrier and I frequently had to translate for him. I told him to quit worrying about spitting out game and to just keep dancing. The girls loved the fact that he and I were making John Travolta look like a beginner. We kept on grinding all five of them down on the dance floor without pause. They kept having to take breaks from the action but we were like machines and never stopped.

At some point in the night, we became so popular that a local guy started buying our drinks. The way he was dressed and carried himself made it obvious he had money. It would turn out that he was a mid-level cocaine smuggler who was well known to all. He was a nice guy and cool to hang out with, though. We decided it probably wasn't in our best interests to discuss business with him since I was a drug agent and he was a drug smuggler. It's really funny as hell when you stop and think about it for a minute. People with the exact opposite beliefs, mentality, goals, and objectives, coming together like brothers over music, beer, dancing, and bitches. As the night began to close down, he invited us to roll with him.

That would have been quite an adventure but we respectfully declined. We cited the ho's and the immediate fight to get in their panties as the conflict. As a fellow player, he understood. We all shook hands and he left the club with a couple of hotties in tow.

As we got ready to leave, I was more than excited because I was hooked up with Jesse's beautiful ass. However, I didn't have time to properly feel her out as to whether or not she was going to spend the night with me. We spent most of the night dancing rather than talking. Her body language was telling me yes but at that point we'd made no firm arrangements or plans for her to roll with me.

Meanwhile, a problem had presented itself. The Hoy Dog was studying one of the slim chicks in the group but the ringleader named Vivian had already staked a claim and called dibs on him. Unfortunately for the Hoy Dog, Vivian was a big girl. The Hoy Dog can't stand thick women and wasn't having any of that shit. He's a terrible wing man in the bars because he is so damn picky. It was a problem because Vivian was the one with the car. No one was going to cross her. That could mean being declared *persona non grata* by their only friend with transportation. After a quick discussion, Hoy and I decided to just break contact until we could evaluate the situation and see what our next move would be. We got their phone numbers and told them we would call them the next day. I kissed Jesse goodbye and we all parted ways.

About fifteen minutes later, while standing out on the sidewalk contemplating what to do next, a 1987 Hyundai Excel rounded the corner squealing tires. The entire right side of the car was crushed in as if a huge tree had fallen on it. We were both amazed at the fact it was still running and able to drive down the road. It pulled up in front of us and stopped. We quickly realized that it was packed out with our girls. Apparently, they weren't ready to give up yet.

The driver's door opened and all six chicas poured out of it as the passenger side wouldn't open. They convinced us to get in and let them drive us to our hotel. Now, the Hoy Dog is about six-foot-two. It took some effort for him to shimmy across the driver's seat and the stick shift and wedge himself into the front passenger's seat. A chick climbed onto his lap. Four girls and myself climbed into the back seat. I was sitting on someone's lap with Jesse on top of me. I was in heaven. The smell of cigarettes permeated the air and I thought I detected a hint of menthol. That's the smell which indicates someone is going to get laid in the immediate future. I've smelled it many times.

Vivian fired up the Hyundai and we headed toward the hotel. When we arrived, everyone got out so we could say our goodbyes. I asked Jesse point blank if she wanted to stay the night with me. *Fuck it.* I gave her the option. She looked at Vivian who gave her the nod and the go-ahead. Cool! I was in Guatemala for less than twelve hours and had already found a beautiful girl. Life couldn't have been better for me. I looked over and saw Vivian eyeing the Hoy Dog like he was a piece of meat dangling above a pack of wild Iraqi dogs. She said something to Jesse which I didn't understand. Jesse then slowly explained to me that Vivian wanted to stay with the Hoy Dog. I knew that was coming. I hate it when a nice girl gets her feelings hurt but Hoy was out of her league. She had set her sights a bit too high and didn't realize it.

Now, if I were the Hoy Dog I would have said, *Hell yeah I'll tag that big bitch. It's late and I'm lonely.* But, I knew him and his picky ways.

"Yo, dog. She wants to stay the night with you. She ain't no beauty queen, that's a given. But, it's better than going to bed with a hard dick. She's a sweet girl. What do you say?"

I already knew the answer.

"Hell no. You know I ain't down with no fat chick," he replied.

Picky motherfucker.

"Alright, but Jesse's staying with me. Your ass is gonna get pretty lonely listening to us go at it," I advised.

"I just can't do a fat girl," Hoy said quietly.

"That's cool. We'll find you a chick tomorrow."

I broke the bad news to Jesse who relayed it to Vivian. I felt sorry for that big girl but I can't speak for Hoy. Had it been me in his shoes, I would have loved to rock her out all night. As they say, you can lead a horse to water but you can't make him drink. In this case, as with many situations before, I had led the Hoy Dog to a horny fat girl but I couldn't make him sleep with her.

● ● ●

As the car pulled away, the three of us rolled into the hotel. I was on top of the world until the desk clerk abruptly stopped us. He was only about twenty-two years old and was skinny as a rail.

"What's the problem?" I asked.

"She cannot go up to your room," was the reply in good English.

"What the fuck you mean, she can't come up to our room?"

"Because she's not on the guest registration."

"Ok, then add her to the registration. How hard is that?" I snapped.

"I can't do that. She had to be registered when you paid for the room. It's the hotel's policy. Many hotels here in Guatemala City have the same policy," the clerk advised.

"Are you fucking kidding me? That's crazy."

I started to go off on the kid but he obviously wasn't the policy maker. He was only doing his job per the rule book. The problem was that the security guard was looking on so he wasn't about to bend any rules for a couple of gringos. I decided to attack the situation diplomatically and relaxed my tone.

"Look, my friend, I understand. If you could just let her stay tonight, we'll add her to the registration tomorrow when we pay for the next night. I'm sure the manager won't have anything bad to say about that. We'll tell him that you were such an accommodating host we changed our travel plans and decided to stay another day in this fine establishment," I advised.

That was the carrot. I followed with the stick.

"However, if you don't let her stay, I'm going to be an unhappy guest. I'm not going to stay another night and I'm going to explain to the manager face to face exactly why. Unfortunately, I'll have to bring you up by name. So, what do you say?"

"I'm sorry sir, but she cannot go up to your room."

This lousy, straight-laced, snot-nosed shit-head was standing between me and a beautiful Nicaraguan girl's naked ass. It was a nice, thick, ghetto booty of an ass I must add. We were wasting time. My heart was pounding and I was beginning to sweat over how beautiful Jesse was.

"Ok, I'll play your fucking game. Let me pay for my own room and you can list the both of us on the registration."

I'd raise hell about the situation the next morning but at the moment I wasn't really worried about having to pay another fifty bucks.

"I can't do that, either."

"What's the problem now?"

"You're already a registered guest."

The situation had turned from surreal to, *What the fuck is going on here*? But even in my drunken state, subliminally, I understood the policy. It was a fairly respectable-looking hotel and they obviously valued their image with the guests. The policy was designed to prevent exactly the situation we had presented to the poor desk clerk—the scenario where a couple of drunk gringos like ourselves come rolling in at three in the morning with a drunk hooker in tow, with intentions of rocking her out like porn stars while Mr. and Mrs. Kettle try to sleep next door. The hotel staff had seen this situation many times before. Under no circumstances was I taking the girl up to our room. By the way, Jesse wasn't a hooker. I just used that as the example.

"Look dog, I'm tired of arguing with this asshole. I gotta find a new hotel for the night. I'll meet you back here by noon tomorrow."

"Alright, dog. Be safe and have fun."

"You know I'm going to have fun. Fuck the safe part."

We knocked taters and with one last mean look at that skinny fucker behind the desk, Jesse and I rolled out of the hotel. Not sure which way to go, I took a left. It was a good call because in no time I found another hotel and was speaking with the male desk clerk.

"Hola mi amigo. Neccessito un cuarto para me y mi esposa para un noche," I said.

I told him I needed a room for me and my wife for one night. The kid smiled and almost broke into laughter. I knew I wasn't fooling anyone but just in case they wanted to play the policy game, I would argue to the end of time that Jesse was my old lady. While the clerk was completing the paperwork, I looked around the lobby and realized that all of the bell hops and the security guards had their eyes fixed squarely on my girl's ass. Now, most men would have probably gotten upset about the obviously overt gawking and staring. Not me. I just nodded my head and said, *Oh yeahhh.* Why have it any other way? If other men don't stare at your chick with lust in their eyes, it might tend to indicate you're with an ugly bitch. Personally, I like it when people stare at my girl. It reminds me of how lucky I am to be living my life as a king.

The clerk handed me the room key and it was off to the races. We got settled into the room and immediately went at it like savages. There was no time for a shower as too much time had already been wasted. Within seconds, my boots, her high-heels, and all of our clothes were shed. As the game progressed, Jesse uttered that buzz-killing word which brought the music to a screeching halt.

"Condom?"

"No tengo," I said.

"Es necessario. No quiero niños."

"No problemo," I said, trying to reassure her and avert a crisis.

"Es necessario," Jesse insisted, sticking to her guns.

Fuck. Where the hell am I going to get a condom at four in the morning?

I had to think quickly. I had just dropped fifty bucks for another hotel room which wasn't in line with our principles for traveling on the cheap. I looked around the room as if by some magical chance there were condoms next to the Gallo inside the mini-fridge. I suddenly had an epiphany and picked up the telephone. I got the desk clerk on the line and pleaded my case.

"Look, I've got a big problem here. I need some condoms. Can somebody run to the store and buy some for me? I'll be glad to pay them for the trip?" I explained.

"Sorry sir, but there's nothing open right now," was the response.

Damn it! Think man, think!

"Ok, ok. Can you ask around and see if any of the guys has one they can spare? Tell them I'll give them ten dollars for it."

"Ok, sir. Let me see what I can do. I'll call you back."

I hung up the phone and told Jesse not to worry. Her beautiful, tan skin and tight body was torture to look at. To keep the mood going, I grabbed some lotion from the bathroom and started giving her a royal rubdown. In a crunch-type situation like that, you can always buy time by flipping over to romantic mode. Women love that and it keeps them in the mood. You can maintain the momentum for an hour or more by dishing out a quality massage to a girl. Just make sure you do it energetically or you'll put her to sleep.

After about ten minutes I started to get concerned. Then, the phone rang. *Could it be? Is there really a Santa Claus?*

"Sir, Jorge is on the way up and he has what you asked for."

"Holy shit! Thank you very much, my friend. I owe you one."

With a knock at the door, I was standing in front of Jorge with a towel wrapped around myself trying to conceal a hard dick. Jorge couldn't keep from giggling like a school girl. He was only about twenty years old and probably hadn't knocked out his first piece of ass yet. He was clutching a rubber which looked as if he'd been carrying it in his wallet since he was fourteen. I didn't care. He had exactly what I needed at exactly the right moment. He had the supply and I definitely had the demand. I handed him a ten-dollar bill and he looked down at it while still giggling.

I snatched the condom out of his hand and said, "What's so damn funny? This is a serious situation, man. Get the hell out of here!"

I said it in a joking manner so he would have a good ending to the story for his co-workers. We both laughed. I closed the door and got back to the more pressing business at hand. There's no need for graphic details but I can assure you I had a much better night than the Hoy Dog. And if you're wondering, the answer is yes, you can re-use a condom if it's the only thing standing between you and another round. I don't recommend it, but it will work. This entire predicament was due to a complete lack of preparation on my part. From the snafu at the first hotel to the lack of condoms on hand, I had just been plain lazy.

At about 11:00 a.m., we took one final shower and got dressed. It was time to get on with the day and link back up with the Hoy Dog. As we strolled into the lobby, still wearing our club clothes from the night before and reeking of cigarette smoke, I realized that all eyes were on us. Smiles, snickers, and gossip kicked off in all directions. The funny thing was that a crew of ladies staffed the day shift, rather than the male-dominated crew on the night shift. Apparently, the story of my desperate quest for a condom had made the rounds to everyone in the hotel. I'm sure those ladies were saying, *That must be the gringo who paid ten dollars for Jorge's six-year-old rubber.* I was thinking, *Laugh all you want to bitches. I guarantee you Jesse had a better night than you did.* We rolled out of that lobby like rock stars. Early on, it seemed like going international was indeed the right call.

● ● ●

We met back up with Hoy and got some breakfast. As we contemplated our next move, Jesse got on the phone with Vivian. They suggested we let them take us to an old Spanish colonial town about an hour outside of Guatemala City, called Antigua. That's not to be confused with the island of Antigua. We discussed it briefly and decided it sounded like a great idea. What a way to start a trip. We had walked out of the airport with no lodging, no transportation, and didn't know a soul in the country. In less than twenty-four hours, we had established communications, hooked up with some bitches, had transportation, and were going on a free tour, guided by locals. Not to mention the fact that the body count was already at one, right out of the gate.

While most people try to pre-plan their travel down to a tee, I personally find that extremely boring. If you know exactly where you're going to stay and your sightseeing and touring is scripted, how is that exciting? Where's the adventure? The adventure is not knowing where the road will take you. Adventure is moving forward without rules. It's about taking chances.

Vivian picked us up in the crushed-in, lopsided, permanently tilted, piece-of-shit Hyundai. Now, I really shouldn't refer to that fine machine as a piece of shit. That little thing had taken a licking but was still driving us down the road. As we got underway and headed out of Guatemala City, I looked at the Hoy Dog and started laughing. He was sitting in the front passenger seat and because he was so tall, he had to lean hard left. The body language and positioning made it appear as if he was really into Vivian and was trying to get closer to her. It appeared as if he was hanging on to everything she was saying and trying to woo the chick. It appeared as if they were a couple.

However, it had nothing to do with that. He had to lean hard left because the car's crushed-in A-post and the door frame wouldn't allow him to sit up straight. The black trash bag and the duct tape over the window kept flapping back and forth and sounded like someone was beating on a drum. The plastic occasionally slapped Hoy on the right side of his face. Scenes like this cannot be bought no matter how much money you have. Being part of these scenarios always makes me feel sorry for the rich and privileged who can never imagine nor appreciate the hilarity of the moment.

After sucking on dark smoke and fumes being emitted from an armada of chicken buses, we finally got out of the traffic and started making good time. For reference, the chicken bus is how the locals get around in the country. Once a school in the U.S. auctions off their old school buses that aren't fit for operation, at some point down the line they make it to Central America. There, they become the equivalent of a Greyhound bus transporting everything from people to chickens up and down the road. As they were already mechanically wore out when they left the States, their emissions are terrible. When you get behind one you'll swear that it's powered by burning coal.

The drive to Antigua was filled with questions and answers as we tried to learn everything we could about Guatemala from the girls. By the time we pulled into town they were exhausted from our questioning. Antigua turned out to be a nice, quaint, little town with cobblestone streets. For me, it had an almost magical vibe to it. It reminded me of a place that could have been written about in a child's storybook.

We spent the day exploring and doing touristy-type things. That evening, I made Hoy sit in the lobby and entertain Vivian while I rocked Jesse out for about an hour. Later on, it was decided that Jesse would stay the night but Vivian had to go home and take care of her kids. After

Vivian left, we decided to saddle up and go hunt down a girl for Hoy. Here's where I really started to like Jesse. She told me she just wanted to stay in the room and watch some religious channel and for me and Hoy to go without her. She'd be waiting on me whenever we got back.

What? The girl just told me to go party with my friend and have a good time? There was no jealousy, attempts at control, or back talk involved. I didn't have to remind her or educate her on the principles of *Kingdom Rule*. She had already conformed to my way of life without any education on the situation.

"Cool, brother. She says she just wants to stay here and watch television. That will save me some funds by not having to buy her drinks all night. Looks like it's just the two dogs rolling out."

"Are you sure you trust that bitch to stay here by herself?"

"Bro, you know I don't trust no bitch. But what's she going to steal? Your clothes and that shitty bag of yours? My backpack with a pair of dirty drawers? I'll tell the clerk to keep an eye on her and call us if she tries to dip out."

On that trip, we had packed light. We hadn't brought so much as a camera because we knew we'd be in high-risk adventure mode. We ended up buying a disposable camera in Antigua but other than that, our only valuables were in our front pockets—a passport, a credit card, and an ATM card. That's the best way to travel. Don't take anything with you that you're worried about getting stolen while unattended at a cheap hotel or hostel. When you're constantly worried about a laptop, expensive camera, jewelry, etc., you can't focus on just relaxing and enjoying the environment. I love traveling like that. *What? You want to rob me? No need for violence.* Here's the cash out of my other front pocket and my backpack. This way, the only reason I'd have to fight someone is if they try to take my passport, credit card, or ATM card. If you just throw your bag at them and run, they're not going to come after you and get your passport. They'll be too busy seeing what goodies the bag contains. Tricks of the trade. While my travel now always generates material for my blog and therefore, pictures and video are a necessity, it's just not as relaxing as rolling with no valuables. Back to the topic at hand.

We rolled out of the little hotel and hit the streets. Before long, we had stumbled onto a packed-out club playing salsa music. As we took our first steps into the club, we both got sick to our stomachs. There were nothing but gringos and European chicks up in there. *What the fuck? Are we still in Guatemala? Where's all the Guatemalan girls?* We decided to give it a run and ended up trying to spit game (converse) to some white chicks. After getting snubbed a few times by girls who were far from being pretty, we stopped and asked ourselves exactly what the hell we were doing in that particular establishment.

"Fuck! What the fuck are we doing in here? We didn't come all the way down here to look at these nasty-ass white bitches. We came here to get away from these hogs!" Hoy exclaimed.

"I agree. Let's get the hell out of here," I said.

We roamed around but kept running into commercialized places packed out with gringos. Finally, we ended up off the beaten path at someone's house which doubled as a bar after hours. We found it by accident in the same way we've found a lot of cool spots. If we walk by a place and hear music, we knock on the door to see if we can come in. That's exactly what happened in this situation.

The home had a nice, walled-in courtyard out back where a bonfire was blazing. There was no neon and no expensive sound system. There were candles and a Guatemalan kid playing an acoustic guitar. Local chicks were in abundance. The rudimentary wooden bar was rickety as hell but had character. A bartender was mixing drinks and a fine-ass chick was serving bottles of Gallo out of a cooler. There was a cool breeze blowing which gave the night a bit of a chill. The moon was almost full and only added to the romance of the place. The scent of the smoke from the fire set the tone at an even more rustic level. We had found what we had been looking for all along.

Almost immediately, we hooked up with three girls who looked as if they were business types. They were locals, but they were upscale. We started chatting and entertaining them. They spoke English so Hoy was able to have a good time without worrying over the language barrier. They were respectable ladies with careers. I knew early on they probably weren't going home with either of us. They had jobs to get to the next morning. Still, it didn't matter. Getting laid is always important but this trip was about much more. The objective was to identify potential replacement wives. The girls were definite prospects we could continue to cultivate during our trip.

Hanging out at that little speakeasy was one of the best nights I've had while traveling—just a laid back atmosphere, a cool setting, and some beautiful Guatemalan girls.

The party eventually ended and we started to hike back to the hotel. As it was dark and we were obviously less than sober, we couldn't find the right street the hotel was on. I think we walked in circles for an hour until we finally found it. Upon opening the door to the room, there was Jesse in the same spot I left her. She was wide awake and still watching the religious channel. So far, she was presenting herself to me as a contender in the race to be my next queen. Could it be that easy to find the perfect wife? In my experience, if something is too good to be true, it usually is.

● ● ●

A couple of days passed by with the same nightly routine. We both kept striking out in the bars but at least I had Jesse to come home to. I was doing some serious planning about what to do with her. I finally decided I would take a chance and set her up with her own place and see how she did for a few months. The best way to know if a girl is on your team is to give her enough rope to hang herself with. Don't try to be controlling because you'll mask her true intentions and motivations. When we all went for breakfast, I decided to see how well she could follow some simple instructions.

"Girl, listen. I like you. I like you so much that I'm going to set you up in your own place and take care of you for a while. That way, there's no stress and we can see where things go between us."

Jesse was listening but I think she thought I was full of shit. I already knew she would and was prepared to make her a believer. I pulled out $200 dollars from my pocket and laid it down on the table. Her eyes perked up as that's a ton of money to a poor Nicaraguan girl. With the Hoy Dog looking on and sipping his coffee, I continued.

"This is what I want you to do today. I want you to take a taxi to Vivian's house and get your belongings. Pay her any money you owe her for rent and let her know you're leaving. Then, take a taxi and be back by tonight so we can go out to dinner. Tomorrow, we're going to go rent an apartment for you."

She acknowledged what I told her and I then repeated the instructions with one final, clear directive.

"Listen, I know Vivian is your friend. But unfortunately, Hoy isn't into her at all. He doesn't want to have to entertain her tonight. Therefore, under no circumstances should you bring Vivian back with you. That may cause some friction but you'll just have to explain it to her as nicely as you can."

She again acknowledged my instructions. I looked over at Hoy who had a look of relief on his face. I'm sure he was going to reiterate that part but I had taken care of it for him. We finished eating and I ushered Jesse to the taxi stand. Armed with $200 dollars in cash and tasked with a clear, simple mission, she kissed me goodbye and departed in the taxi. I thought about how sweet she looked.

"Yo dog, you think you should have trusted that bitch with a couple of Benjamins?" Hoy asked.

"Absolutely. If she fucks up on any part of that, it will be the best two hundred bucks I've ever spent. If she gets it right, she's my girl. If she gets it wrong, she just saved me a lot of money and bullshit later on. I just gave her the rope, now let's see if she hangs herself."

"Good point, but we'll see," said Hoy, not convinced.

"Ah, fuck it. Let's go drink some Gallos down at the market with the locals. I'm tired of running into gringos."

To be honest, I wasn't so sure either about whether or not Jesse would just run off with the money. I'd only known her for less than a week and I was certain she'd heard bullshit promises from gringos before. I'm a pretty charitable person and I knew that her poor family would benefit from the money if she decided to skip. The only thing I was concerned with at that point was getting an ice-cold Gallo.

We hiked toward the local fresh market but stumbled onto a little hole-in-the-wall bar a block down. The only customers in there were a couple of old Guatemalan men. Guatemalan folklore-type music was coming from the jukebox. There were no signs of any gringos so we decided it would be a nice, tame place to do some planning. We ordered a couple of Gallos and they arrived at our table promptly. I pulled out my trusty little journal that goes everywhere with me and started to jot down some notes.

"Dog, it looks like I may be hooked up already. As long as this bitch makes it back here tonight, I've got to go find her a crib tomorrow. We've got to find you a bitch, quick."

"Yeah, I just ain't having no luck. For starters, the damn language barrier is killing me. I can't spit no game to these bitches," said Hoy.

"I feel for you, man. My head's been spinning since we got here because I'm constantly trying to find the right words. I've got to kick it up a notch on studying my Spanish books. This is what we need to do today: Since we don't have Jesse in tow, let's concentrate on getting you a couple of phone numbers. No need for me to be hunting at this point. I'm working as your translator today. We ought to be able to come up with something," I said.

"Where we going to go in the middle of the day?" Hoy inquired.

"I don't know, but let's start at the market," I offered.

"Ok," agreed Hoy.

After finishing off a few beers we strolled through the market. While there were many beautiful girls there, most of the time they were busy working or with their families. Guatemalan girls are pretty shy and religious to begin with, so trying to talk to them in a crowded market didn't work out so well for us. After making a few rounds and talking to several chicks, we had no phone numbers and no potentials. We were beginning to believe that we just needed to go back to Guatemala City and kick it in the same club where I met Jesse.

"Hey bro, let's go get something to eat. I'm tired of getting nowhere. I want some American food. I want a cheeseburger. Let's hit Burger King," said Hoy.

"No problem, my man. It's about time for a break."

We strolled up to Burger King which was located near the town square. It's kind of comical when you think about all of the places in the world where you can go and get a Whopper or a Big Mac. We strolled up to the counter to place our order and realized that all of the beautiful chicks had been working at Burger King the whole time! Who knew? We both immediately started joking around with the girls as we waited for our food. We also took note of something you typically don't see at a Burger King in America—pride in your work. While most fast-food employees in America seem to hate their jobs and could care less about whether or not they get your order right, the Burger King employees in Guatemala are the exact opposite. They appreciate the fact they have a job in the first place and treat the customer as such. The place is clean and everyone looks and acts professional. Eat at a Burger King in another country and then immediately eat at one in America. The difference will make you sick at how lazy we Americans have become.

"That chick right there. That's the one," Hoy said, as he pointed to a beautiful young girl.

She was about twenty-one years old, with her hair put up in a bun. She was some type of manager because she had on a different uniform than the other employees. I watched her as she helped another girl wipe down tables and tidy the dining room. She looked in Hoy's direction which gave him the opportunity to smile and acknowledge her. She smiled and got somewhat embarrassed by the gesture. She quickly disappeared into the kitchen.

"Oh yeah, bro. It's on now," I said.

"Yeah, I think so. But I still don't know how to approach her. I can't fucking speak the language," said Hoy.

"No big deal. She's apparently the boss so this ain't exactly the place for her to be playing grab-ass, anyway. How about this idea. I'll write your name and number on a napkin and give it to that chick right there cleaning the tables. I'll tell her to deliver the napkin for you."

"Alright, do it. I'll watch and see where she goes."

With that, I scribbled down Hoy's name and number on a napkin and wrote a quick, *I think you're beautiful*, in Spanish. I got up and walked over to the chick scrubbing the tables. After a few minutes, I got the message across as to what I needed her to do. She was smiling and giggling the entire time. I turned and walked back to the table.

"What's she doing?" I asked.

"Bro, she disappeared into the kitchen the second you turned around," said Hoy.

"Ok, that's a good sign. She didn't waste any time or possibly lose the damn napkin," I said.

A few minutes later, Hoy's girl emerged from the kitchen, briefly smiled at him and held up the napkin. She then made a gesture with her hand indicating she would call him. Hoy nodded and the chick again disappeared. The stage was now set for him to move forward.

"God damn that was easy. That bitch is fine, too," I said.

"Yeah, I hope this works out. She's fucking hot," said Hoy.

We left Burger King, excited about what had just happened. Not only was it good for Hoy to hook up with the girl but it could potentially be good for me as well. We walked toward the town square to see if anything was going on. As we turned the corner the phone started ringing.

"Holy shit, that was quick!"

"Answer it dog. You gotta translate for me."

I answered the phone and sure enough, it was her. I found out that her name was Ariana and that she was single with no kids. Coincidentally, the next day she was off from work so she was free for the night. I told her we'd meet her at the town square around seven that evening. She was ok with it because she finished work at six. The Hoy Dog had a solid date.

"Bro, she's meeting us in the park at seven. She'll call when she gets close by. I told her that we'd take her to dinner and that my girl was coming, too. She sounds like a quality chick and is probably a keeper. I'd say it's one hundred percent that she shows up tonight."

"That's good news, dog. Damn good thing I had a craving for a cheeseburger," Hoy said laughingly.

● ● ●

Back at the hotel, we laid out our clothes for the evening's events and tried to relax a bit in case it was a long night. Hoy acquired an iron and begin pressing his jeans. Now, here's where he and I differ somewhat. I can be ready to hit the club in about five minutes. Taking a shower is included in that time frame. On the contrary, it takes Hoy about two hours to get ready to roll. That's not saying anything bad about either of us, just that we have different views on fashion and club preparedness. Hoy is very particular about his clothes, his hair, and manner of dress. He always looks stellar when we go out and routinely makes me look like a hobo. He's always tried to teach me a few things about fashion and how to dress but I'm just from too far back in the woods. A pair of jeans and a t-shirt is usually my attire if we're going dancing. If I want to get fancy, I've got a nice, long sleeve silk shirt. Add my signature white jacket into the mix and now I'm formal. But, when you spend a lot of time out on the dance floor, long sleeves just make you sweat. I like to be comfortable when I'm cutting a rug and breaking bitches down like shotguns.

"You heard from Jesse?" asked Hoy.

"Nope, not yet. She should be calling anytime."

"Hey, just make sure that bitch ain't bringing Vivian back over here. I don't want that bitch showing up and fucking things up with this new girl," Hoy reiterated.

"I hear you bro. You heard what I told her this morning. I think I made it pretty clear to her. All she had to do was go pack her suitcase, say her goodbyes, and get back in the taxi. If she can't pull that off, I gotta drop the bitch for failure to follow directions."

"Alright dog, just don't let that fat bitch show up here."

I sat there sipping on a Gallo and jotting down notes in my journal while Hoy ironed. In a way, I was hoping that Jesse came back. In a way, I was hoping she fucked something up. You see, I knew that Hoy's girl had to have a bunch of beautiful friends in and around Antigua. If I could hook up with one of them instead, it would be a better situation. Two friends dating two friends. It would help out with logistics on down the road. As I continued to scheme, my cell phone started to ring.

I answered the phone and found myself speaking with Jesse. She said she had packed some of her clothes and that she would have to go back and finish the next day. She was on her way to the hotel for the night. As she advised me of her progress, I detected a familiarity in the noise and hum of the car she was riding in. The music sounded eerily familiar as well.

"Wait a minute. Are you in the taxi?" I asked, reluctantly.

I knew what was coming. A blind man could have seen it coming.

"No, Vivian said she would bring me back to the hotel. We're in her car," Jesse said quietly.

"What? What did I tell you this morning?"

The tone of my voice suddenly caused Hoy to stop with his ironing and stare at me intensely.

"Yo bro, is she bringing that fat bitch back here? Please tell me she's not doing that. Please!" Hoy pleaded.

"Dog, you know that's exactly what's happening. Apparently, she has an issue with following simple directions. I'll handle this shit."

With that, I engaged in a brief conversation with Jesse. I was fair, yet firm and up front. I told her to turn the car around and go home. She could keep the money and use it to help her family. However, she had failed my test by disregarding some simple instructions that could have easily been adhered to. Because of her inability to follow instructions she was potentially screwing up our plans for the evening. On a larger scale, she had shown me that I wasn't her priority. Without going any further into the details of the conversation, it ended with me dropping Jesse like a hot potato. I had no other choice in the matter. If I couldn't trust her to do a few simple things, how could I trust her with an apartment and money? I wished her good luck and hung up the phone. Deep down, I felt sorry for her. I still do. But, I couldn't depend on her so she had to go.

"Well, that's the end of that bitch," I told Hoy.

"Damn dog, that quick? You're not going to let her come back tomorrow?" Hoy asked.

"Fuck no. If she's that damn stupid then I don't need her. I gotta stick to the principles," I said.

"That's cold, dog. But oh well. She should have listened," said Hoy.

"Yeah, but enough about her. Looks like I'm going to be a third wheel tonight on your date. I'll translate for a while and eat with you guys, but then I'll disappear and give ya'll some quality time together. How's that sound?" I asked.

"That'll work. If she doesn't speak any English, I may have you just stay the whole time," Hoy advised.

"Whatever you want to do, my friend. I'm at your disposal tonight."

In both Hoy's life and my life, things are subject to change drastically at a moment's notice. It's always been that way and probably always will. We adapt to change easily and look at it optimistically. Most people, naturally, fear change and the unknown. To us, it's just the way we do business. Less than eight hours earlier, I was planning on looking for an apartment with Jesse. Now, I was hoping that Ariana had some friends at the Burger King who wanted to meet King Marcos.

● ● ●

Hoy finally got himself ready and we headed out for the park. A few minutes later we had hooked up with Ariana. First of all, the Burger King uniform didn't do her any justice. She was standing before us in a pair of tight blue jeans which displayed a beautiful, firm ass. Titties were bursting out of her blouse. Her hair was long and flowed halfway down her back. She wasn't a bad pull for a Burger King chick. Who am I kidding? Ariana was fine.

We went to dinner as a trio and I acted as the translator. It was apparent she was into Hoy from the start. Early on, I had to be selfish and inquire about her having any friends. Specifically, friends that were bonita (pretty). She said she had a friend named Paola who would love to meet me. It was good news since I suddenly found myself single toward the end of the trip. Dinner ended up being a wonderful occasion at the quaint little restaurant we had picked out. It was one of the best dates I've ever been on as a third wheel.

The next day, true to her word, Ariana introduced me to Paola. She turned out to be a petite girl from a very poor family. She didn't have a job because she had to help out with her brothers and sisters. After a quick evaluation, I was digging her more than old thick-headed Jesse.

Since we only had a couple of days before our flight back to gringo land, we didn't have much time to get to know the girls. We decided to make our way back to Guatemala City the day before our departure so we wouldn't be rushed. Ariana somehow scored an extra day off and both girls rolled with us. When the time came, we all crammed in a taxi and headed for our hotel near the airport. After getting checked-in, we ventured to a commercial area filled with restaurants and bars. There were numerous restaurants which Hoy and I wanted to try out. But, after asking the girls where they wanted to go, the answer was T.G.I. Fridays. After we said ok to that request, you would have thought we'd just bought them both a new car. As Americans, sometimes we really take the simple things in life for granted. Eating at T.G.I. Fridays for most people would seem routine or even mundane. For these two chicks it was the trip of a lifetime. As we settled down at our table, they seemed to be surprised when the waitress handed them each a menu. They began to browse the pages and discuss things among themselves. They didn't know how to act when we told them to order anything they wanted off of the menu.

Now, as I've said before, Hoy and I are a couple of cheap bastards. But, there is something that will neutralize our frugal ways. That something is gratitude and appreciation—two subjects American women know nothing about. The sense of entitlement ingrained in American women will make anyone want to be cheap. Why would any man in his right mind want to reward that type of attitude? *What? You think I owe you something? Fuck you, bitch. You ain't getting a dime of my money and I damn sure ain't taking your fat ass out to dinner.* When you're with girls like Ariana and Paola who will forever be grateful for us taking them to T.G.I. Fridays for a hamburger, you actually want to share your wealth with them.

"Fuck it, dog. Let's show these girls a good time tonight. There's a casino next to that first hotel we stayed at. I bet they've never stepped foot in there, much less gambled a few bucks," I said.

"I'm down with it. I've never been around girls this damn appreciative. I don't even know what to think," Hoy replied.

We paid the bill and beat feet over to the casino. Those two girls must have felt like royalty when we strolled through the door and past the security guards. We showed them around and then explained how some of the games worked. I sat down at a roulette wheel with Paola and threw a few bucks down on a number. I promptly lost, as is the case with all of my attempts at casino gambling. After making sure that Paola understood the concept, I handed her a five-dollar bill to put down on a number. She took the five-dollar bill and stuffed it in my front pocket. When I asked her what she was doing, she told me she couldn't take a chance on losing that much of my money. She said she didn't want to cost me more money, especially since I had just taken her to a nice, expensive dinner. It was a shocking exchange of words.

I had dated a few Hispanic girls before in the States. None came across like Paola. The reason for this is because of Americanization. No matter how good a girl is, once she starts living in America she becomes Americanized. She starts getting tainted by *The Union* and Dr. Phil and is introduced to the concept of entitlement. Before you know it, she's no different than a fat, pasty, white chick.

Hoy had a similar conversation with Ariana. They just didn't want to spend our money. We had to insist that they play one time to experience the thrill and excitement of gambling. They both must have got the ultimate high when that roulette wheel started spinning. The high of putting five dollars on the line. When they both lost, we thought they were going to have heart attacks. They were so hyped up over what just happened it was comical.

Back at our hotel, it was time to get some sleep because of an early morning flight. The girls crawled into bed with us but with one major difference we weren't used to—they kept their clothes on. From a standpoint of getting laid, that was not a good sign. However, from the perspective of a wife-replacement-hunting trip, we chalked it up as a good thing. We had accomplished our mission by identifying two potentials to work on for the long-term plan of dismissing our American wives and breaking free from American women in general.

We woke up a few hours later and said our goodbyes. We told the girls to sleep as long as they wanted and gave them money for the taxi ride back to Antigua. They tried not to take it, saying they could just take the chicken bus for a lot less money. We insisted and gave them some travel funds. We left them in the room and headed downstairs.

As we tried to speak to the desk clerk, there was an error in communication. I just couldn't figure out what he was trying to tell me. I called the room to ask Paola to figure out what the problem was, via the telephone. She wasn't having it and two minutes later the girls were at our side ready to do battle. They hadn't even taken the time to put their shoes on and were standing there barefooted. Hoy and I just laughed. We only needed some help with translation but there they were—present and dedicated.

On the flight back to the U.S., we discussed our situations. We were definitely on the right path. Life was so much better with girls who had never heard the words *child support* and *alimony*. We would keep good communications with Ariana and Paola and plan for a second trip. We had plenty of time to scheme and strategically plan.

Meanwhile, it was time to get back to being slaves to the machine we call America.

CHAPTER 6

RIDING BAREBACK

Several months later, we began to plan for our next excursion down to Guatemala. Hoy had put some serious time in with Ariana and things were looking good for him. Between e-mails and sneaking calls to her on a cool phone he kept concealed in the trunk of his car, he had cultivated a pretty tight relationship with her. They were both looking forward to some face time. As for me, I hadn't had the opportunity to court Miss Paola as I would have liked. I was predisposed and without good communications in the beautiful country of Iraq. Regardless, I was looking forward to spending time with her and seeing if things might work out between us. If not, I was going to take my ass straight back to the local club in Guatemala City. That place was a smorgasbord of beautiful girls just begging for attention.

When I spoke to Hoy, he advised he had a friend who was interested in rolling with us. His name was Pablo. According to Hoy, Pablo was straight and would make a good addition to the *Dog Pound*. He was fluent in Spanish because his family was from Mexico and he grew up in El Paso. I told Hoy a third player would be a plus for security and logistics and that I thought it had been a good idea to invite him. Besides, if Hoy decided to true-love Ariana the entire trip, I would have someone to hang out with. We finalized the plans and agreed to meet up in the ATL (Atlanta) for the journey down south.

I got off the plane in Atlanta and beat feet over to the international terminal. Hoy and Pablo were already there waiting on me. After introductions, we hit the bar to prepare for the ride. For some reason these days, I have to drink a few before I get on an airplane. In my younger years I jumped out of them. Nowadays, they worry the shit out of me. I think it's because someone else is suddenly in total control of my destiny and not me. When I go out, I want it to be on my terms—not because the pilot was still drunk from the night before or the maintenance guy forgot to tighten a screw. After several grande-sized draft beers, I was ready to rumble. I like to get the Ron White attitude from drinking before flying. *Fuck it, take her down. Just make sure you hit something hard because I don't want to limp away from this bitch.*

● ● ●

The jaunt down was uneventful and soon we were at the rental car place. We had decided that on this trip we would acquire transportation in order to venture out of Antigua and see more of the country. In no time, we had secured a chariot and were heading out of town. Hoy and I collectively remembered the route and navigated while Pablo drove. Before too long we were pulling into Antigua.

Somehow during our search for accommodations we had stumbled onto a three-bedroom crib for rent at a good price. After some negotiating with the *owner* we had secured it for the week. I use the word *owner* lightly because I eventually figured out the girl's scam. As far as scams go, it was a pretty-damn-good one even though it still infuriates me. (She was a typical American chick who lived in Florida, by the way.) You see, when we discussed the method of payment, I told her that I would just put the deposit on my credit card and pay the balance via my credit card when we got there. She wasn't cool with that and wanted me to Western Union the deposit to a guy named Jose down in Antigua. We could pay the balance in cash upon arrival. At first, I just figured that like everywhere else in the world, cash is king. But after looking at the professionalism of her ad, I pondered why she wasn't set up to accept credit cards. She wasn't living in Guatemala. She lived in Florida. Therefore, why in the hell would she want me to give a thousand bucks in cash to the gardener? After a brief investigation later on, I understood why. And no, it wasn't because she was cheating the tax man. You see, this vixen was the chief financial officer of a pretty-good-sized charity based in the States. They were doing work down in Central America. Apparently, the woman had purchased a nice house in Antigua with the charity's funds and labeled it the Guatemalan headquarters. In reality, she was renting the thing out for a grand a week and putting the cash in her pocket. If anyone had legitimate business in Guatemala, she would just clear the calendar of tourists and nobody was the wiser. There's no telling how much money she's made off of that little *investment* in Antigua. *Shame on you, girl!*

The house turned out to be a small palace. It had walls that were about two stories in height. It had an old Spanish feel to it. In the living room, there was a nice fireplace which just added to the coziness of the space. Upstairs, the bedrooms were decorated in a rustic Spanish style theme. Outside, there was a small rooftop patio with a nice seating area. It turned out to be a really nice place which couldn't have been more romantic. Any girl we hooked and walked through the door was definitely going to want to stay for a while.

We decided to drive over to the market and pick up some groceries before we got to partying. As Pablo pulled the car into the lot, we all had to laugh for a moment. In Guatemala, security guards are cut from a different cloth. I would never call one of them a rent-a-cop because they're far from that. The reason? Well, it could be the fact that they're strapped with a 12-gauge, Mossberg 500 pump shotgun on a sling. They only have the pistol grip attached and not the stock because most Guatemalan men are short like me. Therefore, it's too long and too hard to shoot if it has a stock attached. No problem. Besides, a Mossberg 500 looks more menacing with just the pistol grip. Anyway, the old comandante in charge of the lot was actively directing traffic, blowing his whistle, and giving orders. As he would turn his body, that Mossberg would swing around like a Louisville Slugger. After we parked and got out, we thanked the old guy for his service. We first addressed him as *Comandante*, but we later changed his name to *Mi Grande General* (The Big General). He was quite the character and took his job seriously. You certainly didn't have to worry about your ride getting broken into while you shopped at this particular store. That lot was more secure than Fort Knox.

Inside the grocery store, we discovered a plethora of beautiful girls. Whether they were working there or just customers, they all looked good. It was hard to focus on shopping as we spent most of our time trying to get phone numbers. We stocked up on basic provisions and beer and headed back to the crib. Pablo immediately went to chopping up some avocados and ended up making the best damn guacamole you've ever tasted. I'm not exactly sure why it was so good. Obviously, all of the ingredients were fresh and not some shit that came out of a can. But, he had a recipe that's probably a family secret. I'll never forget the sight of his ass standing in the kitchen just working away. I had no idea that he possessed some serious cooking skills. Like a pig, I stuffed myself with chips and dip until I could eat no more. I could have lived off of his guacamole the entire trip.

• • •

For some reason, me and Pablo decided to take a quick walk to the local market while Hoy took a shower. On the way back we hollered at some girls on the street and ended up running some game on them. Now, most Guatemalan girls from the country are pretty shy as I've said before. These girls fit that mold but somehow we talked them into stopping by the crib for some of Pablo's cooking. When they stepped into the house through the courtyard, it was apparent they were in awe. Most people in poor countries believe that if you're from the United States you must be rich. While that's far from reality especially in our cases, there was no way to convince them of this after they saw the crib. We ushered them into the kitchen and threw some of Pablo's guacamole down their necks. A big girl named Elsa was immediately in love with Pablo and ravaged the last of the chips and dip. We moved to the living room, laughed and joked, and drank a few beers. They turned out to be good, respectable girls. *Damn.* It was obvious they weren't going to stick around and let us run a train on them. Oh well, it was a nice start to the trip, nonetheless. We were just getting warmed up.

When Hoy finally emerged from primping, he was dressed to kill.

"Yo dogs, ya'll ready to kick it?" he asked.

"Bro, I'm always ready to kick it. I thought you were going to call Ariana. She knows you were coming in today, right?" I replied.

"Fuck that. Tonight I'm gonna kick it and not worry about that bitch. I'll hit her up tomorrow during the day. Get ready and let's roll. Fuck it," Hoy countered.

"No problem. Give me ten minutes and I'll be ready to roll," I said.

"Yeah, I'll be ready in ten," said Pablo.

In no time at all, the three amigos were rolling out of the crib, en route to the center of town. We wanted to show Pablo the town center so that he could get his bearing on where we were. We discussed some contingency plans in case trouble should find us during the night. The first rally point would be the town center if we became separated and the backup would be the house. Once that was established, we headed over to the club that had been full of Europeans the previous trip. Nothing had changed. It was still full of Europeans. We had already been drinking and said, *Fuck it, let's party.* We rolled in strong and before too long we were dancing with some girls on the crowded floor. While I was having a good time, I seriously wanted to go back to the speakeasy we'd stumbled onto the first trip. We just couldn't remember where it was located. That haunted us the entire trip because we couldn't find it.

After a few hours of no solid prospects at *Club Europe*, we rolled out and ended up at what reminded me of an Irish bar. Since I was hammered by the time we made it there, it might not have had anything to do with the Irish. Either way, it was packed out with women. We ended up having a pretty good time but still had no girls in tow. As we departed the bar I decided to resort to drastic measures.

"Yo dogs, I need to speak to this fucking taxi driver over here. Give me just a minute," I said.

I walked over to the taxi stand and asked the gentlemen if they could take us to a whorehouse. Since I didn't exactly know how to say whorehouse in Spanish, I literally asked them to take me to the house of ladies. It was close enough and they understood the concept. A driver by the name of Felipe said he would take care of us. He would even stand by and bring us back to town. He gave me his card and told me he could be our driver anytime night nor day. Just call. Sounded like a solid guy and we needed someone to drive us while we were drinking, anyway.

"Hey, come on! We're outta here!" I yelled to the other two amigos.

"Where we going, dog?" Hoy asked.

"This dog's going to take us to a nice bar off the beaten path," I replied as seriously as I could.

Back then, Hoy wasn't as adventurous as he is today. He was quite the security-minded, straight-laced, don't-trust-anyone, everyone's-trying-to-kill-me type. I've always been the *Fuck it, let's go* type. I didn't know Pablo that well but he didn't object to the journey and hopped in the cab without any hesitation.

About twenty minutes later, we pulled up in front of a large house with a big, steel gate. It looked dark from the outside, as was the entire street. I have to admit that for a minute, I thought I had gotten us into a robbery. We all suddenly went on *Ponte Trucha* alert status to see what was about to transpire. When the door opened and a guy spoke to the taxi driver, we felt better—at least Pablo and I did because we spoke Spanish. Hoy was still on edge and on high alert. The man inside the house motioned for us to come in.

As we walked inside, we realized that what appeared to be a big house was nothing more than a bar. It just didn't look that way from the street. There were girls, couches, a dance floor, other patrons, music, etc.—just like a small nightclub. I knew right then Felipe had brought us to the right place. So did Pablo. Hoy was still looking for the escape route. We plopped down into some plush easy chairs and ordered three Gallos. Once the Gallos arrived and I had a drink, it was time to get the party started. I motioned for a couple of ladies to come over to our table. Fortunately for me, I grabbed the skinny one before anyone else could lay claim to her. The bigger chick who came with her plopped down right next to Pablo. Me and Pablo suddenly were hooked up. Hoy was still struggling with the strangeness and dirtiness of the joint and couldn't focus on the girls at all.

Pablo and I were in heaven. There's nothing like being drunk in a Guatemalan whorehouse, drinking cold Gallo beer, with a half-naked bitch sitting on your lap. The girls wanted us to go upstairs for some action but we both vetoed that idea. We broke the news to them that they were coming back to the palace with us. That was their only option. After some drunken negotiations, they agreed and decided to go get dressed. As they left to locate their clothes, we tried to reason with Hoy.

"Come on dog, just pick one out," I pleaded.

"Dog, you know me. I've got high standards and I just ain't seeing any bitches in here that I'm studying," Hoy said.

"Fuck studying any of these bitches! We're just going to take them back to the crib and party. Maybe do a little dancing. Grab you one or you'll regret it," I said.

"Nah. I'm cool, dog. I'm straight," Hoy insisted.

"Your choice my man but me and Pablo's gonna rock these bitches out all night long," I advised.

We just couldn't talk any sense into him. Once the girls got dressed and ready to go, we walked out of the establishment and hopped in the cab with Felipe. True to his word, he had waited on us the entire time. The four of us in the back seat were laughing and joking and playing grab-ass the whole trip back to the house. Poor old Hoy was all alone in the front seat. Upon arriving at the crib, the party immediately kicked off. Before ten minutes had passed, I was down to nothing but my underwear and so was my chick. We were putting on a pretty good dance exhibition for Pablo, his girl, and Hoy, until drama erupted.

● ● ●

For some reason, bitches always seem to fall in love with us. It's because we're gentlemen, we're crazy, we're good dancers, and we're fun. Whatever the cause, the effect is always the same. Some chick will end up getting too territorial or jealous over one of us and start showing her ass. It was no different on this occasion. Jealousy struck Pablo's girl when she caught him eyeballing my girl's naked ass. The next thing we knew, she had twirled around and was giving him hell about it. We were all thinking the same thing—*Damn girl, you're a hooker and he just met you. Lighten the fuck up.* Either way, it was the end of Pablo's socializing for the night. It was time for him to take the chick upstairs and make her regret her redneckness. A good pounding was in order for her due to that loud mouth she kept running.

I rolled my girl up to the room and we went at it. After a good session, I got up to take a piss. She jumped in the shower. When we met back up in the bed, I was ready for round two.

"Propina?" she asked.

The word propina in Spanish means tip. I understood very quickly that she was trying to charge by the nut and not by the night.

"I don't speak Spanish very well," I said in English.

She knew better because I had been spitting game to her all night. However, she understood my displeasure with the situation and my sudden inability to communicate. There was no way I was going to tip the girl for every session. She had lost her damn mind. It was time for her ass to go. I got dressed and ushered her back down the stairs. As soon as Pablo's girl emerged, they were both promptly bounced out the door and into the street. A quick point in the direction of the taxi stand was all the courtesy they received. Hey, we're nice guys. We'll be nice to you as long as you act like a lady. If you act like an ungrateful whore, that's the way your ass will get treated. Jealousy, loud mouths, and trying to gouge us for money will get you dismissed, quickly.

Pablo, Hoy, and I sat down in the living room and enjoyed the ambiance of the fire in the fireplace. I was starving and hoping Pablo would get proactive and make something to eat.

"That bitch of mine was fucking crazy," Pablo said.

"Yeah, what the fuck was her damn problem?" Hoy asked.

"She got upset and jealous because she said I was looking at Marcos' girl's ass. I told her to relax but she just kept on like she was my damn wife. I just met her. And, oh, by the way, she's a fucking whore."

"That bitch of mine tried to charge me by the nut. I told her I didn't speak Spanish. She got the hint that it was time to go," I added.

"I hammered that fucking bitch in her ass. I had to, dogs. I had to corn hole that bitch after she ran that big mouth down here," Pablo continued to elaborate. You had to have been there, but it was funny as hell listening to him tell the story.

"I hope you wrapped up, dog. Please tell me you had a condom."

"Dog, I had a condom—in my bag. Bro, I ain't gonna lie. I stuck it in that bitch raw," Pablo admitted.

After eyeballing one another suspiciously, laughter broke out. I was beginning to like Pablo more and more by the hour. He was definitely a good wing man to party with. But nailing a Guatemalan whore in the ass without a condom? Now that's classic.

"Man, I take a lot of risks in life, but riding bareback on a whore in the ass? That's crazy, dog," I said.

It may be apparent by this point that I'm not exactly a model advocate for safe sexual practices. Ok, who am I kidding? I've hardly ever used condoms. However, I wouldn't ride bareback in the same manner Pablo did. Anal sex isn't my style at all to begin with. But, if it presented itself to where I had to perform, I wouldn't do it without a condom. I don't want to have to clean shit off of my dick. My dick doesn't deserve that type of treatment. It's too valuable of a body part to allow it to get shit on. You know what I mean? Pablo's one crazy *motherfucker*. I've often pondered something, though. Pablo was scared of his American wife. He allowed her to rule over him with an iron fist. He was scared to leave her. He was scared to make changes in his life. He was scared of divorce. However, he was not afraid of sticking his unprotected cock in the asshole of a hooker. That defies logic if you evaluate the situation for a minute. If you're not afraid of riding bareback and potentially catching something you can't wash off, how can you be afraid of a fat, lazy, uneducated, American bitch? Somebody please explain that one to me.

● ● ●

The next day, Pablo and I met up on the rooftop patio. He had a cup of coffee and I drank a Gallo for breakfast. While we were sitting there discussing various philosophies, we commented on how beautiful the volcano was. We had a perfect view of it from our vantage point. It was something I hadn't paid any attention to at all on my first trip. It was absolutely mesmerizing. While we were gazing upon its beauty, it suddenly began to spew ash out into the sky. We weren't quite expecting that. We began to panic.

"Holy shit! What the hell do we do?" I yelled.

"I don't know, dog. Call Jose!" Pablo replied.

I quickly, nervously, and drunkenly dialed Jose's number. He answered calmly with an *Hola*.

"Jose! The fucking volcano is erupting, man! What the hell do we do?" I yelled into the handset.

"No se preocupe. Don't worry. It does that every day," Jose said while chuckling at my craziness.

"Are you sure? The volcano is spewing shit into the air. It looks like Pompeii's about to go down," I reiterated to make sure he understood the gravity of the situation.

"No problem. Relax. It always does that. If you want to take a tour up there I can arrange it," Jose advised.

Jose eventually got us calmed down to where we started to believe death was not imminent. Who the hell knew? I've never seen a damn volcano up close before—much less one that erupts. Have you? Sure, maybe if you live in Hawaii. I'm from the South. We don't have active volcanos and therefore I know shit about them and their behavior. I'm an expert in several things but volcanology isn't one of them.

With the crisis over, Hoy emerged from a session of kissing his American wife's ass on the telephone. He had no idea that we'd almost been wiped off the face of the earth due to Volcano Del Fuego. In reality, his telephone conversation had probably been more painful than the near-death experience Pablo and I temporarily endured.

We discussed our game plan for the day and decided to check out the real estate situation in Antigua. I made some calls and ended up talking to a guy named Quincy. He was from the States but had been in Guatemala for several years. He agreed to pick us up in an hour so we hustled to get ready. We spent the day hanging out with him and his partner looking at land and homes in the area. No matter where we travel to, we always spend a portion of our time researching the local economy and the property market. It turned out to be a productive day.

● ● ●

That night, we partied as usual and at some point ended up bringing some girls back to the crib whom we'd met while walking down the street. The chick I hooked up with turned out to be a holy roller. Everything she talked about had something to do with a guy named Jesus. I listened to her talk about not believing in sex before marriage, love, commitment, and several other topics that made me queasy. There was, as usual when it comes to religion, an air of hypocrisy in her game. You see, that bitch started drinking wine like she was a fat kid on a Big Gulp. Before I knew it she was drunk off her ass. I started to think for a slim minute my luck was beginning to change and that she may be spending the night. However, the wine just intensified her preaching. All three of us were wishing she would just shut the hell up.

Hoy kicked off the dance music with some heavy bass to try and drown out *Ms. Religious*. I immediately grabbed her up off the couch and we hit the dance floor. All of a sudden, she was transformed into *Baby* from *Dirty Dancing*. I was grinding on her like a cheese grater and she just kept throwing her thick ass back at me. I started laughing at the situation and how it was unfolding. Why do people try to portray themselves as someone they're really not? When men and women get together in this manner, the purpose is not to discuss theology. The purpose is to talk, laugh, drink, dance, and probably knock boots. This chick had just put us through hell for damn near an hour trying to establish her reputation as being a good girl. I think Margaret Thatcher said something like, *Being powerful is like being a lady. If you have to tell people you are, you aren't.*"

We were all enjoying a good time downstairs when my girl and I started getting a bit more serious. I motioned with a nod of my head that we should take the party to my room. She smiled and up we went. I threw her on the bed and clothes began to fly. She was a bit aggressive and started biting and scratching me like a hungry lion on a gazelle. My back was bleeding from the carnage. I was getting prepared to bring her my A-game in what I suspected would be a marathon session. If rough was what she was into, then rough was what she was going to get.

...She reminded me of a girlfriend *I had when I was in my early twenties. I want to note that back then, I was a bit more refined and timid than I am today. This particular chick was a wild child. She drank like a fish and would snort lines of cocaine like her nose was a vacuum cleaner. I knew she drank but didn't realize she was a coke-head until later on in the relationship. The point of the story is that she was an absolute freak in the sack. We would rock it out for hours at a time until we were physically exhausted. On occasions when we got tanked up on margaritas at the Mexican restaurant, she would get violent during sex. She would scream at me to hit her while I was pounding her from behind. Initially, I would spank her ass until it was red. As time progressed, that wasn't sufficient. She would beg, yell, and scream at me to hit her. At first I thought she was just drunk and being stupid. She wasn't. She wanted to endure some physical pain before and* *during orgasm. It got to the point that I was bashing her in the back of her head with my fists, slapping her face, choking her, and blistering her ass with a belt in order to satisfy her. Afterward, she would tell me what a rush it was to come while feeling that pain. Ok, I know. That's some freaky shit. I thought the same thing at the time. Maybe the tequila and cocaine cocktail was what brought it on. I don't know. Either way, my initial reluctance turned into a sense of duty to the girl. That's what she wanted and that's what I gave her. I promise you that after any one of our romps, had the police shown up, I would still be in jail today. Who's going to believe that she asked for that type of treatment? Actually, they would because I was smart enough to get some video to prove consent. Maybe one day I'll release it for your entertainment. Back to the Guatemalan chick...*

She got all the way down to her panties when the music came to a screeching halt. She suddenly sat up, looked into my eyes, and started preaching. As I sat there naked, she began to lay out our future. She began by telling me that the next day I would have to come to her home and meet her parents and take them all out to eat. We would then go to the church and talk with the priest. We would have to wait until after the wedding before we could have sex. It was very important to her that she was still pure for the wedding. *What the fuck is going on here? Am I in a bad dream? I must be. Now I finally understand what the Twilight Zone was all about.* A few minutes prior, I was getting bloodied up by this girl's fingernails digging into my flesh during the throws of passion. Now, I was thinking about floral arrangements and renting a tux. I looked off into space to escape reality. The crazy bitch then grabbed my face with both hands and physically held me in place to where I had to make eye contact with her. She started talking in sort of a low growl with anger reserved for the worst of enemies. I ain't going to lie. I got scared. She was an athletic girl with what I call BSA's (big strong arms). She was obviously as crazy as a shit-house rat. She had already got physical and was now holding me against my will. I started to cry out to Hoy and Pablo for assistance but they couldn't hear me because of the music bumping downstairs. No, I'd have to either negotiate or fight my way out of this one.

"You know, you're right. We shouldn't be doing this. It's just not right and I don't believe in it, either. Let's get dressed and go back downstairs before my friends think we're up here doing something bad," I said in a somber tone, as if I was at a funeral.

It made me absolutely sick to have to say that. It was one of the best undercover roles I've ever pulled off. It was still up in the air as to whether or not she believed that bullshit and was going to let go of my face. We sat there in silence with our eyes locked for what seemed like an eternity. Then, she kissed me as if nothing had happened. She let go and started to get dressed. I had my pants back on in no time and opened the bedroom door. I put my shirt on as I was scurrying down the stairs.

"Yo dogs, this bitch is fucking crazy! She's trying to kill me! You gotta help me get this bitch out of here," I advised.

"What's wrong?" Pablo asked.

"Tell you later. Just help me convince her that she's got to go."

With that, we were able to get the girl to exit our hacienda and head for home. I told her that I would call her the next day to arrange dinner with her parents. When I was certain she was traveling in the right direction, I locked and dead-bolted the door. I had narrowly escaped a bad situation. I was physically ok other than some minor flesh wounds. Psychologically? The chick scarred me forever. Why does shit like this happen to me? The answer? It's because I play the numbers. I always go with quantity rather than quality. I've probably gotten laid a hell of a lot more times than the average man. With the numbers, incidents like this are highly probable and unavoidable—at least in my life.

● ● ●

The next day we decided to take a road trip. We had heard from a few locals about a little beach town on the Pacific side of Guatemala called Monterrico. They said a lot of people go down there to party on the weekends. It sounded like a good time and would give us a broader perspective on what the country had to offer. We packed some overnight bags, a cooler full of Gallo, and headed out. The trip turned out to be picturesque. We passed right by the volcano which had scared the shit out of me and Pablo. It was beautiful. After traveling through a few rough-looking towns where we were the only gringos, we found ourselves driving parallel to the beach. There were quaint little homes and rudimentary shops along the way. I began to fall in love with the place all over again.

We pulled into Monterrico and found a parking spot near the beach. The little town was nothing more than a few blocks with restaurants and a handful of hotels. There were houses that sat right on the beach and I thought I saw a *For Sale* sign. I was thinking, *Cool, another house-hunting trip.* Not knowing anything about the place, our initial instinct was to check out the beach. We soon found ourselves sitting under an umbrella at a table in the sand. Immediately, two young girls arrived to be our waitresses. They were only about eleven years old. They had us served up with cold Gallos and some badass food in no time. The black, volcanic sand of the beach was nothing we'd ever seen before. I didn't even know a beach could have black-colored sand. Again, I'm not an expert in volcanos so I didn't know. It was a beautiful scene.

We found a cheap hotel and checked in. Now, when I say cheap, I mean cheap. The beds were old mattresses on a piece of plywood sitting on cinder blocks. The shower was a pipe coming out of the wall. It was fine for me and Pablo but Hoy wasn't too happy about the accommodations. He's just too picky. We secured our belongings and headed out to look at the homes for sale on the beach. After a few hours of real estate research it was time to party. We ended up hitting a night club situated right on the sand. After many prospects, we all three struck out and went back to the room without any female company.

The next morning, Hoy realized he was about to take some heat from his girl, Ariana. She knew he was in the country and I'm sure was perplexed as to why he hadn't made her his priority. He hadn't even stopped by to say hello to her yet. I think Hoy began to suspect he was screwing up his best option. He needed to get back to Antigua to try and salvage the relationship. As with all three of us, we always put the bro's before the ho's and it ends up causing problems with the bitches. Ah hell, we'd already had a good time, anyway. Hoy needed to dedicate the rest of his time to Ariana. Pablo pointed the car in the direction from which we came and off we went.

• • •

When we got back to town, Hoy made arrangements with Ariana to meet at her home later that evening. He asked for us to be ready in case he needed some backup. We told him not to worry and that we'd be standing by to help with anything he needed. Hoy finally got himself looking presentable and had me call the cab for him. I dialed up old Felipe and in twenty minutes he was honking the horn out front. Hoy and Felipe soon disappeared around the corner, headed to Ariana's house.

Pablo and I chilled out in front of the fireplace, talked, and sipped on some Gallos. About a half-hour later, my phone rang. It was Hoy. He sounded frantic.

"Yo dog, I'm inbound to the house with a carload of people. I need some help, quick!"

"What's the deal, bro?" I asked.

"Dude, I'll explain later but I'm inbound with Ariana, her mom, her sister, and her two brothers. I've got to feed them dinner. Can you call and get some pizzas on the way? They like pizza," Hoy advised.

"Yeah, bro. No problem. We'll have the crib ready to go. We've got a fire going and drinks on ice. Bring 'em on. I got one question, though. What the fuck does her sister look like?" I asked.

"Dude, she's fine. But ya'll gotta help me. I'm overwhelmed here. I thought I was just picking up Ariana. That ain't the case," said Hoy.

"We got your back, brother. Come on and we'll entertain them. Pablo and I will flip a coin to see who gets the mother and who gets the sister. I don't care either way," I advised.

With that, Pablo and I tightened up the palace and got ready to entertain the family. It wasn't a big deal because we were always ready to receive guests. We never knew when we'd pull some ho's back to the crib. All I had to do was freshen up my cologne and cut up a few limes. Pablo and I laughed at the situation Hoy suddenly found himself in. It sounded like Ariana was punishing his ass for blowing her off the first half of his trip. When the crew arrived, Pablo and I became outstanding hosts.

Introductions and greetings were exchanged. I think Hoy got some points with the mom right off the bat because Pablo and I spoke Spanish. Everyone grabbed a seat in the living room and drinks were soon served. The younger sister turned out to be a fine little bitch but old mom was on my radar as well. She was a tight forty-year-old who looked damn good, especially since she had popped out four kids. It was a good thing because Pablo and I didn't have to flip a coin to see who got the sister. Either one of us was cool with either one of them. No competition.

The pizza man arrived and everyone chowed down. It turned out to be a nice, low-key evening. There was good conversation and a little bit of dancing. I ended up teaching the mom how to two-step. I had a great time as did everyone else. The two brothers just sat their droopy asses on the couch and picked their noses. Fine with me. They weren't benefitting any of us anyway. The night concluded with me calling Felipe and having him come pick everyone up. Hoy and crew rolled out while Pablo and I picked up the place. An hour later, Hoy returned via the Felipe express. He looked exhausted and plopped down on the couch.

"You ok, bro?" I asked.

"Dog, they ambushed me the minute I walked in the door. I thought I was picking her up and taking her out to dinner. The first thing she said was, *Ok, we're ready to go.* I'm thinking, *What the fuck do you mean we?*

They poured out of the house like a pack of wolves. They knew they were getting a free meal on old Hoy. I wasn't ready for that shit."

"Fuck it, dog. We had a good time and the night's still early. Don't sweat it. You're only out the bill for a couple of pizzas. No big deal. You ready to hit the club?" asked Pablo.

"Yeah, I'm ready but I think things are fucked up because I just now hooked up with her. She's pissed because I've been down here for four days and didn't go see her," replied Hoy.

"She should be dog. What did you think she was going to say? She knows we've been partying like rock stars," I said blatantly.

"Damn. I've put a lot of time in with that girl over the past few months. She's a good girl, too."

"Maybe you can patch things up tomorrow. Let's kick it tonight," Pablo said, trying to reassure him.

● ● ●

With that, the three amigos rolled out and into the night. We danced, drank, chased women, and tore up the town in typical fashion. The next day, Hoy found out that his premonition was correct. Ariana wanted nothing to do with him. She was a girl of principles and her principles were firm. He snubbed her for his friends and for the sake of partying. Therefore, she clipped him for a couple of pizzas and some drinks for her family and then dropped him. He was back to square one like the rest of us. It wasn't until later that we determined one slight, minor, rookie fuck up on my part. Actually, I can't take all the blame because no one else thought about it either.

You see, we had allowed a major blunder in operational security to occur. This is a lesson learned if you are running multiple ho's in any given situation. When traveling, our typical modus operandi is to establish communications by purchasing a local cell phone and then lock down reliable transportation. I had found us a reliable set of wheels with my man Felipe. That *motherfucker* was on time, every time. He charged us a fair price and was a safe driver. He always had plenty of gas in the car to take us anywhere we wanted to go. Therefore, he stayed on speed dial. There was only one major problem that we were unaware of. He happened to be Ariana's cousin. *Fuck!* Imagine his surprise when Hoy directed him to Ariana's house. All this after he had taken us to several nightclubs and a whorehouse. Needless to say, he had informed Ariana of all our exploits and destinations. She knew everything the minute he dropped Hoy back off at the house that night. The lesson? Don't use the same *fucking* cab driver to take you to your girl's house that you used to take you to a whorehouse. Slight risk of trouble. Learn from our mistakes.

We all left Guatemala with good memories and stories to tell. It would end up being our last ho-hunting trip down there. There was a new adventure that was about to rear its ugly head and change all of our lives forever. That adventure would be the Kingdom of Thailand.

CHAPTER 7

THE TRIP OF
THREE DIVORCES

Let's discuss the trip which ultimately resulted in Hoy, Pablo, and me ending up in divorce court. While it was no laughing matter at the time, we can at least share it with you, the reader, for your entertainment and evaluation. It is quite a long story so bear with me. As I mentioned before, I was in Iraq on some business with the U.S. military. Being in that environment, you look forward to your vacation time. There was a lot of discussion between Hoy and I about where our next destination would be. At the time, I had befriended a beautiful girl on the Internet who was from Tegucigalpa, Honduras. She and I were communicating on a fairly regular basis, strictly in Spanish. I was becoming even more fluent in writing Spanish due to all of the e-mailing and her correcting my grammar.

My vote was for Honduras. I had e-mailed a real estate agent about looking at some beach-front property that was up for sale on the cheap and was looking forward to checking out the market there. As far as I was concerned, we were heading back to Central America. Hoy wasn't exactly sold on the location after striking out with Ariana. He kept bringing up other options. Prague came back into play. We could resurrect our trip to the Czech Republic. As time passed, coincidentally, Hoy found out that he had to take a business trip to Eastern Europe. He suggested it would be easy for him to launder a couple of weeks on the back end of his legitimate business trip in order to fool his old lady. Since he would be on the same side of the world as me, we should take advantage of the situation and go back to Central America later.

At some point during our e-mailing and limited phone contact, the subject of Bangkok came up. I knew nothing about Thailand and neither did he. We'd heard the wild stories about Bangkok but really didn't believe them. We both loved Asian chicks so it was a subject that we both couldn't seem to let go of. My Honduran girl was holding me back because I really wanted to go see her. Then, something happened that would change my life forever.

● ● ●

An incident occurred on my forward operating base (FOB) in Iraq. The incident itself is irrelevant to the story, but sad nonetheless. A poor kid from Sri Lanka had hung himself because he wanted to go home but couldn't. That's a long story which I will save for another forum. Anyway, I had to go help work the case and ended up meeting a guy named Erik. He was a civilian contractor of sorts and had an office on the FOB. When I sat down in front of his desk so we could get together on some paperwork, I noticed he had a picture of himself and a beautiful Thai girl sitting on an elephant. He elaborated that he had taken a trip to Thailand on his last vacation and absolutely loved it. He told me that if I went, I wouldn't regret it. I kept asking him if his girl on the elephant could hook me up with one of her friends. He just laughed and said it wasn't necessary. When I kept pressuring him about it, he uttered four infamous words that have changed many lives.

"Just go to Pattaya," he said calmly.

"Yeah bro, but it would be nice if your girl could hook me up with one of her friends, first."

"Just go to Pattaya," he said again, while shaking his head.

I couldn't sway him. He wouldn't budge. He wouldn't provide any further information. All he would say was, *Just go to Pattaya*. Now, Erik was a black gentleman, very refined, and somewhat elegant in his mannerisms. The guy had more class than I've ever thought about having. He wore circle-rimmed glasses which added to your perception of his educational background. To put it in simple terms, for some reason I just trusted the guy. I can't explain it. Maybe he has that effect on everyone. He was cool, calm, collective, and had an air of confidence about him. Regardless, those words of advice had already stuck. I immediately booked a flight to Bangkok and got Hoy on the phone.

"Dog, I just e-mailed you my flight information. We're going to Thailand. There's your warning order. But, we're not going to Bangkok. We're going to a town called Pattaya," I said.

"Where the hell is that? What's wrong with Bangkok?" Hoy asked.

"I don't know, dog. But I met this cat named Erik and he told me to go to Pattaya. I can't explain it to you right now but I've got to go with his advice. If it's fucked up, it's on me. I'll take full responsibility for the adventure," I said.

"Ok, bro. I hope you're right," Hoy replied.

● ● ●

Soon after that conversation, Hoy had worked out his scheme of maneuver to get to Thailand. Once Pablo was notified of the operation he quickly booked his flight as well. But immediately, there was a huge operational security problem with this adventure. You see, Hoy's wife and Pablo's wife had met one another on a previous occasion because Hoy and Pablo worked for the same company. While the wives weren't friends, they knew all three of us had taken a previous trip together. My wife was friends with Hoy's wife but they would only talk once or twice every couple of months. Therefore, there was a loose network between the three of them. Pablo's wife didn't know me as we had never met. Hoy's wife knew me very well and was well-versed in my evil ways. She looked upon me as a corrupter and bad influence on her husband. I'd held that title for around ten years because Hoy and I had been friends before they even met.

The problem was that Hoy and Pablo's company had planned a family barbecue and their wives were looking forward to attending the event. Pablo was going to utilize the cover story that he was deep-sea fishing with me down in Central America. Hoy was using the cover story that he was working in Eastern Europe for an entire month when actually he was only working there for two weeks. I was going to have my wife come to Thailand to spend a week with me and then clandestinely party with the boys for a week on the back end. All of our stories would stick, but only if their wives didn't run into one another at the damn barbecue. If they got to talking they would quickly put two and two together, call my old lady, and we'd all get busted out. The fucking barbecue was the crutch! But, suggesting that two American bitches not attend a barbecue with free food? We all know that can't be done. Food and American bitches go together like, well, food and American bitches. American women aren't the fattest chicks in the world for nothing. It was finally decided that only Hoy's wife, Dixie, needed to be derailed to accomplish the task at hand.

Now, Hoy could have told his wife the barbecue was cancelled himself but it would be more credible if the host called her direct. She would be less adept at asking questions if it came straight from the source. Hoy and Pablo cornered the host of the barbecue at work and had a man-to-man talk with the guy.

"Hey look, dog, we've got to ask a favor of you," Hoy said.

"Sure, guys. What's up?" the gentleman asked.

"We need you to call Hoy's wife and tell her the barbecue has been cancelled for some reason," Pablo advised.

The gentleman just stood there and looked puzzled. I'm sure the wheels in his mind were turning, just trying to figure out what the hell this little meeting was all about.

"Listen, we know it don't make any sense but we need you to do this for us. We're trying to take a trip on the sly and we don't need our bitches talking to one another at the barbecue. Shit could get fucked up if they end up face to face," Pablo advised.

After working on the guy (who we'll call Albert) and hammering him for about an hour, he finally gave in and said he'd do it. The problem was that Albert was a devout family man and a Christian. He was a nice guy, respected women, and…wait a minute. *Who the fuck am I kidding?* The guy was a spineless, *pussy-whipped jackass* who was his wife's puppet. He despised Hoy because he considered him to be a womanizer. Albert knew about all the girls within the company who Hoy had slept with. He also didn't like Hoy because he thought that Hoy was the reason for Pablo's infidelities and bad behavior.

However, it was one small *fucking* request. It would have amounted to him grabbing a set of balls and making one simple phone call to Hoy's wife. A few weeks later, this asshole's weakness would manifest itself.

● ● ●

I rolled into Bangkok and spent a week with my American wife doing the touristy thing. We looked at temples, rode elephants, held a tiger by the tail, and got nice massages. We stayed at a five-star hotel, only because they had a huge promotion going on and I got it on the cheap. We went to the floating market, the night markets, and explored the city. When I kissed her goodbye and sent her on her way back to America, I found myself outside the airport looking for a taxi.

I was on the level of departures but the taxis were on the ground level. I was about to hit the escalator when I was approached by a young Thai man who was wearing a newspaper boy hat (you know, like Fred Sanford used to wear).

"Taxi?" he asked.

He was dressed in a pair of jeans and a collared shirt. While most people shy away from these types of entrepreneurs, I find them motivating. I asked him where his car was and he pointed to the curb. He said we had to hurry. The reason we had to hurry was that he wasn't supposed to park there and he didn't have the necessary government permits to be a taxi driver. Again, most would find that a negative thing and a risk. I look at it as if he's just saying, *Fuck the government and their taxes,* and keeping all of his money to himself. I loved that guy.

He wrestled my bag into the trunk of his green Toyota four-door that had dark, tinted windows. I jumped in the front passenger seat and off we went. A quick stop at 7-11 and I was working on downing a six-pack of Singha beer while the stereo was thumping. We were hauling ass south, headed toward the City of Pattaya at around a hundred miles per hour. The guy, named Tui, would end up being my personal driver for years to come. In no time at all we were pulling into the city I would ultimately end up calling home. I put Tui on the phone with the manager of the house we had rented and he received the final directions.

We pulled into a gated community that was obviously upscale. A couple of turns and we stopped in front of a walled-in home. The door opened and I was met by an older American guy named Ed. He welcomed me to the villa while Tui and the manager named Sunet started grabbing my bags. I walked through the door of the place and immediately fell in love. It was like walking into a tropical garden with two beautiful swimming pools in the middle. To the left was the main house which contained two suites upstairs. To the right were two suites which were ground level, adjacent to the pools. A stack-stone water wall served as a huge backdrop for an outdoor couch that looked comfortable as hell. I was absolutely speechless. I had never been inside a home so beautiful. Ed had definitely created paradise on earth. I didn't even know what to say.

After a quick tour of the villa, I chose one of the suites next to the pool on the ground level. Since I was the first one there I didn't feel a bit guilty about cherry-picking the room. Ed introduced me to the maid and the pool boy. He suggested we take a walk and a quick tour of the city so he could acclimate me to my surroundings. That's exactly what we did. After a couple of hours, Ed had educated me on the pros and cons of sin city. You see, Pattaya was a small fishing village until the Vietnam War kicked off. Due to the fact that American soldiers were being sent on rest and relaxation in Thailand, a huge sex industry was born. Yes, my fellow Americans, we are responsible for sex tourism hot spots the world over, whether you want to admit it or not. The City of Pattaya, Thailand was born a whore due to us gringos. Ed explained that since the Vietnam War, beautiful Thai girls from the countryside had been flocking to the city to sleep with foreign tourists. For about $30 dollars, a girl would go home with you for the night. *Are you fucking kidding me?* I thought he had lost his damn mind when he told me that. Besides, I hadn't traveled to Thailand to pay hookers. I was there to chase and woo them bitches with my charm. Ed explained that it didn't matter with the bar girls. It didn't matter how much game you had. The only thing that mattered was the $30 dollars in your pocket. You could trade that for a night of sexual escapades with no questions asked.

Ok, whatever. We had our own game plan which didn't include having to pay a bunch of money to get laid.

• • •

We had already been conversing with some beautiful Thai chicks on a singles website we had come across. Hoy had e-mailed me a spreadsheet of about thirty-five girls who were waiting to meet us. After Ed left me alone in the villa, I immediately shed my clothes and hit the pool with a cold beer in hand. I enjoyed my solidarity for about an hour and just looked up at the sky in deep thought. I finally snapped out of my trance and got out of the pool. I opened up my laptop and scanned the spreadsheet Hoy had prepared. It was chock full of names, phone numbers, e-mail addresses, height, weight, beauty rating, etc. I decided to start dialing and see where it took me. The first girl I called was named Annie. When I explained to her that I was Hoy's friend, she could hardly contain her excitement. She told me she was busy working but would be free later on. However, she had a friend named Kate who had the day off. She told me to talk with Kate and handed her the phone. I spoke to the girl and discovered she was at the mall doing some shopping. She said she would be available to meet me later on in the afternoon.

Fuck that. The king is more important than a shopping trip.

"Listen, I'm going to have my driver call you in about five minutes. Just tell him where you are and we're coming to pick you up. You're going to spend the day with Marcos over here in my pool," I told the girl.

"But I go shopping now," she responded.

"No, you *were* shopping. Now, you're waiting on Marcos and his driver to come pick you up."

With that, I hung up the phone and called Sunet.

"Yo dog, I need you to call this chick and find out where she's at. Come get me so we can go pick her up," I told him.

"Kop," was the only thing he said in response, which basically means yes or ok or cool, in that context.

A few minutes later, Sunet was honking the horn. I jumped in and we rolled toward the mall.

"Listen man, here's what I want you to do. I'm going to sit in the back and duck down low. When you drive by where she's standing, I'm going to take a gander. If that bitch is dog-ugly, I want you to hit the gas and roll out. If she's beautiful, hit the brakes and I'll grab her. Cool?"

"Kop," he said.

We drove over toward the mall and approached the corner where she said she would be waiting. Sunet slowed down in order for me to pick her out of the crowd. Once I did, I couldn't believe my eyes. Standing before me was a twenty-one-year-old chick who was an absolute perfect ten. She had to be one of the most beautiful girls I'd ever seen.

"You want me to go?" asked Sunet.

"Stop! Stop! Stop!" I yelled and almost ripped the door handle off trying to get out of the back seat.

Sunet eventually got the car pulled over and unlocked the doors so I could get out. I composed myself and tried to contain my excitement. I got ready to spit some game like I'd never had to spit before. Now, I've been with some absolutely stunning American bitches during my travels but none come close to Kate. I was ready to bring my A-game to the table on this little opportunity. Luckily, I was half-drunk from hanging out solo in the pool so my creative side was in play.

I strutted up to her and introduced myself. She offered her hand for me to shake but instead, I immediately dropped down on one knee and kissed it, ever so gently. She laughed. *Mission motherfuckin' accomplished.* I knew right then we were going to hit it off and have a good time. My friends, never underestimate the power of laughter when it comes to trying to get into a girl's panties. It has worked for me the majority of the time. Hey, I'm just an average-looking guy who's only five-foot-five-inches tall on a good day. I've always had to rely on my wit rather than my looks to get girls to jump in the sack with me. Now, once I do get them there my sexual prowess ensures they keep coming back.

Kate and I hopped in the back seat and Sunet drove us to the villa. When we walked in, Kate was just as mesmerized as I had been. I gave her a tour of the place and then we settled in the kitchen. I mixed up a rum and Coke for her and we sat down on the sofa. The water wall helped set the tone from the get-go. I cranked up Kid Rock on the box and we began to chill. After a couple of drinks we found ourselves in the swimming pool. For some reason, she had a bikini with her. I can't remember if she had bought it while shopping earlier or if she just happened to have one in her purse. Regardless, I was staring at the sexiest and most toned body I'd seen in a long time. Her gingerbread skin was killing me. It was time to get the party started.

"You like Jack Daniel's?" I asked.

"I never try before," she said.

"No problem. Let me mix us up some Jack and Coke. You'll love it," I insisted.

...Allow me to say a few words about Jack Daniel's whiskey. And no, they're not paying me anything to say this, either. If you really need to get a party started quick, Jack Daniel's is the answer. If a situation is stalling out and people are starting to get bored, Jack Daniel's is the cure. If a party needs creativity, just resort to Jack Daniel's. It's just like pushing a reset button. Why? I don't know the science behind it but it works every time. It has certain properties which make a person not have a care in the world. Yeah, you can argue that alcohol in general does that, but it's just not the same. I would venture to say that more redneck children have been conceived due to the effects of Jack Daniel's than from any other cause. Jack beats out love and family planning as the cause of children being created within this demographic of folks. Hey, I'm a redneck so I can attest to this.

Two Jack and Cokes later, we were going at it like rabbits in my bedroom with the door wide open to the courtyard. Between the earth-shattering sex, the music, the view, and the sound of falling water, it couldn't have been a more perfect afternoon. We ended up rocking it out for about three hours. I wasn't about to let her get the best of me and had to put a little extra on her at the end to establish who was in charge. We showered and dragged ourselves to the couch where romance kicked back in. I blamed her for taking advantage of me in my drunken state. She laughed and blamed me for serving her Jack Daniel's whiskey. We chilled out together like we'd been in love for years. It was an afternoon I will never forget.

She suggested we roll to her crib so she could pack some clothes for the night. She wanted to stay with me but she had to get up and be at work at 7:00 a.m. the next day. I was all about her spending the night. We grabbed a motorbike taxi and headed over to her pad. As we walked in, she introduced me to her two roommates. They were beautiful girls as well, but only about 9.0's. It's kind of funny how I say they were *only* about 9.0's. In the States, you have to struggle to find a 9.0 who will give you the time of day.

I told her my buddy Pablo would be at the villa in a matter of hours and suggested we invite her roommates to come over for a while. They didn't have to be persuaded and immediately saddled up. An hour later, we were back at the villa. Only, at that point, I had *three* beautiful chicks I was kicking it with.

At around 9:00 p.m., Pablo's taxi pulled up out front. After giving his ass a big hug I began the introductions. He didn't know what to think. I helped him get settled in and then poured him a drink. Kate's roommates advised they needed to get back home because they too, had to get up and go to work. After they departed I told Kate we needed to go find Pablo a woman.

"No problem. We go Walking Street and find him lady," she said confidently with a smile.

● ● ●

We took a taxi to Walking Street and were immediately overwhelmed by what we saw. There were thousands of people among the dozens of beer bars and go-go's. Beautiful women were everywhere. They were scantily clad. Kate told Pablo to pick one out. Pablo and I just laughed until we realized she was serious. He eventually said hello to a girl named Apple, who stopped in her tracks and locked in on him. After two or three sentences from Kate, Apple agreed to roll back to the villa with us. I'm sure Kate basically said, *Listen, these motherfuckers are staying at a badass crib and they're nice guys. You're stupid if you don't come with us.*

With Apple in tow, we took the party back to the villa. Pablo was true-loving Apple while I was true-loving Kate. The next morning, Kate got up and put on her business suit. *God damn that bitch was beautiful!* The best thing about the situation was that I'd been in Pattaya for only an hour before I hooked up with her. She wasn't a bar girl nor a hooker. She was a businesswoman with a college degree. She would end up being the best Thai girl I've ever met, though at the time I didn't realize it.

Apple said she had to go home so we put her on a motorbike taxi and told her we'd see her later. Pablo and I sat by the pool reflecting on the night's events. We decided to go out and scrounge up some grub. Maybe we'd take a walk along Beach Road while we were at it. Hoy was coming in later that evening and we wanted to try and have a chick on stand-by to hang out with him. After seeing Walking Street the night before, we didn't think it would be a big deal to pull that off. A couple of hours later we were trolling Beach Road in search of some new girls. It didn't take long until we had stumbled upon three cuties sitting by themselves. After a quick conversation, two of them agreed to roll with us. As we were walking away, I happened to glance back and saw the third chick with a sad look on her face. I felt bad so I motioned for her to come along as well. We really only needed two because I figured Kate would be back after her shift.

Back at the villa, we started partying. Hoy's taxi finally arrived and we met him at the curb. After hugs and handshakes I introduced him to the three girls. He wasn't sure what to say. One of the girls latched onto him and wouldn't let go. She had staked out her claim. Hoy had no problem with it. As we were walking in, old Apple showed up. At that point there were two chicks who weren't being attended to. *Fuck it*, I thought. I'll take them both and that's what ended up happening. Nothing like two chicks in the sack at the same time. We refer to it as *Rolling Deuces*. That afternoon, I rocked it with those two girls in my suite and booted them out just in the nick of time before Kate showed up. It was a close call but it was well worth the risk of getting caught.

• • •

Over the next few days we ran bitches in and out of the villa like they were cattle. The villa had been transformed into a stockyard. Most of them came off of Hoy's spreadsheet and were good girls. We didn't pay any of them because they weren't hookers. They obviously wanted American boyfriends to take care of them–that's a given. But, when they stepped foot into the villa, they fell under the spell of romance. They fell in love with us. No money was involved.

Think I'm naive for saying that, my seasoned Pattaya travelers? *Up to you*. However, the three amigos are actually decent-looking guys, we're fun to be around, and we treat the ladies well. The typical asshole who frequents Pattaya has a beer gut that lops over his belt, has at least eighteen tattoos, is ugly as a mud fence, and has no social skills. Maybe that's why all of the Thai chicks who are actually good girls fall in love with us. We're the anomaly.

We were slaying bitches and partying like rock stars. We were all having the time of our lives until about the fifth day. Hoy received a strange e-mail from his old lady and knew something was up. He walked out to the pool area with his netbook in hand and a concerned look. Pablo and I knew immediately there was a problem. I wish I had a picture of Hoy at that particular moment in time because the look on his face was absolutely priceless.

"Dogs, I'm not sure what's going on but something's up," Hoy advised seriously.

"What's going on, bro?" I asked.

"Not sure right now. I got a strange fucking e-mail from the old lady. Going to put a call in to her and see what's going on. This shit might not be good," Hoy said. "Pablo, you need to go check your e-mail and see if anything's going on in your camp."

Hoy got on the phone with his old lady and quickly figured out the problem. We were all stone-cold busted by the American bitches. Want to guess what happened? Yep, it was that *pussy motherfucker* named Albert and his damn family barbecue. Apparently, old Albert didn't call off Hoy's wife like he had promised. Whether he did it out of spite or just out of being a spineless *pussy*, we'll never know. Regardless, the exact scenario they had worked hard to prevent occurred at Albert's get-together. I wasn't there, but it went something like this...

"Oh hey, Dixie. How are you?"

"I'm fine, how are you?"

"I'm good. Where's Hoy?"

"Oh, he's in Eastern Europe on a business trip. Where's Pablo?"

"Oh, he's down in Central America deep-sea fishing with Marcos."

"Are you fucking kidding me? With Marcos?"

"Yeah, why?"

"Those no good *motherfuckers*! They're all going to hell!"

After that brief exchange of revelations, Hoy's wife got on the phone to my wife. It probably went something like this...

"Hey girl, what are you up to?"

"Oh, I just got back from a wonderful trip to Thailand with Marcos. We rode elephants, petted tigers, and went to the temples. We had a really good time."

"Where's Marcos right now?"

"Oh, he was going to go backpacking for a bit and then head back to Iraq. He wanted some alone time."

"Those no good *motherfuckers*! Those three dick-heads are in Thailand chasing slant-eyed Asian bitches! They're all going to hell!"

It was as simple as that. A well-coordinated plan had fallen apart due to a bible-thumping, holier-than-thou, *pussy-whipped hater* named Albert. That poor bastard will die and be thrown in the grave after having fucked only one woman—his fat-ass wife. Albert, you sir are the dick-head of the decade. Congratulations to you and your shitty existence.

Hoy ended up doing battle on the phone with his old lady for what seemed like an eternity. That redneck bitch threatened him with everything she could think of. A short time later, Pablo was engaged in the same type of battle with his wife. I was too drunk to even give a shit at that particular moment in time. When the phone calls died down, we all re-assembled around the couch and kicked on the water wall. Deep thought and conversation ensued while we proceeded to get tanked up.

"Fuck it, dogs. What's done is done. There's nothing we can do about it from here. You know you're getting *Pearl Harbor'd* as we speak. That's a given. Ya'll have two options. Either change your flights and go back now to face the music or continue the path. It just means that we have to party even harder to properly honor those bitches and the situation. Let's party tonight like it was 1999," I said.

"That *motherfucker* Albert!" Hoy yelled.

"Fuck him!" exclaimed Pablo.

"Forget about that *pussy*, Albert. We're in paradise right now with a house from an episode of *Cribs*. Let's get our heads straight and get ready to chase bitches. I'm breaking out the pimp-suit and the combat boots tonight. It's on," I advised.

"He's right. Whether we go back now or in three days, it's still going to be a plane right straight to hell. We might as well enjoy the rest of our time here," said Hoy.

"Yeah, dog. You're both right. I'm not ready to go back right now. I don't want to have to deal with that bitch. I'm staying here and enjoying myself. Let that bitch do what she's going to do. I'm sick of her fat ass, anyway. Fuck her," Pablo elaborated.

With that, we continued with the drinking. By the time night fell we were ready to rumble and tear up the town. I decided it was time to debut my new white suit I had bought in Iraq. For some reason, I had wandered into a small bazaar in Ramadi and found myself talking with some Turkish tailors. I had no intentions of buying a suit when I walked into their shop. I was just killing time waiting on the convoy to leave.

The Turkish gentleman was trying his best to sell me something when I stumbled onto a photo that he had hanging on the wall. It was a picture of about twelve U.S. Marines, all dressed in suits, wearing combat boots and sunglasses. They were posing with their weapons while standing on top of a T-72 tank. It was one of the coolest photographs I've ever seen. Screw all of the pictures of blood and gore associated with war. A photo of twelve *motherfuckers* wearing pimp-suits and carrying machine guns, with a tank as a backdrop, just can't be beat. I was sold. I ordered two suits right then and there—one white and one pin-striped. About a week later, I picked them up in time for my trip to Thailand. Since it was a special occasion (all of us getting busted out) it was the appropriate time to sport the white suit.

● ● ●

We hit Walking Street with a vengeance. Before too long, Pablo and I had run into a couple of cuties at a club called *The Candy Shop*. One chick was a bit older and the other was only about twenty. Pablo was on the old bitch and I was running my mouth to the younger bird. For some reason I wasn't studying the girl. I chalked it up as a lack of motivation on her part but later realized it was only her lack of English skills. Regardless, Pablo asked me point blank if I was declining her company. I told him he was cleared hot to roll with the both of them if he so desired. Pablo's next words were, *Ok dog, we're outta here*. That sorry *motherfucker* grabbed both of them bitches, made a hasty exit, and headed toward the taxi stand. I can't say I blame him but I found myself all alone for some reason. To save my life, I can't remember where the Hoy Dog had disappeared to.

I found my way down to Soi 6 which is basically a street full of whorehouses. It's one of the most erotic places in Pattaya, yet classy at the same time. I've made many friends on that Soi over the years and feel right at home there. I have to admit that I'm just attracted to that type of environment. *What man wouldn't be?* Within no time I was rolling out with deuces. To be honest, I don't remember their names, nor where I pulled them from. Once I made it back to the crib I realized that the posse was already there partying. Pablo was in the pool with his two girls, Hoy was true-loving some nineteen-year-old chick we named Chili, and there I was with two of the most disreputable women the world could offer. *Life was good!*

The party lasted until the sun started to come up. I didn't feel like cuddling so I bounced my two ladies out the front door sometime around

7:00 a.m. I gave one some simplistic instructions before she left. I told her that for the next three days, she needed to report to my room with a different friend every night at 3:00 a.m. She was down with the program and advised she would see me promptly at three. That little arrangement turned out to be rather interesting over the next few nights.

I ended up bouncing whatever girl I was with at 2:45 a.m., just in time for my two girls to arrive at three. Yeah, most of you reading this can only dream about that scenario. However, you can live it if you so desire. All it takes is the courage to take control of your life and do what makes you happy, rather than being a slave to your ungrateful wife. I'll say it again my friends, life if short. Live your life while you have the chance.

• • •

After three days of killing ourselves with booze, dancing, chasing women, and unadulterated sex, it was time for Pablo to head for the airport. It was a somber time. When the taxi arrived, we all hugged one another as if someone had died. All three of us shed tears as Pablo reluctantly sat down in the back seat. As the cab pulled away, three grown men were full-on crying. *Hey, fuck you if you think we're weak. We're not weak. We're romantics.*

Hoy and I sat down on the old couch and had a drink together.

"God damn, dog. Pablo's about to be on a flight straight to hell. In two days, I'm going to be on a flight straight back to hell," Hoy offered.

"Yeah, man. My heart goes out to you guys. I'm probably going to suffer the same fate, but right now I've got to get back to Iraq. To be honest, I really don't give a shit about anything except not getting blown up by a damn bomb. Fuck a bunch of American bitches," I said.

• • •

At that point in time I really didn't give a shit about much of nothing. Normal everyday problems did not factor into my thought process. The only thing I thought about was living and dying. That's it. Everything else was a nuisance to even consider. Right before I left for Thailand, an up-armored SUV (sport-utility vehicle) had ran over an improvised explosive device in the road, just outside of Fallujah. The bomb blew the car into pieces and killed a U.S. civilian sitting in the back. That incident happened only days before I rolled out on leave. It was, to say the least, fresh in my mind. The poor gentleman who died didn't even have a chance. He never saw it coming. He wasn't even a combatant. He was a civilian helping out with construction projects. The incident had reinforced my mindset that I was going to live every day as though it were my last. In Iraq, that was a strong possibility. I was going to make every minute with my friends count.

My American wife's opinion of me partying with my buddies didn't even rate. I was merely concerned with Hoy and Pablo and the ramifications they were about to face upon returning to the machine. It definitely was not going to be a pleasant experience for them. However, things often have to get worse before they can get better, right?

• • •

A few days later, Hoy and I shared a cab to Suvarnabhumi Airport in Bangkok. He boarded his flight to hell while I began my journey back to Fallujah. He told me to be safe and keep my head down. I laughed. It wasn't me that needed to watch out for danger. It was he and Pablo. They were the ones going into harm's way. By the time Hoy returned to his crib, his bitch had already cleaned out the bank account and fled to her mother's house with the kids. He found himself inside the walls of a huge, quiet, broken home. Pablo had suffered the same fate. However painful it was at the time, it was the beginning of their journey to happiness.

CHAPTER 8

GETTING PEARL HARBOR'D

I certainly hope no veterans group takes offense to me using this term. We don't mean to hurt anyone's feelings over it. It's just the term we've been using for years to describe a sneak attack on a man from an American bitch. We typically use it to refer to when a woman steals every dime out of your bank account, abducts your children and flees to her mother's house, and max's out all of your credit cards. Or most commonly, it refers to when your old lady backs a damn U-Haul up to your front door and steals all of your worldly possessions while you're at work.

I can promise you that in some form or fashion you will get *Pearl Harbor'd* if you decide to split with your wife. It has happened to all of us in the past on several occasions. Aside from finding your wife in bed with your best friend, it will piss you off more than any other issue. It's pretty much the same as being robbed or burglarized. In all cases, you, the man, will certainly end up being the victim. That's of course, unless you pull a *Booger Red*. That will be explained at the end of *The Art of Divorce* chapter as an extreme alternative to my sound advice and guidance.

Getting Pearl Harbor'd with Drama

Hoy returned home from the *Trip of Three Divorces* to a quiet house. His redneck bitch had cleaned out the bank accounts, took all of the jewelry and valuables, and anything else she could cram inside her mini-van. She took the kids and rolled down to her hometown of Redneckville, Alabama. There was nothing he could do but drag his ass to work and try to keep paying the bills. As he did this, his redneck bitch was living large and partying like a rock star. As the summer concluded, Hoy found himself around $30,000 dollars in credit card debt because of her lavish spending. A couple of weeks before school in his town was supposed to start, the bitch tried to have her cake and eat it, too. In her case, it's closer to having her cigarette and smoking it as well. Anyway, the phone rang and she lay down her demands for him to meet in order for her to come back. Much to her chagrin, the conversation didn't exactly pan out as she had planned.

"Are you ready to straighten up and be a better husband to me and do right?" she asked arrogantly with the utmost of southern twang, while simultaneously exhaling a cloud of menthol.

"Well, to tell you the truth..." Hoy began to reply.

"And I'm gonna tell you right now that you're going to counseling or I just don't think I can live with you. And, you're going to start going to church. All you have to do right now is say you're sorry," she harped again as she exhaled another round of cancer.

At that point in time the old girl had absolutely no idea she was about to have her world rocked. It is perplexing how she ran up a $30,000 dollar credit card bill and still thought Hoy would take her back with open arms. How could she even fathom that? Redneck bitches aren't very intelligent to begin with but their thought process is even stranger. *Hmmm, let me see, I'll party all summer, max out the credit card, make some new demands, and then return home in time for the kids to go back to school.*

"Dixie, I think you just need to stay where you are. I'm ok right now and I don't want you back. You've been partying with your friends down in Alabama and you've spent all of our money. I'm $30,000 dollars in debt because of your little vacation. I'm happy now and you're not welcome here anymore," Hoy advised.

The conversation turned to verbal violence (from her) at that point. Want to drive a redneck bitch damn near batty? Just tell her you don't need her useless ass anymore and leave it at that. Ignore her calls and go about your business. The problem is, she wants you to argue with her. She's looking for a good fight. She is begging you for some drama. It's what the culture thrives on. When you don't give her a Jerry Springer performance in which she can cite to her family and brag about, you have disrespected her in the worst possible manner imaginable. Hoy unknowingly just set the timer on the bitch. At some point, she was going to explode. Since the minute Hoy dropped the news on her that she wasn't coming back, the girl and her redneck friends began planning a *Pearl Harbor*. Right on time, the attack came a week later.

...*I wish that I could have been a fly on the wall* *at those strategy meetings. It probably went something like this: I appreciate everyone coming.*

It's nice to have a dozen friends show up when you need help. Ok, now who's got a valid driver's license? Who can borrow enough gas money to get us up there? Who's got any warrants? How many packs of cigarettes do we have on hand? Anybody got a credit card with enough credit to rent the moving truck? Who's got a cooler big enough for the Sundrop and the Natural Light? Anybody got any minutes left on their cell phone? Ok, we've got thirty-two kids between all of us. Whose grandmother can we leave them with? Is there a sale on Macaroni and Cheese? Each kid needs three boxes a day. How many boxes is that? Anybody got a calculator? Who all has an appointment with their probation officer this week? Who all has an appointment with their parole officer this week? Community service? Appointment at the welfare office? Shit, that only leaves four of us.

It had to have been funny. I hate that I missed it. If you put that bitch and all of her friends together they would barely have enough brain power to plan a trip to Walmart or the grocery store. Contrary to what I just said, they did manage to plan out the attack and start maneuvering north toward Hoy's house.

A week later, the bitches implemented their sinister plan. For some reason, Hoy had called in sick to work that day. His cell phone rang and it was his wife on the other end.

"Hey, I was just calling to see what you were up to. Where you at?" she inquired, trying to sound nonchalant.

As she said this, Hoy was hearing strange noises in the background. He quickly deduced that it was her shifting gears in a big-ass truck. He knew the fireworks were about to begin. A *Pearl Harbor* was in progress! His radar had detected a big-ass bomber inbound. Hoy sounded the *Ponte Trucha Alarm* for Pablo to get his butt over to the crib as soon as possible for backup.

"Ponte Trucha dog! Ponte Trucha! I'm under attack! Pearl Harbor in progress! Get over here quick! It's about to get ugly!" Hoy screamed.

Before Pablo could arrive, a full-sized box truck drove over the curb and onto Hoy's lawn. It managed to crush a few decorative lawn ornaments in the process. With the engine revving, it backed toward the front door. The truck almost crashed into the house before coming to an abrupt stop. Who was the captain at the controls of this pirate ship? Hoy's redneck wife. After grinding the gears down to a pulp in order to get the truck properly positioned, she exited the cab like a grizzly bear on the attack. She had a menthol hanging out of the corner of her mouth as if it were velcro'd in place. Now, the first instinct of any man is to protect his home and property. It's only natural for someone to protect things they've worked hard for. However, the laws of the West are not designed to allow you to do this. Especially if the man is trying to protect his property from a woman.

In typical redneck fashion, the encounter soon turned near violent. The first act of aggression on her part was to grab his cell phone and put it down the front of her pants right next to her twat.

"Just come over here and try to get it from me," she challenged.

As I've said before, redneck chicks are looking for you to either fight with them or at least argue. If you do neither, you are robbing them of their dignity and their reputation with friends and family. Hoy deduced that his cell phone was lost forever and not worth trying to retrieve in its current location. He decided to just grab his laptop, cut his losses, and get the hell out of there. Pablo finally arrived in the driveway as Hoy was walking out with the computer.

"Let's just go dog. This bitch is crazy. Let's roll," Hoy advised.

As Hoy was about to get into his car his wife emerged from the house and tried to snatch the computer out of his hands. Hoy had to hold it above his head to keep her from getting it. Pablo's first observation upon arrival was the crazy bitch jumping up and down, tugging at Hoy, cussing, and trying to take the laptop. Now, Pablo is a lover. He is definitely not a fighter. If it comes to fight or flight, Pablo is going to soar out of a bad situation like Air Force One. That's exactly what he did.

After Pablo rolled out of the driveway and headed down the street, Hoy called him and told him to cut the block and come back. He needed a witness. Pablo finally grabbed a set of balls and returned to the scene of the crime in progress. When he got out of his truck for a second time, the redneck bitch began preaching to him as well.

"You're going to hell, Pablo! You're going to hell just like Hoy! I'm praying for you, Pablo. I'm praying for your family because you're going to hell. I know about you and those girls in Thailand. I know about Radchad Porn," she said in between puffs.

For reference, Radchad is the name of a friend of ours in Thailand. We call her Brittany but her Thai name is Radchad Porn. Her name has nothing to do with pornography. A lot of people in Thailand are named Porn. Brittany is twenty-six years old and is a very nice girl. Hoy's wife went absolutely ballistic when she found a picture of Brittany on Hoy's e-mail. Hey, it's not our fault that Brittany's a fine-ass chick who looks nineteen. Most all of the Asian girls look a lot younger than they really are. That's a difficult concept for American women to grasp. It's just pure jealousy because American chicks usually look *older* than they really are.

Hoy was finally able to get loaded up into his vehicle and he and Pablo removed themselves from the volatility. They sat at Starbucks Coffee while Hoy's wife stole everything he owned out of the house with the assistance of three of her trashy friends. The bitch even took all of his gear he needed for work. Gear which served her no purpose. Gear that he made a living with. Think about that for a minute. What does a bitch think she is accomplishing by sabotaging your livelihood? A woman doesn't seem to think far enough ahead to realize that her child support or alimony payment depends on the man getting his check first.

After the attack was over, Hoy returned to a trashed-out home that looked like it had been ransacked by wild animals. That's not far from reality. You can only imagine the range of emotions that went through his head when all of his worldly possessions were on a one-way trip to Redneckville, Alabama. I know it was devastating because I've been there before, too. Many American men have been in that position. However painful, it's where you have to start rebuilding. It's the beginning of a better life. That's not to say that things won't get worse before they get better. They always do. But, you have to look at things in a positive light.

...*The positive is that Hoy's wife and her friends* broke their backs and shot hemorrhoids out of their asses while lifting that heavy furniture. Better them than us. They just lightened the load for Hoy. He didn't need all of that shit, anyway. Americans base too many decisions off of their personal belongings. Americans can't live in a smaller, more affordable home because all of their lamps, chairs, and what-nots won't fit. Personal property is an anchor that costs you more money than it's really worth. Hoy's bitch did him a favor by pulling that Pearl Harbor. We've laughed at her and her friends on many occasions for what they did. I must extend to them a special thanks due to the fact that Hoy and I didn't have to lift a finger or even break a sweat over that junk. Ya'll did all of the manual labor and for that, I'm appreciative.*

What is even more comical about the situation is that a few weeks later, Hoy loaded up the rest of the junk himself and drove it halfway down to Redneckville. He gave it to his wife voluntarily in accordance with our principles and philosophy. She had once again failed to invoke any drama, violence, or emotion in Hoy. That was killing her. Even though she wanted the rest of the property, I'm sure it fucked with her head because he just gave it to her without a fight. It had to have taken the wind right out of her sails. All of that planning, money spent, drama, and driving was all for nothing. She could have had it delivered for free! She was suddenly marginalized to the point that no one in Redneckville even cared to listen to her story anymore. It just wasn't at all interesting. Nobody was in jail or had to take a trip to the hospital. Therefore, there was nothing worth gossiping about.

Getting Pearl Harbor'd without Drama

A few weeks later, Pablo became the next victim. Since he is the most passive person you'll ever meet there wasn't much to his incident. The bitch showed up with a big-ass truck and stole all of his belongings. End of story. Let me extend a thank you to his bitch and her friends as well. It saved me and Hoy from having to move all of that shit. We've been laughing at you, too. Was breaking your back over a fucking couch really worth the trip? Your efforts were definitely worth it to the three amigos. Thanks for your hard work.

Getting Pearl Harbor'd via Sabotage

We discussed a full-fledged *Pearl Harbor with Drama* in detail with Hoy's situation. That's what will happen if you're actually married to a woman. But, what if you're not married and it's just some live-in girlfriend who you have to dismiss? Chances are she's not going to be bold enough to back a truck up to your front door, especially if it's your crib and not hers. However, don't think for one minute you're not going to get fucked with in some form or fashion. It's coming. It's up to you to figure out when and how it's going to take place.

    I want to share a couple of my experiences so we can critique how they went down and what the appropriate response is. I'll start off by talking about an incident that happened to me when I tossed out a freeloader who was dragging down my kingdom. It wasn't really too nasty of a breakup. I rented the truck. I loaded her shit. I delivered her shit. We went our separate ways. What I underestimated was the strength of her desire for revenge. I temporarily forgot that she was an uneducated, lazy, free-loading, redneck. To make matters worse, she was a damn smoker. I had really gotten myself into a fix with this particular girl. It was merely because she and I would rock it out like porn stars in the bedroom. I can't lie. She treated me better than most in that one aspect of the relationship. It was definitely some of the best sex I've had during all my days. But, it just got to the point where it wasn't worth putting up with her bullshit. I finally grabbed a set of balls and made the command decision that she had to leave the *Chateau de Moi*.

• • •

Back then, I had a nice boat named the *1 Muff Diver*. She was a twenty-four-foot walk-around with a small cabin at the front. When I say nice, she was nice in my eyes. Anyone else would have thought her to be less than seaworthy. She was a 1988 Chapparal with a 1989 Johnson 200HP outboard on the back. I only paid $4,200 dollars for the boat, motor, and trailer. I bought her while I was down in the Miami / Fort Lauderdale area and spent many days at sea on the old girl. She never let me down while I was out in the Gulf Stream all alone. We motored in and around the Florida Keys in some of the most beautiful water you could imagine. I started to sell her when I left Florida but I just couldn't bring myself to do it. She came back to Atlanta with me after I parted ways with my Miami girl. The trip up to the ATL was a mini-adventure all in itself that's worth mentioning for entertainment purposes.

I had flown back down to Miami to tie up some last-minute loose ends and pick up the boat. Coincidentally, I had spoken to a former co-worker who had a three-quarter-ton truck for sale. The price was reasonable and he assured me it was a solid ride. I figured that a three-quarter ton should be able to pull the *1 Muff Diver*. I knew she was too heavy for a half-ton. After picking up the truck from my buddy I headed over to the boat yard where she was stored. I had ordered a brand new aluminum trailer to sit her on and it looked stellar. The yard crew quickly had her hooked up to my newly acquired truck and properly secured. I pulled out of there slowly because it was the first time I'd ever had to trailer her. She had been kept at a marina up on a rack. All I had to do was phone ahead and a forklift would set her in the water for me. As I cut the first corner I realized just how long and heavy the rig was. Regardless, in no time at all we were trucking along on I-95 North with Fort Lauderdale in our wake. I was jamming to Jimmy Buffett as we blew past West Palm Beach. I was thinking to myself about what a smooth ride it was considering the situation. The old truck had been a good investment. *Wrong motherfucker.*

Suddenly, there was a loud *BOOM* followed by a plume of smoke and mist that filled my rearview mirror. It was so thick I could barely see the *1 Muff Diver* for a few seconds. I started losing speed and noted that the temperature gauge was rising. I limped over to the side of the interstate and got her shut down. A quick inspection revealed that there was transmission fluid all over the boat. I popped the hood and started to look around. There was only one problem at that point. I'm not a mechanic and I know shit about fixing an automobile. I looked in and under the truck until I perplexed myself. Since I had just broken up with a chick I spent several years with and quit my job in Florida, had no home or job yet in Atlanta, and was all alone on that interstate, my world seemed to be crashing down on me. I pondered several courses of action to resolve the situation. After a quick rundown of my options I made a command decision. I grabbed the cooler out of the back of the truck and wrestled it up into the *1 Muff Diver*. I climbed aboard, kicked on the battery, and cranked up the stereo. I unfolded one of my lounge chairs onto her deck and then shed my shirt and shoes. I cracked open the cooler and popped the top on an ice-cold can of Natural Light. I was chillin' like a villain in the back of that boat under the hot Florida sun just watching the cars go by. Most of the big trucks would give me a honk as they passed by the comedy. *Fuck it*, I thought. I got nowhere to go and no place to be. I ended up hanging out in the back of my boat for four hours on the side of that interstate. I was just waiting for the Florida Highway Patrol to show up and ask me what the hell I thought I was doing. I didn't think they would take me to jail considering the truck wouldn't run and there wasn't any water within a few miles to float the boat in. Maybe I could have went for Boating Under the Influence but I'm not sure that would have stuck in court. Was I in control of the boat? Sure. But had I started the damn engine and put it in drive, I don't think I would have went anywhere. It wasn't like I was going to crash into a cargo ship where I was sitting. Either way, at that particular moment in time I just didn't give a fuck. Sometimes you have to put things in perspective before you can think about moving forward.

 I eventually ended my reign as the only boat captain on I-95 and began to address the problem at hand. I filled up the radiator with water from the cooler and then topped off the transmission fluid. I got in the old truck and fired her up. She cranked on the first turn of the key. No problem. *Ok, that's good. Doesn't seem to be anything wrong with the engine.* I dropped her down in drive and soon we were making forward motion at around forty miles per hour. I made it to a gas station about fifteen miles up the road. I deduced that the transmission had blown a seal. However, I figured that as long as I stopped every twenty miles and filled the transmission with fluid I might be able to make it. That's exactly what happened. I bought every bottle of transmission fluid the gas station had and headed out. The old truck would go about twenty miles before it started slipping. I would then pull over and fill it up. That trip ended up taking two and a half solid days of driving to make it to the storage lot north of Atlanta. When I got the *1 Muff Diver* settled in it was time to get an estimate on fixing the truck. The first shop I pulled into quoted me a rough estimate of $1,500 dollars. I was standing there with the manager and the hood up talking numbers. I was trying to negotiate the price down but the guy was hard. I figured I would resort to threats of leaving and getting another estimate.

"That's a little steep, my friend. I think I'll check a few more places and get back to you. I think I can get it done for a grand," I said.

"No problem. I can't do it for any less than $1,500," the gentleman responded by saying.

At that precise moment in time, as we stood there facing one another, the main radiator hose on the old truck cracked open. Steam and radiator fluid began to spew out in front of us. We both just stared at the spectacle in silence. My ass wasn't going nowhere in that piece of shit. The negotiations were over. When it finally stopped erupting, we turned and faced one another again.

"So, you did say that a one-year warranty is included in that $1,500 dollar estimate?" I asked casually, in an attempt to downplay the fact he had just won our little game of negotiation. It was check and mate.

"Yep," the manager replied.

"Can you fix that hose while you're at it?"

"Yep."

"Sounds like we've got a deal. When can you have it ready?"

My buddy Dave had to come pick me up and take me to get my other vehicle. Shit like that only happens to me. I tell that long-winded story to prove that the *1 Muff Diver* was very important to me. I loved that damn boat. Now back to the point...

● ● ●

I had bought a little cabin out in the woods soon after returning to Atlanta. I nicknamed the estate the *Chateau de Moi*. It was a quaint little place I must admit. It was fenced in and there was a little red barn out back. The *1 Muff Diver* sat on her trailer out in front of the cabin. Sometimes I would hang out on her all day long. I'd barbecue, drink cold beer, and make my female guests help me with various maintenance projects. They all knew I loved that boat. The girl I am about to speak of was no different. For various reasons, I ended up putting her redneck ass out to pasture during the winter time. She departed without too many fireworks. That should have been a clue within itself.

When the weather finally warmed up I was anxious to fire up the *1 Muff Diver* and start getting her ready for the summer. It was the first winter she had ever sat through so I figured there would be some issues to resolve. As hard as I tried I could not get the engine to crank. I ordered a fuel pump and replaced that in an attempt to correct the problem. She still wouldn't budge. I was concerned because she had never let me down and had never failed to fire up when I turned the key. Eventually, I had to break down and take her to a boat mechanic back at the original storage lot. The mechanic was a typical Georgia redneck and just a good ol' guy. He said he'd have the problem diagnosed in about a week. True to his word, he had identified the issue and was on the phone.

"Hello, this is Mark," I said.

"Hey man, I figured out what's wrong with your boat," he said with a heavy southern accent and a chuckle.

"Ok, cool. Lay it on me, my man," I said.

"Ok, but first, I got one question for you."

"Shoot."

"I want to know what woman you pissed off," he inquired, while laughing and barely maintaining his composure.

When he asked me that, it struck a chord because I had just dismissed *another* crazy bitch. My first instinct was that somehow he knew this particular girl and was somehow related or an acquaintance. It momentarily pissed me off that he was trying to get involved in my personal business. *Who the hell does this guy think he is?* I was about to tell him to mind his own damn business and just fix the boat. His next statement made me realize he was just being the good ol' country bumpkin he was and trying to make light of the situation.

"Apparently, you pissed a woman off. Ain't none of my business but I've seen it before. The reason your boat won't start is because the gas tank is full of water. That's a one hundred and forty gallon tank on there and I pumped out about a hundred and thirty gallons of water. That was the problem. It didn't get in there by accident," he advised.

Multiple suspects began going through my head. There were just so many women I had slept with and somehow pissed off that I couldn't immediately identify who did it. I thought about the girl who I moved out over the winter. But honestly, I couldn't be sure that it was her.

"Are you kidding me?" I asked.

"Nope. Serious as a heart attack. When I get done cleaning out the tank I'm going to have to clean the carburetors as well. Should be able to get her back up and running by next week," he said.

● ● ●

They say that revenge is a dish best served cold. This little meal ended up costing me $1,200 dollars. Whoever the culprit was had used a water hose to violate the only woman in my life who loved me unconditionally. It was a dastardly act of cowardice and terror. Ever since that incident the *1 Muff Diver* was never the same. She broke down on me every time I took her out. I eventually gave up and sold her on the cheap. To this day, no one has come forward to admit their transgressions and seek my forgiveness. While I have several suspects, I can't definitively say who did it. I may never know. This is a perfect example of getting *Pearl Harbor'd* via sabotage. It's kind of ironic that this *Pearl Harbor* incident actually involved an attack on a boat.

Getting Pearl Harbor'd via Theft

Another way a woman will *Pearl Harbor* you is through plain old thievery. This pertains to girlfriends you've scorned who have absolutely no legal right or claim to property that you own. I want to share one quick incident to highlight how cruel they can be and to call out a certain bitch.

I had been letting a crazy-ass girl stay with me for about a month. While I had met her at a bar, it was under different circumstances than I'm accustomed to. I was sober, she was sober, and she was with her dad. Her dad seemed like a nice guy and the three of us ended up eating a meal together. One thing led to another and we started dating. She eventually brought a suitcase full of clothes and was hanging out at my crib.

That's when I started realizing her true colors. I would come home from work, open the refrigerator, and go to grab a cold Natural Light. To my dismay there would be none. I first thought the two of us had just drank too much the night before. I quickly realized that this chick had a drinking problem and was cleaning out my stash during the day. She had to go. I came home late one night and she was tanked up. Along with that, she was running her mouth non-stop. I gave her several chances to quiet down and let me get some sleep. She didn't heed the warnings so I got up and told her to pack her shit. She refused. I packed her suitcase for her and headed for the car. She finally got in while still running that flapper. I was going to drive her home but I just couldn't take it anymore. I pulled over at a McDonald's and put her suitcase out in the parking lot. When she got out to yell at me, I jumped back in and hit the gas. That bitch was still raising hell as she faded from my rearview mirror. *Hey, sometimes you gotta take drastic measures to get the job done.*

I called Dave and told him to do a drive-by of the McDonald's on his way to work. Several hours later he reported that the silly chick was still sitting in the parking lot next to her suitcase. *Oh well. If you mess with the bull, sometimes you get the horn.* I thought that would be the end of the drama with this girl but she just had to get the last laugh. It came in the form of a petty theft. You see, I had just bought this miniature Dachshund puppy that wasn't even as big as a kitten. It stayed on my nice, covered, front porch most of the time because it seemed to like it outside better than being cooped up in the house. About a week later I had to go on a business trip and asked my buddy to stop by and feed the puppy. He promptly called me and reported that she was gone.

Now, the vixen I had dropped at McDonald's was the only one who knew I was rolling out of town and knew about the dog. My house was secluded and the entire place was fenced in. It didn't take a rocket scientist to figure out who did it. I mean, what kind of monster steals a man's miniature Dachshund? That's downright cruel. That woman has no heart whatsoever. Getting dumped at Micky D's is one thing. But stealing my damn dog? *Come on, girl!*

• • •

The moral of these stories is that you will get *Pearl Harbor'd* in some form or fashion during a divorce or breakup situation in America. That's especially true if you're married to a woman in the demographic I constantly refer to. Accept that it's going to happen and control your anger. When it begins to go down just get the hell off the scene and let her do what she's going to do.

If you stay and try to protect your property you will probably end up going to jail. Trust me when I tell you this. I used to be a cop. Back in the day when I worked the road, I took many men to jail because of domestic disputes. I seldom took a woman to jail. Not because I was biased but because of how the situations played out and the way the laws are written. They are designed to protect the women and children in the situation. The man will almost always go to jail and be deemed the *primary aggressor*. If you simply remove yourself from the equation you can avoid problems with law enforcement.

If you go to jail, the girl can actually take her time stealing all of your belongings and the money out of your bank account. If you're married to her, she's going to get all of it awarded to her in the courtroom later on, anyway. Therefore, don't let her take your freedom as well. As long as you remain a gentleman, she can't take that away from you. Do not forget that the laws and culture of the West will always side with the woman.

The *1 Muff Diver* getting ready to set sail from North Miami Beach. A lot of good times were had on the old girl while cruising the Florida Keys and the Bahamas.

The flag the *1 Muff Diver* sailed under. The ladies loved that flag for some reason. The truck that let us down on I-95 just north of West Palm Beach. Back in service after a new transmission.

Hanging out with four hotties in the Philippines. Below, two beautiful Thai girls slave away in the kitchen to prepare a feast. Should you go for a Thai girl or a Filipina chick? If you're not sure, just get one of each.

Option #1: Get bossed around by an ungrateful wife in America.
Option #2: Hang out in the pool with ladies who appreciate the king.
I'll take Option #2, please. I'm not real sure what the "T & A" stands for.

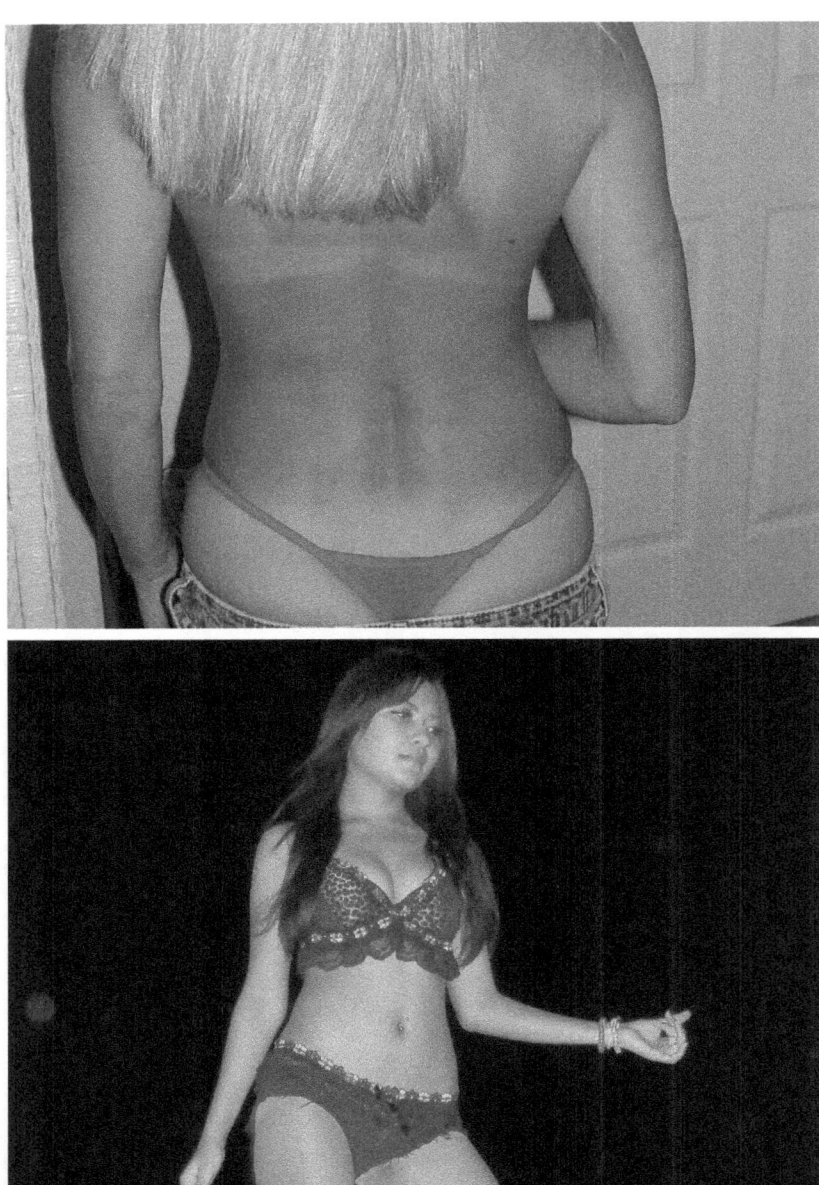

Which do you go for? The blond American chick or the dark-haired Thai girl? Do I really need to provide the answer to this question? Both are beautiful, but the blond will make your life miserable.

Me and *Booger Red* chilling at a family reunion. Just a couple of outlaws. Having a hard day at the office trying to finish the final round of editing. Nothing like a working lunch to maximize your time and productivity.

It is difficult to find a fat, out-of-shape Asian girl. They're all beautiful. Hanging out with my friend Noi from Cambodia. Hard to believe the girl has two kids. I'd love to meet the dumb-ass who left her.

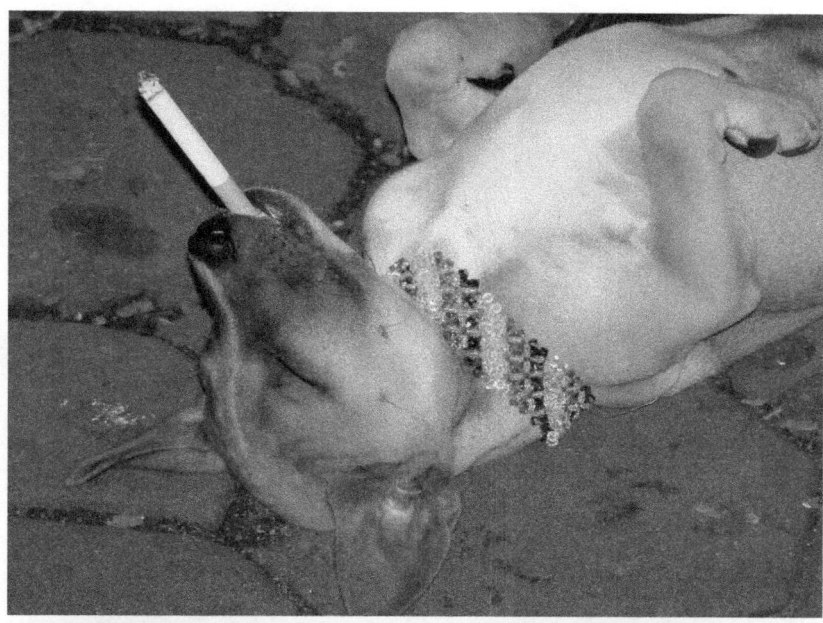

The Hoy Dog after a good night of partying. (not really the Hoy Dog) I've been sporting a white suit since the first episode of *Miami Vice* aired back in the eighties. Always wanted to be Sonny Crockett.

CHAPTER 9

THE ART OF DIVORCE

It is inevitable that this manuscript will touch a nerve in a lot of men. I hope it inspires the reader to make changes within his kingdom and his life for the better. However, some men are married to the laziest, most self-centered, blood-sucking bitches that America has to offer. These particular women are too damn sorry to recognize the value of their husbands, much less the value of these principles. It is with these vixens that divorce is in order.

I have said numerous times already that you cannot be afraid to make changes or to be alone. Remember that life is short. You only have a limited number of years on this earth. You have to make them count and live them happily. So once you decide to grab a set of balls and establish *Kingdom Rule* because your home is a *fucking* disgrace, be prepared for threats. I'm talking about the threat of divorce. That may be a frightening prospect to some of you because of the kids and property which has to be divided. There is no sugar-coating a divorce. It is a shit sandwich that you as the man will always have to eat. You are going to lose a lot of money and a lot of time with your kids. This is what the American system of family law has come to.

The only way to deal with divorce is to take it head on. Once you decide to do it, be firm in your decision and be prepared for what's about to come down the pipe. If your wife threatens to divorce your ass, do yourself a favor and hold her to it. If a woman threatens divorce, she is trying to control you. Let's evaluate this. A woman with no job and no education is threatening to divorce you? The appropriate course of action is to encourage her to do so by filing yourself. Grant her wish and set her ass free. Tell the bitch that next time she should be more careful about what she asks for and might want to keep that big mouth shut.

Let me explain my philosophy on how to handle a divorce. It's going to be shocking to you at first until you think about it for a while. It goes against all of the traditional tactics of how a divorce is handled in America. My way is cheaper, less stressful, and much quicker. If you follow this advice, you'll suddenly find yourself riding in the express lane on the way to becoming a king. It basically boils down to four key areas: emotions, child support, property, and attorneys.

Emotions

First of all, let's resolve the main obstacle to making sound decisions during a divorce. Yes, I'm talking about your feelings. If this is your first divorce the emotional and psychological aspect of it can be traumatic. It can possibly even cause you to have suicidal thoughts. I've been there on many occasions, my friends. Obviously, you didn't plan on ending up in divorce court when you married the girl you fell in love with. None of us did. You're feeling like a total loser because something you put together failed. You've invested a lot of time and money and you stand to lose even more. If you're a businessman, shit like this doesn't happen to you in the business world. I can empathize with you but you need to remember that housewives are not businesswomen. They're basically shitty maids who have been given too much authority because of the laws in America. Don't beat yourself up because most of the time, you *can't* reason with them. No one can. It would be easier to convince me to swear off of drinking—it just ain't going to happen.

We all have this pipe dream that our lives are suddenly going to be perfect with the girl we decided to wed, and we never contemplate anything to the contrary. Guess what? It doesn't always work out. Shit happens. Welcome to the real world. You can't turn back the hands of time or make a lazy bitch be energetic. You can't make your wife want to treat you good. You can't undo her getting fucked in the ass by the neighbor down the street. As early as you can you need to accept that it's time to move on and stop quarterbacking what went wrong.

The bottom line is that you have to check your emotions at the door. If you think with your *heart* and not your brain, you're really just wasting time. As a side note, that made me sick to have to use that term. Suppress the burning feeling inside of you along with any feelings of jealousy or revenge. It's not going to make things any better. Your emotions will lead you to make the most idiotic decisions you could ever imagine. Many of you will end up destroying every single bit of your dignity before you accept the situation. Some of you will do some stupid shit and end up taking a ride in the back of a police car. That's counterproductive to the ultimate goal of becoming a king and has to be avoided at all costs. Divorce has to be looked upon as a business transaction and nothing more. Hey, don't hate the player for telling you how to play the game. Hate the game of the American civil justice system and the *pussies* who allowed it to become what it is today.

So, how do you cope with the emotional roller-coaster ride you've found yourself on? Your friends are the answer. The saying, *Bro's Before Ho's* will suddenly become real to you. I'm not kidding. When all hell breaks loose with your bitch, you have to rely on your friends to get you through the situation. Your family is not going to fill that void. Only your friends can get you drunk, hook you up with a cheap fuck, and remain by your side whether you're right or wrong. They will listen to your whining, your crying, and your indignities. They will comfort you. Simultaneously, they will break down the nasty truth about your soon-to-be ex-wife. If she fucked her boss at work, your friends will remind you of it constantly so that you do what has to be done. Your family will lean more toward forgiveness which is not always the best policy. Only a friend can remind you that your wife hasn't slept with you in over two months. Only a good friend can look you in the eye and tell you that your wife is a whore if you caught her sleeping with the neighbor.

Before the ordeal is over, your friends will be so damn tired of your shit they'd rather kill you than talk to you. You will owe them for being there for you. However, at some point they will probably suffer the same fate. You will then become their support network and pay back the debt.

More steps are detailed in the next chapter which will assist you in dealing with the range of emotions you will find yourself going through.

● ● ●

At some point during the madness you will end up hooking up with a new woman. This is commonly referred to as the *rebound*. A rebound is dangerous because she ends up being there for you in a dire time of need. She will fill a void whether it be sexual or by just helping you take care of the house. Due to this, you will feel as if you owe this particular woman. You should, because her presence will help you get over the departure of your wife. However, realize up front that rebounds never work out. Why? Because the rebound is the first piece of ass that you stumbled onto during a time of loneliness and despair. She's not what you're really looking for, nor what you need. Accept the fact up front that the rebound is only going to be a temporary arrangement. That relationship will fail—I promise you. If you get too emotionally attached to her you're going to get hurt all over again. When it happens don't say I didn't bring it up. I've had several rebound relationships that all ended in disaster. The only good thing is that after some time, we've all ended up being friends because there was just so much history between us. Now, we laugh about all of the bullshit we put one another through. It's just part of the healing process.

Child Support

Let me share my views on the subject of child support. It will conflict with all of the propaganda and programming you've ever heard on the subject. Personally, I consider child support to be a form of extortion. If you break down the word *extort*, the *ex* means out, and *torquere* means to twist. The definition of extort means to get money from someone by force or threats. Isn't that exactly how child support in America works? A judge, who knows absolutely nothing about you, your wife, or your kids, issues an order that allows a government agency to take your money by force. If you're unemployed or don't have the money to pay, they threaten you with arrest and jail time. Or, they actually do put your ass in the slammer. This is the textbook definition of extortion.

Over the years, due to our inaction and lack of organization as men, we have allowed laws to be passed which have legalized this type of criminal activity. Instead of looking upon ourselves as victims of a crime, we have been programmed to believe that we are noble if we pay our child support in an efficient and orderly fashion. The term *Deadbeat Dad* was generated and promoted as a public relations tool in order to quell any dissent among those brave enough to speak out against this debacle. An extremely flawed concept that kept getting worse by the minute was justified and covered up by this new buzz word. Suddenly, if you couldn't afford to pay a woman damn near every dime you made, you were labeled a *Deadbeat Dad* and an arrest warrant was issued for your ass. *Shame on you, Mr. Deadbeat for not taking care of your children.* How about let's put some truth in advertising here. In reality, child support should be referred to as *Lazy Bitch Support* (LBS). That's a much better description and accurately depicts what the money is really used for. I think that the men of America should all unite and refuse to pay any more *Lazy Bitch Support*. The time for reform of this broken system is now.

The money you get ordered to pay does not benefit your children in any form or fashion. Your marriage has ended in divorce possibly due to your wife's inability to understand finances in the first place. Now, a judge is going to order you to give the redneck bitch your money in lump sums and trust her to properly allocate it for the benefit of the children? That defies logic. Now she's got her grubby little paws on the money and is suddenly unsupervised. To most American girls, *Lazy Bitch Support* is the same as Christmas coming every month. The money will really go toward her new clothes, makeup, beer, cigarettes, lottery tickets, nights out on the town, trips to Panama City Beach, Florida, fake tits, new car, etc. I can pretty much guarantee you through experience that no matter how much you pay the bitch, you will still have to buy your kid new shoes when he comes for the weekend. Welcome to America.

● ● ●

As far as the term *Deadbeat Dad* goes, I want to re-brand that one as well. I now consider *Deadbeat Dads* to be revolutionaries, regardless of the reason they're not paying. Their persecution is in line with that of political dissidents and they should therefore qualify for political asylum in other countries. *Oh, I'm just getting more terrible by the minute, aren't I?* After enduring the quantity of bullshit and paying the money that I have due to the fucked up system in America, I've got every right to be angry. Most men paying *Lazy Bitch Support* feel the same way but just don't have the balls to speak out for fear of getting re-evaluated by the court and then having to pay more.

When you get to court, it is inevitable your wife will get custody of the children. This obviously doesn't happen in all cases but don't bet against it. The American system of family law in its infinite wisdom has decided that a child is always better off with the mother. That's fucked up, but is another topic in itself. Accept the fact that when you get a divorce you are going to become a weekend, every-other-holiday, and one-month-out-of-the-summer type dad. Your wife is going to get between thirty to sixty percent of your take-home salary. Yes, that is devastating to give a bitch most of your hard-earned money while she sits on her ass every day. There's nothing you can do about it if you choose to call

America home. Just accept the fact that your world and your income has changed and go on living your life.

Here's some light at the end of the tunnel for you. In the end, the man usually has the last laugh. Unless you're one of those unlucky fools who has to pay alimony for life, at some point your youngest child will surpass the state's age limitations and the child support order will end. All of a sudden, you're rich! You get to laugh while watching your ex-wife fall *hard* off the gravy train. You can go out and buy a brand new car while old girl is filling out job applications at the Department of Labor. She'll be working two jobs just to keep her lights turned on while you're on easy street. The woman will win every battle playing the child support game but in the end, you will win the war. Child support is only temporary so don't get too pissed off. Besides, you can't do a damn thing about it.

Children these days are looked upon by American women as eighteen-year paychecks and nothing more. In most cases, the children are better off with the father who probably wouldn't even ask the mother for a dime of child support. However, as they say, *You can't beat a woman in court.* In America this is true about ninety-nine percent of the time.

Dividing Property

When it comes to fighting over household belongings, don't fight. Give the bitch everything in your house. The only real exception to that would be your big-screen television. That is the only piece of furniture worth bickering over. If she causes a stink over the big-screen, give it to her with a smile on your face. It's probably several years old anyway. During the divorce, if you continuously haggle over who gets a thousand dollars-worth of old furniture, realize that you just paid the lawyer ten grand because of the issue. Give her everything in the house and save the money you would end up having to pay the attorney. You can buy new shit with these funds. Don't waste your time bickering over who gets the ice trays and the good towels. Give everything to the woman and move on. This might not make sense to you now but just keep reading.

Attorneys

Let me educate you on the reality of most divorce attorneys in America. First, I want all of them to know that I consider them to be extortionists—those who specialize in extortion. They engage in fraudulent and unscrupulous practices by stealing from the poor and less fortunate. I consider divorce attorneys to be on par with common thieves. They're all a despicable lot who have contributed to, advocated, and encouraged the breakdown of traditional American culture. Congratulations to all of you for your efforts in destroying my faith in the word *justice*.

These criminals are going to charge you about $5,000 dollars up front as a "retainer" just to take the case. This is basically payment up front for only twenty hours or less of *work*. Twenty hours of work multiplied by $250 dollars per hour equals $5,000 dollars. Now, I am no math scholar but a typical contested divorce case is going to take more than twenty hours of work to settle. So don't think you will only be out $5,000 dollars. That is just to get started and get you locked into their billable-hour scheme.

● ● ●

The best thing for both you and your wife is to sit down and divide up your property on your own. Settle on who gets what. Just give her everything. Calculate the child support at the top of the scale. Once that is done, you only need someone to type up the settlement and then you both can go before the judge without an attorney. That is, if you are dealing with a reasonable bitch. Most of the time this is not the case. So be aware that $5,000 dollars to the lawyer is just for starters. Be aware that attorneys are motivated solely by money. They will drag your case out for as long as they can so that they can bill you for as many hours as they think you can afford to pay. And don't worry, they will let you make monthly payments if they bleed your bank account into the quick. So no matter how good you think your attorney is and how well you think he is looking out for you, don't bullshit yourself. Those *motherfuckers* are out to make money so they can take off on Friday and play golf. Don't forget this. Also realize that every time you get pissed off at your wife and run to your attorney, the billable-hour clock starts ticking to the tune of $250 dollars every sixty minutes.

You have to look at the positive things in life rather than the negative. We could sit here and discuss how the American system basically fucks all fathers. We know that already. Attorneys are only out for one thing and that is your money. They could give two shits about the outcome of your case. So don't get too worked up over the legal system. Just break divorce down to simplicity. Simplicity is simply, how much am I going to have to pay this sorry-ass bitch? At the end of the day that's all a judge cares about as well. Determine the amount, get temporarily pissed off, and then get over it. Once you accept the fact that you are going to have to pay, you are on the road to happiness.

Divorce Case Study - King Pablo's Gross and Negligence

Pablo got depressed because his wife had taken the children away from him. His life was relegated to working sixty hours a week, voluntarily sending the bitch $2,000 dollars a month, hanging out with his dog, and drinking every night. This began in 2009.

We tried to give Pablo advice but he would not take any action. One reason is because he was sitting around the house feeling sorry for himself. How do I know this? Because his lazy ass was sitting at home drinking a bottle of Vodka every night for no apparent reason. He didn't have any ho's at his house with the music kicking trying to get laid (thereby having a valid reason for the drinking). No, his butt was sitting in his easy chair getting drunk and petting his damn dog. What are the results of this? The results are that as I write these words in 2014, his ass still has not gotten a divorce! He also hasn't been allowed to see his children freely even though he's been *voluntarily* shelling out $2000 dollars per month to the fat bitch.

Drinking too much and feeling sorry for yourself during a break-up situation only leads to one thing. That one thing is inaction. You can't formulate a strategic plan, negotiate with an uneducated woman, nor make decisions when you're constantly drunk or hung over. During a divorce situation you've got to sober up and make some tough decisions quickly. That's the only way to get the ball rolling. Pablo is the perfect example of exactly what not to do. I'm not casting any stones at him because it's exactly the same thing I did during my first divorce. I stayed drunk, felt sorry for myself, and as a result I let that bitch get one over on me. I learned the hard way as well.

● ● ●

I hate to air out anyone's dirty laundry but that's what this book is about. We want others to learn from our drama, especially the younger players who are just entering the game. Therefore, I asked Pablo and received his blessing to publish his wife's deposition here in this manuscript. It is quite comical and theatrical, but is lacking one important element—

the truth! This is an important lesson for men who choose to do battle with women through the U.S. court system. Bitches can lie their asses off during the whole process without repercussion or fear of prosecution. The shitty side of it is there is nothing you can do about it. Trust me. Even if you try, it is a waste of your money. These nasty-ass ho's will lie to the judge and get away with it every time. Welcome to America, my friends—the land of the most fucked up domestic law on the face of the earth. Enjoy the read from the testimony of Pablo's ungrateful, fat-ass wife. She laughed the entire time she was lying and swearing to these words, so let the men of the world now laugh at her.

Declaration of Ungrateful Bitch X: I, Ungrateful Bitch X, declare as follows: I am the Petitioner in this matter. I have personal knowledge of each of the facts set forth herein, except as to those matters stated on information and belief, which matters I believe to be true...

Ok, so to begin any typical legal document, she is stating she is the complainant and that she's certifying everything she's about to say is true. Keep that in mind as we break down her statements. I'm going to skip around a bit to keep to the pertinent parts.

I request that the court make the following orders: Respondent, PABLO ESCOBAR pay child support and alimony, retroactive to February 21, 2011, the date I filed the Petition for Dissolution, and pay $20,000 toward my attorney's fees.

Damn, with all the money this bitch is asking for, you'd think that Pablo Escobar was Pablo's real name. Who the hell has $20,000 dollars just lying around in which to give a damn attorney? Not this guy nor most of the men in America. What the fuck is going on here?

PABLO ESCOBAR and I were married for twenty-two years. After our children were born, he began drinking heavily. Over time, his drinking habit got worse. Around 1998 he started spending most of his free time in nightclubs. In an effort to save our marriage, he agreed to go to marriage counseling. Unfortunately, after one session, he refused to go again to counseling.

Maybe you should stop and ask yourself about why your husband was hanging out in nightclubs. Is that his fault? Or could it possibly be that you were a shitty-ass wife? Maybe, just maybe, if you had been handling business properly, your man would have been at home fucking you instead of the whores at the club. You need to go back and read the chapter *Honey, I'm Home!* to learn where you went wrong.

• • •

Any man who has ever gone to one session of counseling is a *pussy*. If he went back for a second session, he is a fucking moron. Luckily, Pablo saved himself from being categorized as a moron. Women in America think marriage counseling is the cure-all solution for their problems. In actuality, the concept can only be seen as comical.

Let me get this straight—you wanted Pablo to pay some stranger a hundred dollars or so of his money to listen to you bitch about him? *You've lost your damn mind*, would have been my response. *How about we end your unhappiness through a nice, quick divorce. Then we can both be happy.* That should be the standard response from any man who is ordered to go to marriage counseling.

You mean to tell me that neither one of you had any friends who could mediate a conversation for free? A family member? The family dog? Is the world so short on people to where you had to make Pablo pay someone to hang out with you for an hour? What the fuck? I would have objectively been the referee if you'd asked me.

• • •

I spoke with Pablo and found out the ground truth about what happened at that one and only session of marriage counseling. To begin with, the counselor was a fat-ass bitch who was ugly as a mud fence. He knew he was doomed from the start when he sat down in front of that troll. The counselor allowed his wife to tell her side of the story first, which turned out to be a plethora of exaggerations. After the counselor listened to his wife's bullshit she went on the attack without giving him a chance to speak.

"So, why do you drink too much?" the counselor asked Pablo.

"I don't drink too much. She just said that I drink too much and you took her word for it," Pablo replied.

"From what she's telling me, you obviously drink too much," the bitch countered.

"Listen doc, what's your definition of drinking too much? Do I come home after working all day and have a couple of beers? Sure, I do, but I don't think that's drinking too much. I should be able to do that, shouldn't I?" asked Pablo.

"It's also apparent you're addicted to sports."

"What are you talking about? I like to watch football like any other American. How can you say I'm addicted to sports? I turn on the TV at night like anyone else," Pablo offered, trying to defend himself from the feminist shrink.

"I think I already know what the problem is with this marriage. The problem is that you are addicted to alcohol and sports. Maybe you should turn off the TV and stop drinking. You need to spend your time with your wife and your family," the troll ordered.

Pablo told me he began to think about who was going to have to pay for the session. Once he realized in his mind that he was the one paying for the gang-bang, he started to get pissed off. Since he is a gentleman he patiently endured the attacks for the rest of the time and waited quietly for it to be over. He had seen enough to know his ass wasn't going back for another hour of tampons, Vagisil, and man hating. As an independent observer, let me break down what Dr. Nut-Nut was accusing him of. She said he was addicted to sports. Just what the heck does that mean, exactly? If a man comes home from working his ass off all day to pay the bills, cracks open a cold beer, plops down on the couch, and watches a football game, that's his *fucking* right. That does not make him an addict, you stupid bitch. Apparently you're not too familiar with what addiction is so let me try to educate you. Since I worked narcotics for the majority of my law enforcement career, I think I'm qualified to school you on the subject.

● ● ●

An addiction to sports would be something more like this: Pablo gets up in the morning and instead of going to work, he calls in sick and goes to the basketball courts. There, he plays basketball for eight hours straight without stopping. Afterward, he heads over to the YMCA and plays in a ping-pong tournament for two hours. Once that's over, he plays in a beach volleyball tournament until midnight. He then decides to run the ten kilometers back to his house to get in a bit more cardio before he crashes on the couch from exhaustion. The next day, he repeats the process. If he did all of this, even I would call him a sports addict. But, there's one small problem with this situation and that's the fact Pablo doesn't do any of this. How do I know? Hell, anybody can just look at him and tell you he's not addicted to any sport. He's a wee bit on the cuddly side and isn't exactly an athlete. That's not saying anything bad about him but what it is saying is that he's not even experimenting with sports. If there's any sports around him I can promise you that he's not going to inhale. Therefore, he's certainly not an addict.

• • •

Dear Dr. Nut-Nut: It was very feministic, unprofessional, and downright mean of you to accuse Pablo of being an addict and neglecting his family. The man has worked every day of his adult life to provide for them. How do you think he felt when a bitch who is supposed to be a doctor told him that? He needs counseling from having gone to the counselor. So, from all of the real men of America, we must say, *Screw you and your biased diagnosis.* Whatever school you got your medical degree from, please let us know so we can blacklist their graduates from treating any real men. Sports addict? *Please.*

PABLO'S drinking got worse and he would often disappear at night... In 2006 our marriage took a turn for the worse... In 2007 PABLO began drinking more heavily, often drinking an entire bottle of Vodka by himself. I found inappropriate voice mail messages on his telephone from his female co-workers. His drinking got worse and he became verbally abusive toward me. I asked him to go to Alcoholics Anonymous, which he refused to do.

Why do you suppose his drinking got worse? Could it be that he was forced to live with an ungrateful, fat, lazy bitch who kept insisting he go to Alcoholics Anonymous? Who the fuck made your uneducated ass the psychologist and expert on addiction? You testify to that as if it were a bad thing he refused to attend a self-help organization full of drunkards and chain-smokers, in defiance of your expert advice and direction. Is the word *worse* the only thing that pops into your head?

In 2009, PABLO told me that he was going deep-sea fishing with two of his co-workers. I supported this trip, hoping that it would help him relieve some stress and re-evaluate things. However, I found out that he and his friends were actually in Pattaya, Thailand for two weeks. Upon his return, he told me that he wanted a divorce because American women are ungrateful and greedy and don't know how to treat their husbands right. I did not quite understand what was going on at the time and I begged him to stop. In front of my children, he grabbed me by my shirt and threw me out of the house. He was very cruel to me that year and told me that I was an embarrassment as a wife because I had no education and was lazy.

Well, this paragraph pretty much speaks for itself—*res ipsa*. The thing about it is that he brought all of your deficiencies to your attention for corrective action. Instead of just divorcing your useless ass, he tried to get you to tighten up and get motivated. Obviously, you took no action and continued to be lazy. Deep-sea fishing? It was more like *deep-C* fishing. Pattaya, Thailand? Damn right we were in Pattaya, Thailand. We were living like kings away from the ungratefulness of American women. That adventure is detailed in *The Trip of Three Divorces* for your reading pleasure, my dear. And by the way, you're a liar. Pablo happens to be the most non-violent and non-confrontational person I know. That bullshit about him throwing you out of the house is pure fiction. If he had, your evil ass would have had him arrested. Where's the police report? I want to read it. Don't worry, I'll wait...

In 2009, Pablo took another trip to Thailand. When he came back he said that he would go to marriage counseling and Alcoholics Anonymous. He never went to either. I later discovered that Pablo had obtained a mail-order girlfriend from Thailand. I found pictures of him in Thailand as well as videos of him having sex with a young Thai woman. In spite of his conduct, I did not want to end our marriage for the sake of our children. In 2012 Pablo went to Thailand again.

How did you discover that Pablo had obtained a mail-order girlfriend from Thailand? What exactly is a mail-order girlfriend? Where is he hiding this mail-order girlfriend? Did she actually come in the mail? Thai girls are pretty petite so the shipping costs would be a hell of a lot cheaper than trying to ship a big-ass American chick in a box. Can you let me know where I can get a mail-order girlfriend? Got the website you can share with me? If they're not too expensive, I'm going to order me three or four of them bitches to keep around the house.

You're swearing to this in a legal document but it's pretty apparent you're just making shit up as you go along. Perjury, I think it's called. Isn't that punishable by law? Where are these videos and when can I see them? I need some new material to look at. For the sake of your children?

Please. It was for the sake of your laziness and gravy train that you stayed. By the way, is it illegal to travel to the Kingdom of Thailand? Last I checked, they have always been a close ally to the United States. You may be thinking of Cuba but we didn't go there, now did we?

In 2013, based on my previous experience, I believe Pablo has traveled to Thailand again. With regards to support, I think that Pablo makes $140,000 dollars per year. He has been giving me $800 dollars but that's not enough and won't allow me to move out of my parent's house.

Anytime you can't find Pablo, just assume he's in Thailand and that we're knee deep in naked chicks. Pablo only makes about $100,000 dollars a year, by the way. A little bit off on that belief, now weren't we? You mean to tell me that $800 dollars every two weeks isn't enough? That's more than a lot of Americans make working full time you ungrateful bitch. Why do you suddenly think you're Paris Hilton and are owed a lavish lifestyle? And again, can you elaborate on why you think it's illegal for U.S. citizens to travel to Thailand? I'd really like to know, especially since I've lived here for over a year.

Although I worked part time at a grocery store for a short period of time, I was never employed full time during the majority of our twenty-two-year marriage and have no skills.

Yeah, so you just proved my entire point of this book. You had a twenty-year run on easy street at Pablo's expense. Be thankful that you didn't have to slave away in a factory on the night shift for twenty years. You should be sucking his dick to this day for that benefit. Instead, you and the rest of the feminists think that because you didn't work, he owes you money? That defies logic in all directions. I could see your argument if you said that you had to slave away in a factory for twenty years to take care of Pablo and that he now owes you money. That would make sense. But, you shouldn't be rewarded for being lazy. In my opinion you owe him a fucking refund for the money he spent on you during the past twenty years of his life.

I had no choice but to hire an attorney to handle these issues. I borrowed $8,500 dollars from my parents in order to hire my lawyer. Based on what my attorney has told me, I will likely incur a minimum of $20,000 dollars *in legal fees for this case to be resolved. I do not have the ability to pay that amount. I ask that Pablo contribute $20,000 dollars toward my legal fees.*

Wow. What gives you the impression that Pablo has $20,000 dollars lying around in which to contribute to your legal fees? If you weren't so much of a bitch you could have settled this shit years ago without a damn lawyer. He didn't run up that bill. You did. You and your lawyer are conspiring to commit extortion against Pablo, by definition.

This synopsis of what a bitch will say during the divorce process is actually quite mild compared to some. The little lady obviously lied, made things up, and over-inflated his income in order to steal more money. The reason? Because she has been discarded like a burrito wrapper. Rejected.

One more thing I don't want to leave out. This bitch's attorney is charging $495 dollars an hour. Can you believe that shit? Welcome to America, my friends.

● ● ●

So, where is Pablo now? His ass is still trying to get a divorce. For five long years he has been trying to get rid of this bitch. What is she asking for now? She's asking for $2,000 dollars alimony per month for life. What? *For life?* What gives you the idea that you're entitled to take money from Pablo for the rest of your life? That's ludicrous. Before you met him, your *pussy* wasn't worth paying $2,000 dollars a month for. So, what exactly gives you the delusion that you're magically worth that much money now? Especially since you won't be doing one damn thing to earn it. It must be because of that magical piece of paper called a marriage license. Because of some ink on a piece of paper that the government charged $35 dollars for, you are suddenly worth $2,000 dollars a month? I've got news for you and the rest of the bitches of America who are stealing money in this manner: you're all delusional if you think you deserve one penny of it. I rank that thought process right up there with believing in the Tooth Fairy, the Easter Bunny, and Santa.

Pablo's wife has said on many occasions that he *stole her youth*. Exactly what the hell does that mean? I think it means the women of America have such a sense of entitlement now, they think if they marry a man he is forever in debt to them. Not in my book. Life is about everyone's pursuit of happiness. How the fuck do you think Pablo can continue his life if a judge orders him to pay this useless bitch $2,000 dollars per month for the rest of her life? What about Pablo? How can he afford to pay rent and eat? In America, the courts don't give a rat's ass about that one small aspect. How did we get to this point? It's because men stopped acting like men and allowed this precedent to fester in our society. I can speak frankly on the subject now, but I was scared to speak out when I was being victimized by the system. I should have been raising hell about this for two decades instead of waiting until I was forty years old. But hell, I'm just getting started. I've got plenty to say.

● ● ●

Let me tell you about how the courts in America arrive at the dollar amount you'll have to pay your ex-wife. They do it based upon percentages of your gross salary and not your net. It's figured similar to the method used to qualify people for loans. That's how the entire housing industry crashed in 2008. It was because of the fucked up way we calculated debt-to-income ratios. We ended up approving people for way more than they could actually afford and it bit the entire country in the ass. The courts are doing this to American men every day of the week, even as we speak. The court will take the man's gross salary and start to figure out how much he owes. The court will not take into account taxes being withheld from this amount, deductions for health insurance, 401k's, pensions, retirement plans, repayment of loans, garnishments, etc. They only give a shit about the man's gross salary. In Pablo's case, this lousy bitch has been temporarily awarded $3,400 dollars per month in child support and alimony based upon his gross salary. After this amount is deducted from Pablo's check, he is left with $1,200 dollars for living expenses. His mortgage is $1,600 dollars which the judge was aware of. Now, how in the hell does the judge think he can continue to live on less than what his mortgage costs? The answer is that they just don't give a fuck. When Pablo asked his attorney that same question, the attorney told him that, *Unfortunately, it's just the way it is.* The courts do not care about the man's welfare. Not one damn bit. When the judge ordered Pablo to pay $20,000 dollars to his wife's attorney within thirty days, Pablo told the judge that he didn't have the money. The judge responded by saying, *Well, I guess you'd better borrow it then.* Unbelievable.

● ● ●

God damn it, judge! Have you ever heard the old saying, *You can't get blood from a turnip?* How can you order a man to pay for his wife's attorney when he can't even afford his *own* lawyer to defend himself in the first place? Are you familiar with the word *justice*? I have to say, probably not. Or, maybe you have but you just don't care anymore. You're probably married to that fat, ugly, nasty bitch that I'm always referring to in this book. She probably rules over you like a tyrant, doesn't she? You have no dignity in your home and therefore, you've lost your dignity in the courtroom as well. I hate to do it, but from all the real men of America and the fathers like Pablo whom you have victimized, I must say, *Fuck you*. You sir, are guilty of negligence in your mission of ensuring justice for all. Your man-card is hereby revoked and you will never become a member of *The Players Club*. You will certainly never become a king. I've seen many like you before. I would almost have to guess that you may be a closet alcoholic hiding behind that black robe. How else can you live with your conscience at night after what you just did to my friend. If you did this to Pablo, I know you're doing it to everyone else. *Shame on you*. I'll take a guess that you're a religious man. If you do believe in heaven and hell you can be sure that no matter which one you end up in, there's a line of men waiting to give you a good-old-fashion country ass-kicking. They're probably already lined up and camping out to see who gets the first lick. You're going to be more popular than the release of the iPhone. If you are a religious man, how do you think God will judge you after you just sentenced a good father to a life of slavery and hardship? Never thought about that one, now did you? Even if you leave religion out of the equation it still amounts to the fact you're an evil person. If you believe in Karma, then I wouldn't waste any money on buying lottery tickets—good luck will never come your way.

Divorce Case Studies - The Hoy Dog and his Friend Tray

Yes, there are multiple divorces under the Hoy Dog's belt. *Well, that doesn't exactly make him an expert on love and marriage now does it?* Maybe not from an American woman's perspective, my scorned vixens. However, it does make him a king and a subject-matter expert on divorces wouldn't you think? Let's break down how it panned out for him when he decided to show these ho's the portal to freedom.

We'll begin with the first divorce. It occurred when he was a very young man and entails a lot of what is referred to as TRA (pronounced as Tray), which is short for *typical redneck activity*. If you're familiar with rednecks and trailer-park bitches then you know where I'm coming from. Typical redneck activity includes, but is not limited to: lying, cheating, domestic violence, stealing, chain-smoking, getting drunk off of Jägermeister and Red Bull, breaking items in the home, getting drunk off of Natural Light, burning the clothes of another person in the front yard, squealing tires, intentionally damaging the vehicle of another person by using a key, putting sugar in the gas tank of another person's vehicle, telling lies on another at church, stalking, slashing the tires of another person's vehicle with a buck knife, making false allegations to the police in order to have another person arrested, enticing and encouraging family members to fight with another person, and quoting the bible while drunk and disorderly. That only scratches the surface of typical redneck activity but those are some key points which come to mind.

The Hoy Dog's first divorce was really uneventful. Why? Because when you have no children and no property together, and you're both young and dirt poor, there's nothing to fight over. The woman has no grounds to argue that you owe her anything. You just experience a rash of TRA and then finally sign the papers. Sure, your Camaro might need a set of tires and a paint job by the time it's over, but financially you'll get away unscathed. The only specific advice that Hoy had in regards to his first divorce was to watch out for flying ashtrays made out of marble. Something about getting hit in the head with one over a dispute about who cheated on who first. Moving right along...

● ● ●

His second divorce was obviously a bit more dramatic. As seen in Pablo's case as well, there were numerous lies, libelous writings, and slanderous statements made by his old lady. Once again, she also elected to include me in the mix but for some reason, never by name. Pablo's wife had referred to me only as a friend in her affidavit. The Hoy Dog's wife would follow the same path. Let me explain why these bitches only referred to me as an anonymous friend instead of Mark Blackard, the king. You see, if they had listed me as Mark Blackard, they just identified a witness. That witness could have and would have shown up in the middle of their hearing and disputed most of their testimony from the stand. By not naming me personally, they intentionally and safely left it vague in case it ever kicked off in open court. It's smart from a strategy standpoint in order to conceal the lies and fraud. An early lesson to learn from this is that if you do decide to engage in a legal battle with a woman, pick up on these minute points and capitalize on them. If she wants to make false accusations about what she *thinks* she knows, march some bodies into the courtroom and destroy her credibility in front of everyone.

The Hoy Dog's wife made claims that we were drunks, had gambling problems, and were sex addicts. What? Those are bold claims to make against anyone. That's another reason she didn't identify me by name and referred to me only as a friend. She knew I would show up and dispute or elaborate on her testimony. *Drunks?* Guilty as charged. *Sex addicts?* It depends on how you define that term. We've screwed a plethora of women in their twenties, thirties, forties, and in my case, fifties and sixties. So, *whatever.* That claim is due to pure jealousy because of the fact we're not attracted to lazy, wrinkled, worn-out, nasty women like herself. But accusing me of having a *gambling problem*? Now that's going too far. It's damaging to my good name.

The numbers of this divorce weren't too bad. The Hoy Dog got hit with about $800 dollars per month in child support and agreed to pay the bitch's rent for three years. Between getting *Pearl Harbor'd* and the shit he had voluntarily given her, she already had all of the household property and sentimental belongings.

Divorce Case Studies - King Marcos Gets Macaroni Grilled

Yes, there are multiple divorces under King Marcos' belt as well. My first run was with a redneck bitch that lasted seven years. As I have admitted on many occasions, my actions were the primary reasons for this divorce. While we were married, the girl was actually a decent wife. It wasn't that I didn't love my wife at the time. I loved her very much. The problem was that I loved everybody else's wife, girlfriend, sister, cousin, friend, etc., as well. I was sleeping with so many girls back then I couldn't keep track of them all. The problem was I kept getting caught. It wasn't necessarily because I was always sloppy and careless, it was mostly due to the numbers of chicks I had going. It was too damn hard to keep up with the cover stories I had to tell my wife, the cover stories I had to tell the ho's, and how they all intermingled. I had a few unlucky incidents happen which did me in with my wife. She finally had enough and rolled to her momma's house. That's when the nastiness began which lasted for over a decade. I went from feeling sorry for that bitch to wishing she would get hit by a train.

● ● ●

Let's begin with the early days of the divorce. Against all odds and everything I talk about in this chapter, I beat the woman right out of the gate in the courtroom. She initially left our son with me and went out and got her own apartment. I was being a good dad and being the responsible one for a change. Meanwhile, the old lady got in with a crowd of potheads and was stoned all the time. When we went to our initial hearing the judge gave me temporary custody of our child. I didn't appreciate the impact of that ruling at the time because I was totally ignorant to the ways of the legal system. For several months my son and I lived like a couple of bachelors. The judge gave her a couple of days a week *visitation* which really amounted to the fact I had a free sitter when I needed one.

On one occasion when my wife had my son, I was waiting for her to bring him home as scheduled. I was standing in the kitchen cooking a pot of macaroni and cheese because I knew he would be hungry when she brought him home. He always was. I had the macaroni noodles boiling in the water when she knocked on the door. I opened it and she walked in without our child. He was asleep in his car seat in her vehicle.

When I asked about what was going on, something set her off. I still can't figure out to this day what sparked the carnage all of a sudden. She told me she was taking the stereo and several other items. As the judge had ordered no property to be divided, I politely explained to her it wasn't going to happen. As she started to work herself into a rage, I said *fuck it*, grabbed the phone, and called 911. Before the line could connect, she ripped the phone out of my hand, jerked the cord and the base out of the wall, and slammed it onto the kitchen floor. It broke into a dozen or more pieces.

"Now see if you can call the police, *motherfucker!*" she yelled, and grabbed the pot off of the stove.

With a single heave, she tossed the pot of boiling water and noodles toward me. Luckily, I was able to dodge it. The pot seemed to explode as it hit the wall behind me. Steam, noodles, and hot, buttery water ricocheted and rained down on my ass. Since I was only clad in a pair of cutoff jeans, it hurt like hell. As I was tap dancing around because of the boiling water on the floor, she rolled through the living room like a bull in a china shop. First stop? The bitch reared back and drop kicked my terrarium. The damn thing split into several pieces. Soil, plants, and knickknacks went flying. She proceeded over to the stereo and threw it in the floor. She tore up several other items during her tour of my living room before making her way back toward the front door.

At the time, I had a sport bike which was only about six months old. I always parked it just inside the front door in the hallway. She leaned up against one side of the wall and kicked my motorcycle. It hit the other side of the wall and the grip and the brake lever embedded themselves into the sheetrock. She then hauled ass out the front door, jumped in her car, and left while squealing tires.

● ● ●

I stood there, looking and feeling like an idiot. If she had left my son it would have been the end of this little incident. However, she took my kid. I humped up the stairs and called the police from my bedroom. A few minutes later, a burly cop was walking up to the front door. I invited him in and he looked around the kitchen surveying the damage. I stood in front of him with macaroni noodles hanging from my hair, my shorts, and my back. My hair was still wet and greasy from the butter I had added to keep the noodles from sticking. At that point, I really felt like a moron. There I was, a grown man, standing before another grown man, with burns caused by an assault with a pot of macaroni.

"What the fuck happened here?" he asked in disbelief.

I started to tell him the long, drawn-out story because I didn't know any other place to start.

"Well, I was cooking a pot of macaroni and cheese for my son..."

He cut me off.

"Yeah, no shit, Sherlock. That's pretty damn obvious by the fact you've got macaroni noodles hanging off your fucking head. Get to the who and the why," barked the officer.

I explained to the gentleman exactly what happened. I told him I didn't want her to get arrested and that I only wanted him to call her and tell her to bring my son home. If she wouldn't, would he please go over to her apartment and get him. I didn't want any trouble for either one of us. Unfortunately, I didn't know the law at the time and the cop had already seen too much.

"I've got news for you. It doesn't matter what you want because I'm going to charge her," he advised.

Fuck. Now I had the government involved in my private affairs. That wasn't the intended outcome of calling for assistance. The cop took me to see the magistrate judge to get a warrant for her on the charge of Battery. That's one step up from Simple Battery in the State of Georgia, due to the fact I had visible injuries. She was actually lucky the cop and the magistrate judge went that route. Throwing a pot of boiling water on someone is technically Aggravated Assault—a felony. They locked her up on the misdemeanor charge and I got my kid back.

● ● ●

Again, I didn't appreciate my situation at the time and didn't recognize the value of it. I had an order giving me temporary custody of my son and now the crazy bitch had come over to my house, assaulted me with a deadly weapon, and had been arrested. I was on the one-yard line with a first down. All I needed was one more hearing for her to have to pay me child support for eighteen years. That's when I made a severe blunder. I let the bitch come back. That solved all of her problems and was the beginning of all of mine.

The first thing we did was both go to the courthouse and I petitioned the court to terminate the temporary protective order I had against her. That allowed her to be around me and move back into my house. Then, I attended the criminal hearing with the girl. It was kind of funny because when we got to the courtroom they announced that all of the men needed to go into a side room. I did what I was told. Once inside the conference room of sorts, a lady asked if anyone needed a court-appointed lawyer. That scared the shit out of me. Why in the hell did I need a lawyer? I quickly realized I wasn't supposed to be in that room. Every man in there was a defendant except for me. *This isn't good,* I thought. *What if they've screwed up the paperwork? I've got to get the fuck out of here.* I began to look for the fire escape.

They eventually herded us back into the courtroom. The judge called our last name and my wife and I stood in front of him. We were holding hands in a show of unity. The judge looked at me in a serious, your-ass-is-in-trouble type of way and asked me how I wanted to plea to the charge of Battery. My heart stopped for a split second. My premonition had come true. I was fucked. I kept thinking, *They must have screwed up the paperwork. Why in the hell did I come here to support this bitch? Why oh why didn't I stay my ass at home? He's about to throw me in prison by the way he's looking at me. This ain't good. I'm going to jail.*

I nervously explained to the judge that I was the victim in the case. He could barely hear me as I couldn't seem to get the words out. I had a sudden case of cotton mouth. He kept telling me to speak up. After the judge reviewed the paperwork more closely, he finally realized the beautiful little blond-haired chick standing next to me was the macaroni serial killer and not me. He began to smile and almost laughed. Moments before, he was pissed at me. I'm sure the judge had been thinking, *How could he throw a pot of boiling noodles on such a pretty, petite, innocent-looking young girl? He must be a monster. I'm going to send him to prison. He can eat all of the macaroni and cheese he wants down there. Hope he gets pounded in the ass for being mean to this poor girl.*

"Well, it seems that you are the victim, Mr. Blackard," said the judge while chuckling.

When the judge chuckled it caused the rest of the courtroom to start laughing. I'm sure it was hilarious from the position of a spectator, watching me sweat in front of everyone. My wife plead guilty and got off with probation, anger management classes, and some community service. This incident only reaffirms what I've said about trying to beat a woman in court. The judge was ready to hang me but thought it comical when he found out my cute little wife was the aggressor.

But at that point we had effectively reconciled our marriage. We were back on an even playing field. After the smoke had cleared and I let down my guard; that's when she struck. She borrowed some money from her mother and hired a lawyer. I got blind-sided and suddenly found myself on the other end of the justice system. I was now the defendant. As I had no money to hire my own attorney, I was doomed from the start. Long story short, she ended up with full custody of our son and child support. It was the beginning of a ten-year nightmare for me.

Plan Z - Operation Booger Red

Please heed my recommendations and advice in all other areas of this book. This section is for pure theoretical study based upon a historical event. It's definitely a classic, don't get me wrong. It very well might be the best story I've ever heard. However, do not claim that I told you to pull a *Booger Red* on any bitch. This is venturing into dangerous territory, my friends. What I'm about to share with you is not exactly legal, is not in accordance with my principles of being a gentleman, nor an option if you have children. It is the most extreme course of action you can take, aside from having a woman knocked off by mafia hit men.

I've got an uncle whose real name is Kenneth. However, everyone in the southern states knows him as *Booger Red*. He's sort of the one-percenter of our family—a family which is already chock full of outlaws. Booger Red has done a stretch or two in the big house for various offenses over the years. Don't hold that against him because he really is a good person and would give you the shirt off of his back if you needed it. When I was a young child, we used to go visit Booger Red in the county jail or the penitentiary pretty regularly. It wasn't until I was about six years old that I first heard him called by his real name. When my dad told me we needed to go see Uncle Kenneth, I asked him who that was. After he said, *You know, Booger Red*, I put two and two together. Anyway, Booger Red is pretty infamous around Mississippi and Tennessee to say the least. The act which I'm about to discuss is pure genius and needs to be memorialized before memories fade.

● ● ●

At the time, Booger Red was married to a lady named Patricia, or Aunt Pat, as we all called her. Now, I'm not going to make one claim that Booger Red was a good husband. I don't really know the inner workings of their marriage. Maybe he was in the wrong to begin with. Or, he could have been the innocent victim in this situation. That's probably debatable depending on which of them you listen to. Regardless, at some point, Booger Red caught Aunt Pat rocking it out with another man down at the local juke-joint called *The Showboat*. Like the calm strategist that he is, Booger Red didn't raise any alarms and just played everything cool. He quietly developed a course of action to deal with Aunt Pat's infidelity.

They resided in an apartment which also happened to be in the same complex where my grandmother (Booger Red's mother) lived. Once Booger Red had his master plan in order and everything lined up, he struck with a vengeance. He got up one morning and kissed Aunt Pat goodbye as she left the apartment and went to work. Once she turned the corner, Booger Red rolled straight to the bank and withdrew every dime they had from the checking and savings accounts. He then went back to the apartment and packed up everything of value. These items were sold on the cheap at the local pawn shop for cold hard cash on the barrel. He took all of the items that had little to no value and dropped them off at the local Goodwill-type charity thrift shop. These items included all of Aunt Pat's personal belongings and her clothes. Anything left over went into the dumpster at the apartment complex. Booger Red then rolled out of town with a pocket full of money and a big-ass smile on his face. He never looked back. He certainly didn't leave a forwarding address.

When Aunt Pat arrived home from work that night, she initially thought she had opened the door to the wrong place. She then thought she was losing her mind. Before her, there was nothing but a bare apartment. The only thing left on the floor was the carpet. It only needed a steam cleaning in order to be immediately re-rented. Everything she had to her name was gone. The only thing she had left was her car and the clothes on her back. Since Booger Red had gone on a shopping spree with the rest of the credit on her credit card, she was flat broke. She had no choice but to move in with my grandmother in order to try and get back on her feet. I can't remember how long she lived with her but it was for quite a while.

● ● ●

Two decades later, I pinned Booger Red down on the incident and asked him to give me his side of the story. He went on to give me some advice that still resonates with me today. He said, *Son, if you're going to leave a woman, you've got to leave her high and dry. If you don't, she'll bite you.* Those were, and are, absolute words of wisdom. It was possibly the most compelling thing he's ever said to me. I rank it right up there with the number-one lesson my father taught me when he said, *Son, don't ever turn down a free meal.*

Basically, pulling a *Booger Red* on a woman is a reverse *Pearl Harbor*. The only problem these days is that because of the laws, the man would probably go to jail for something. A bitch gets away with it every time. If a man does exactly what Hoy's wife or Pablo's wife did, he'll get locked up for theft. It's almost a certainty.

CHAPTER 10

KUNG FU FREEDOM

On a trip to Thailand, the Hoy Dog ran into some unforeseen health problems and was forced to roll to the clinic. Don't worry about what the problems were because they're irrelevant to the story at hand. However, if you know what Zithromax is for, then you are familiar with the situation. While he was paying his bill, an old-school player around sixty years old spotted him and called him out in American English.

"Hey, where you from?" he asked.

Hoy turned to see a short little man with a dark complexion. He would turn out to be Hawaiian. The cat was rolling with a smoking-hot Thai girl with a big booty. She was glued to his hip.

"I'm from Cleveland. Where you from?" Hoy responded.

"I used to be from America but now I'm from Thailand. I've been here for seven years," replied the gentleman.

During the conversation, the old man revealed that he had been the typical American caught up in debt, bills, mortgages, and white bitches. A bit of good luck came his way in the form of a small inheritance. He immediately made the move to Thailand and was surviving by using a minimalistic approach. His apartment was around $150 dollars per month and he was eating for about $3 dollars a day. The Hoy Dog explained to the old guy that he too, wished he could move to Thailand and live the dream.

"I would love to make the move, bro. I just can't right now. I've got an ex-wife who's robbing me of most of my money, child support to pay, three mortgages, and credit card bills. Besides, I can't leave my pension. I've got too many years invested in it."

The old player wasn't impressed.

"No problem. You go on back to America, do your thirty years, and be a slave to the machine. I'll stay right here and be a free man," he preached to the Hoy Dog.

Hoy tried to recover from being called out but the old man continued by saying, "When I see people like you, I try to help them. I want to try to help you become a free man. The thing is, if you want to be free you can certainly do it. But, the machine has you convinced that you have to do your thirty years and not question the system."

The old man went on to tell Hoy that when he first came to Pattaya, he moved into a hotel called the Sabai Lodge. He stayed there for over six months and proudly earned the title of being the longest-running guest in the hotel's history. That's a much better claim to fame than working thirty years without taking a sick day.

● ● ●

I start the chapter off with this story to set the tone. If you truly want to change your situation, you can and you will. The old man had heard Hoy's excuses from probably a hundred American men just like him. The truth is, they are all just excuses. Life is too damn short not to live it while being happy, whatever your definition of happiness may be. That is exactly how you should be living.

If you do decide to make a change in your life, you will inevitably end up suffering from what I call *Freed Slave Syndrome*. It will hit you when you finally break free from your wife and find yourself without the daily orders you're used to following. You will suddenly find that you are so free you've become lost. You will temporarily be paralyzed because you don't have some nasty bitch telling you what to do and when to do it. Don't get scared and don't panic. It will subside, I can assure you. Depending on how long you've been married, and therefore programmed, will determine how long it takes for you to adapt. If you've been with a woman for twenty years it's going to take a while to adjust and realize that you are now in control. I've suffered from *Freed Slave Syndrome* after breaking free from bitches in the past. I even suffered from it when I broke free from working around the culture of the U.S. government. For months after I ended my career, I still felt that I had to abide by the useless, mundane policies I had been programmed to adhere to. It took about six months to finally realize I was free to do what I wanted, publish what I wanted, say what I wanted, and not worry about some type of ethics investigation for talking about chasing *pussy*. You will eventually adjust to the change and begin your pursuit of happiness.

I told you during the chapter on divorce that when it comes to fighting over household belongings, don't fight. Give that bitch everything in your house. You probably were reading that thinking, *Is this motherfucker crazy? I worked hard for all that shit. Why would you tell me to just give up and let her have everything?* The reason is simple. It's the first step toward liberation. Now let me explain why.

Make sure she gets *everything* so that you can start over with a clean slate. It's easier that way. As soon as she and her redneck relatives pull away with all of your belongings in the U-Haul, I want you to start cleaning house. I want you to paint the walls, clean the carpet, scrub the kitchen, and throw away any unnecessary junk she may have left behind. Once you get your crib in tip-top shape, it's time to go shopping. Obviously, you will not have a lot of extra pocket change after being robbed by that bitch and her attorney. That's ok because you are not looking for a whole house-full of furniture.

I want you to roll to the nearest Walmart and head over to the lawn and garden section. Find you some cheap-ass folding lawn chairs and a lounge chair to go in the living room. Then, go on over to hardware and pick up a folding table to go in the kitchen. Pick up some red Solo cups and some paper plates. Get yourself one pot for cooking. If she took the bedroom suite and the bed, roll on over to sporting goods. Get you one of those blow-up mattresses to sleep on. This is all you need to start your life over. Trust me, you can live good with what you just purchased.

Oh, I almost forgot. If you have any credit left on your credit card, I want you to stroll on over to electronics and pick out the biggest fucking television they have. Get a nice LCD model, or one with the latest technology–not like the antique your bitch just stole. Choose a nice surround-sound system and charge that as well. I then want you to find some posters of Chuck Norris, Bruce Li, Che Guevara, Thomas Jefferson, Dr. Martin Luther King, Jr., Vladimir Putin, and Edward Snowden. Why these individuals? Because they represent your new-found personality. You can now take your place among real men with balls. And, stop by the liquor store and purchase enough booze to properly stock a full bar.

Once you get home and set up your new furniture in your freshly cleaned palace, you will begin the lifestyle of living stress free. You will be back to living the simple life you once enjoyed before you said *I do* to that sorry-ass bitch you now call your ex-wife. Think about it. There is suddenly no clutter in your house. There is no one to bitch at you. You are in control of your life. You are now making the decisions like a king should. The only thing you have to worry about is what you want to watch on your new big-screen and what drink you want to mix. I want you to hang those posters of Chuck, Bruce, Che, Thomas, Martin, Vladimir, and Edward on the living room wall. If a woman comes to your palace and says anything negative about your choice of wall decoration, I want you to immediately get rid of that bitch. You are the king of your castle. If you decide to hang those posters up then the decision should be respected by any potential girlfriend or wife.

● ● ●

Yes, you may be the only member of your kingdom but that's ok. In no time you'll have herds of bitches coming and going. Yes, I know you're broke and on the verge of bankruptcy. That's ok as well. You can get a part-time job to make ends meet. Yes, I know you're going to miss your children. That is natural and will always make you sad when you think about it. Welcome to the world of divorce in America. Welcome to the world of being a part-time dad, my friends.

Once the divorce is final and you have parted ways, don't believe that you've seen the last of that *cunt* rearing her ugly head. She will still use every opportunity she has to try and fuck with you. It's because you have scorned the bitch. Be prepared for it. If you begged her to come back during the whole ordeal, she might not be so pissed off. But, if you decided to be a king about things and were firm in getting her out, you fucked with her self-esteem. She is down in the dumps because she was the one controlling the situation for all those years you were married. You just upset the entire balance in that poor woman's life. She is used to calling the shots. You are supposed to be subordinate to her. *Who the hell do you think you are to divorce her?* When she yells, you are supposed to kiss her ass. All of these emotions will continue to run through her head for years to come.

So, be prepared to be fucked with. The typical method that a bitch will use to fuck with you is by using the kids. A scorned woman will always resort to this. It is the only control they have over you after the judge's final order. All the numbers have already been set in stone by the court. She obviously made out like a bandit and is stealing most of your money, but psychologically it's not good enough. She didn't make the decision. Someone else did. Therefore, the bitch has to create scenarios where she can personally and directly exercise some control over you. The way they do it is by making it very difficult for you to see your children.

They will show up late to meet you. They will demand that you bring the kids back early because of some fabricated situation. If you live out of state, you may buy your child a plane ticket only to be waiting at the gate to find out the bitch didn't put the kid on the plane. Yes, you may have to eat a few plane tickets. It has happened to me on several occasions. What can you do about it? Nothing. That's the ground truth. But, if you don't want to take it from someone speaking from experience you can go and complain to your attorney. Your attorney will charge you $5,000 dollars to file a motion for contempt of court. Once you pay him the money, he will tell you he will ask the court to fine your ex-wife and to incarcerate her for thirty days for violating the order. *Alright! Now we're talking. That bitch will wish she had put my son on that plane. It's going to be sweet watching the judge lock her up!*

Now come back down to reality. Here's what will actually happen: You will show up in court. Your ex-wife will show up and explain to the judge that the child was sick that day and couldn't fly. The judge will warn your ex-wife that she needs to communicate with you better to get the child to you for *visitation*. End of story. You will walk out of that courtroom madder than a *motherfucker* and $5,000 dollars poorer. That bitch will go back home and laugh her ass off because she lied to the judge, got away with it, and cost you a shit-ton of money. No judge is going to sentence a damn woman to jail time over child custody.

● ● ●

I've already mentioned that the system in America is fucked up. I am not here fighting an enduring crusade to change the child support and child custody laws. (This book is my one and only shot across the bow of the injustice going on.) There are already organizations out there fighting the losing battle for fathers' rights. If you feel strongly about the issue, then join the cause and be heard. But, that will take valuable time away from you being able to live like a king. Remember, this book and the advice herein has your best interests in mind. It's for you, the individual American male. It's an escape plan. It's not about how to go on the offensive and take on a bitch in a biased court system. I'm not trying to change the river. Just learn these lessons so you don't waste your time and money. Learn from my mistakes and the mistakes of millions of other American men. Don't engage in battles that you know up front you cannot win! It will end with you getting twice as pissed as you were before and twice as broke. They say that an ounce of prevention is worth a pound of cure. That's definitely true. The best form of prevention is to never marry an American woman and never have children with one. That could have been the simple solution to prevent all of the problems you now face. Unfortunately, hindsight is always 20/20. However, if you adhere to this from now on, you can save yourself from going through the same ordeal again. I would take it one step further and advise you to never marry any woman. A marriage license is merely a piece of paper that allows the government to get involved with your personal affairs. It allows a bitch to leverage the government to work on her behalf. A marriage license has absolutely no benefits for the man. The bad thing is that all of us willingly signed the fucking document–some of us on multiple occasions.

• • •

Once you get your palace set up, sit back and reflect on what has happened. Think about what direction you want to go in. Set down some goals for yourself. Start thinking about the present and the future and let the past be the past. Do not engage your ex-wife in any type of argument for any reason. That would be stooping down to her level. You are now above arguing with a woman. The king argues with no one. Maintain your dignity as a king. Do the best with the situation as it presents itself.

If she absolutely refuses to let you see your children, then you have to go see the attorney. That's the only exception. For all other issues, you need to realize that they're part of being divorced in America.

Now it is time to have a little bit of fun in your life. Get together with your buddies and start running ho's in and out of your castle. When you and your buddies roll some bitches into your newly furnished living room, the good times will begin. Strange women will party whether you have lawn furniture to sit on or expensive leather. Feel free to serve hot dogs and hamburgers to those bitches. They'll appreciate the free meal and the fact that you cooked it, or they can go hungry. No need for steaks or expensive wine. Whether you've pulled some bitches out of a honky-tonk or from Rodeo Drive, just serve them Natural Light and a hotdog. They're really not there to evaluate whether or not you attended the Culinary Institute of America. They are there to be entertained. They're also secretly hoping to get railed out like a cheap hooker, even though they'll try their hardest to prevent you from knowing this.

Before long, you will start to enjoy living by yourself and chilling on your lawn furniture. Chuck and the gang will be there to keep you company. You'll probably start having conversations with them and sharing advice. They'll help you. You will reflect back on these times later in life and laugh your ass off. I promise. Don't spend too much time being angry. Accept the situation and move forward.

The Den of Sin

Allow me to detail what I've just discussed with some history. Back around 1995 when my first wife and I were going through our divorce, I eventually ended up moving out of our townhouse. I took nothing but my guitar, my clothes, my truck, and my motorcycle. I moved in with a buddy of mine named Scotty. He had a nice two-bedroom house just up the road. Scotty's wife had pulled a *Pearl Harbor* on his ass and took everything in the crib. When I say everything, I mean damn near everything. The only stitch of furniture in his entire home was a coffee table in the living room and a bed in the master bedroom. He had an old stereo system that had somehow survived the attack. That was it. The only other property he owned was an old truck and his Harley. When I moved in, our combined assets were two motorcycles, two trucks, a coffee table, a stereo, one bed, and a guitar. We somehow come up with a gas grill later on for the back deck. That was all we had. We both worked two jobs to pay our bills and basically had little to our names. We both had five-year-old sons that we missed dearly due to the circumstances. We had suddenly been put back to square one in the game of life.

However, we made the best of the situation. As a matter of fact, we made the situation so good we were the envy of all our friends and associates. You see, instead of feeling sorry for ourselves, we decided to kick it like kings. For starters, every night we grilled out. If you opened our refrigerator, there was nothing in there but beer and barbecue sauce. Every night we hit the grocery store and grabbed something to grill. It was cheap but we were still eating like royalty. We would either eat standing up in the kitchen or sit on the floor and eat over the coffee table. To most, that would be considered a hardship. To us, it was living stress free. Paper plates and red solo cups made for easy cleanup.

For entertainment, we immediately started running ho's in and out like cattle. We had a different crew of bitches at the house every night. We would grill out, drink beer, kick up the stereo with some *Coolio*, and dance like fools. What really got the girls' panties wet was that we parked our bikes in the living room. Yep, right on the carpet. Scotty's Harley leaked oil all over the carpet just like a dog marking its territory. When we would get rip-roaring drunk, usually at around one in the morning, Scotty would fire up the Harley in the middle of the living room. It was loud as hell but the chicks loved that shit. There were no rules. There was a lot of free love going on. There was girl-sharing, wife-swapping, and any other deviant activity you can think of. We were sleeping with different girls damn near every night. There were times when I would come home from shagging some girl at her apartment and find a strange naked chick laying on my pallet in the floor of my bedroom. Either Scotty had hooked it up or she was merely a friend of Scotty's girl for the night. It was pure, wonderful madness.

The cops got called on us so many times that our crib was nicknamed *The Den of Sin*. When the police dispatcher would give out the call over the police radio, she never had to use the address. She would just tell the officer to respond to *The Den of Sin* in reference to a noise complaint.

On our days off, we would get together with our buddy Steve who also had a Harley, and go for a ride through the north Georgia mountains. We would pack down Scotty's and Steve's saddle bags with Natural Light on ice. I had a backpack that I filled with the same. The lucky lady who got to ride with me had to wear the backpack full of beer because I had no saddle bags. We would leave *The Den of Sin* and ride toward the mountains. Every thirty minutes we would stop and drank a couple. We would repeat this leisurely cycle until that critical moment when we depleted our supply of beer. At that point, the ride through the mountains was over. It was an all-out road race headed south toward Atlanta. We would always end up at a place called *Cabo Wabo* which was a biker bar on Roswell Road. We would spend a few hours there drinking and hanging out until it was another *Cannonball Run* back to *The Den of Sin* for some more bad behavior.

Point of the story? The point is that no matter how broke you are or how much shit you lose during a *Pearl Harbor*, your life can get better if you allow it to. Scotty and I took a shitty situation and created some of the best memories I can recall. Matter of fact, I found an old video the other day of me and him dancing with a couple of trailer-park girls in his living room. I would not trade those memories for any amount of money. It was pure *Kung Fu Freedom*.

If divorce comes your way, move forward! Stop worrying about what went wrong or how you can possibly salvage the situation. It's over, my friends. The trust is gone for whatever reason. You can't get it back. Move on and create new memories.

• • •

Sometimes as a writer, it is difficult to decide where to put certain sections. I try to put things in chronological order but it's not always that easy. I need to interject some more material that probably should have been part of the *Emotions* section during *The Art of Divorce*. Regardless, here is some more advice on how to move on. We all agree that emotions are a factor in making bad decisions. After a breakup, your emotions can easily lead you to become an alcoholic. How do you mitigate this? Well, my advice is to absolutely conquer your emotions with a head-on attack. You will inevitably have triggers that cause you to go crazy and miss your ex-wife. Those triggers can come in the form of hearing a favorite song, driving by the restaurant you and your wife used to frequent, looking at old pictures, watching your wife's favorite movie, etc. All of these triggers can cause you to either start dialing her number, drive to her new house and act like an ass, or just start drinking. So how do you overcome them? You rewrite the memories.

Imagine your brain as a board with information written on it in permanent marker about your previous relationship. You can't just erase it. What you can do is write over the information so many times that the original material is not legible. For example, if you and your ex-wife went to a Mexican restaurant every Friday night, that restaurant is a trigger. If you set foot in there, it will remind you of those times. They way to wipe out those memories is to go there every night with your friends and drink margaritas. Within two weeks, you will have re-written the original memories and replaced them with newer, more pleasant ones. Now if you pass by the restaurant, you will think of your friends and not the bitch who is now stealing all of your money.

If the two of you had a favorite song, start playing that *motherfucker* over and over. At first, it will sting. After a couple of days of listening to that shit, it won't have the same effect. Another trigger neutralized. If there is a movie the two of you loved together, play it every time a new chick comes over to your house whether she likes it or not. Pretty soon, it too will have no particular meaning. As far as old pictures go, do not look at them alone. Especially, do not look at them at night. Why? I don't know the science behind it but looking at old pictures at night can make your mind think crazy thoughts. Put those pictures away in the back of the closet until several months have passed. Once your mind is straight, you can look through them and reflect on the good times.

If your ex-wife moved out and you are stuck cleaning up the mess, quickly remove all of her belongings from your castle. The easiest way to do this is to get a box of contractor-grade trash bags. You know, the big black ones that can hold a ton of stuff. Go through the house and locate every stitch of personal property your wife left behind. Drop the crap into the trash bag no matter what it is. Tie up the trash bags and put them in the garage. You can deliver them to her mother's house or put them out by the curb on trash day. Your choice. Either way, your home is now sanitized. If you do not do this, you are faced with looking at small trinkets of her property which will remind you of the girl on a constant basis. This will only delay the healing process.

CHAPTER 11

THE SECRET TO ONE-NIGHT STANDS

Want to know how to pull bitches out of clubs in America? Of course you do. If you've been married for more than five years I think it's safe to conclude that you may have forgotten how to meet women. Maybe you were the ultimate player before you got married and aren't worried about it. Most of you don't even know what it means to be a player and have slept with less than ten women in your entire life. That's ok. Once you get to the point of being *Kung Fu Free*, you can begin to focus on the art of pulling ho's. I call it an art, but there is science behind it as well. I'm not a psychologist, so take everything I say with a grain of salt. I'm only going to speak to you based upon my own personal experiences. Let me give you some more background so you can assess my credibility on the subject of hunting women.

First, I've been chasing bitches since I was six years old. Yep, I was on the playground trying to figure out how to get a kiss from the best-looking girl in my class. I had sex for the first time when I was fifteen years old. Since then, I have dedicated most of my free time to the pursuit of getting laid. Why? I don't know. Most guys have hobbies like playing softball, going to baseball games, watching football with their buddies, golfing, bowling, etc. My hobby and that of my close friends is simple—we hunt *pussy*. There you have it. It's a simple mission that doesn't get anymore complicated. We don't give a fuck about football, basketball, fishing, bowling, hunting, religion, going to the movies, etc. We dedicate one hundred percent of our time toward the cause of getting into panties.

If you figure that I've been actively involved in the craft since I was fifteen, that gives me twenty-five years of experience under my belt (no pun intended). If I had to put it into numbers, I would conservatively estimate that I've slept with five hundred girls in America and another five hundred outside of America. A cool thousand might be a little on the low side but it's a safe figure to quote. I'm not trying to brag, posture, or inflate my ego by telling you this. It's merely history. There are a lot of men out there whose numbers make me look like a beginner. I'm not here trying to start a dick-measuring contest—I am only trying to qualify my expertise to speak on the topic.

Maybe you don't really care about trying to slay every bitch that comes your way. Maybe you do. Regardless, you're going to need some entertainment and some downtime before you even think about jumping into a new relationship. You need to live a little and get some of that wander lust out of your system. If you do so, it will help you be a better, more grounded king once you find a new queen. So, how did I talk several hundred bitches into giving up that ass for free? Let's explore the madness and see what worked for me.

Eradicate Standards

First, I had and often have an unfair advantage over most men. No, it's not my looks. I don't have any money. I don't drive a flashy car. I'm not famous. My unfair advantage was that for decades, I had absolutely no standards when it came to women. I did not discriminate on the basis of race, creed, nationality, height, weight, handicap, number of kids, criminal record, overall appearance, or employment status. Those things meant absolutely nothing when I was in the clubs, the grocery store, Walmart, the mall, etc., looking for someone to go home with me. The only standards I had were that they had to be a woman and they had to be motivated. Other than that, nothing else mattered to me.

Now, think about what I just said. You may not subscribe to the same philosophy. The Hoy Dog certainly doesn't. He is a very picky player. All of the girls he's ever been with have ranked from 9.0's to perfect 10's. He cannot fathom the thought of having sex with a fat woman or an ugly bitch. That's his preference. The upside to it is that he's always screwing beautiful ladies. The downside is that I've probably bagged ten times the number of chicks he has. I've seen him turn down so many horny and willing females that it makes me sick. I've never turned down a woman who was motivated about going back to my crib and rocking it out.

When you make it back to your house, apartment, hotel room, or wherever you're staying after getting drunk as hell at the club, do you really want to be alone? If you're already tanked up and feeling no pain, are you really concerned as to what a girl looks like at three in the morning? With the lights off? It's never concerned me at that point in the evening. I would much rather be rocking out a fat girl while drunk as hell than sleeping by myself with a hard dick. All of the times the Hoy Dog went home alone because a chick didn't meet his standards, I can promise you I had a better night with the ugly girl I screwed for three hours straight. It gave me a hell of a story to tell. What's to tell about going back to your room by yourself and watching television? Absolutely nothing. I don't want to hear those stories. Which story would you rather hear?

So, lesson number one is to eradicate any standards you think you have to adhere to. You're looking for a woman who's willing and motivated. That's it. I'm not saying you can't shoot for the stars. As a matter of fact, that's the way I work a club. The minute I hit the door, I'm looking for the finest bitch I can possibly lay eyes on. I'm going to start with her and roll the dice. Sometimes you get lucky with the perfect ten. Most of the time you get rejected and have to start making your way down the ladder. At some point down the line, you'll hook a winner.

Don't lose sight of the fact that you're merely looking for a girl to take home for the night. You're looking to satisfy a sexual urge. You are not looking for a girl to be a potential wife or someone you want to take home to meet your family. Therefore, standards are not necessary.

An Ugly Bird in Hand is Better Than a Beautiful Bird in the Bush

Lesson number two is that an ugly bird in hand is better than a beautiful bird in the bush. If you have a solid chance with a chick who's a 6.0 then stick with her. Don't give up the solid piece of ass because of loose speculation that you can pull the 9.0 across the room. In my travels, I have lost out on many solid pieces of ass due to this rookie mistake. I blame most of this on my attention deficit disorder. I want to caveat this by saying that if you think you can upgrade to a better bitch, then by all means embark on the adventure. Always go for the gusto. The worst that can happen is you go home alone. You've got everything to gain and nothing to lose. Now, there's no law that says you *have* to hook up with a chick every night. But in my case, I was always a man on a mission. I was there to find a girl to go home with me. Mission accomplishment was the only thing that mattered. If I had a 6.0 latch onto me early in the night, I would try to go all-out with the bird in hand. I could relax, drink freely, and sling that bitch around the dance floor. The pressure was off of me at that point. I had achieved my objective. I would have a good time in the club knowing that I was going to sleep with the girl later on. Meanwhile, all of the people trying to maintain their standards were getting edged out as the night progressed. The competition gets tighter as you near closing time. Desperation sets in. If I had pulled a 6.0 at ten-thirty, I had effectively removed myself from that rat race. Stick with the bird in hand or you may go home with a hard dick.

Dress for the Occasion

Lesson number three is to dress for the occasion. If you roll out somewhere looking like a ten-pound bag of dog shit, you're wrong. Women don't want to look at wrinkled clothes or clothes that don't fit properly. They don't want to look at a shirt you're holding onto from the eighties. I'm not saying that you have to spend money on designer clothes in order to pick up bitches. I've never had to do that nor have I had the money to roll that way. But picking out the right outfit for the right environment is paramount. Let's start from the top and work our way down.

Hats? If you're going to a country bar where men wear cowboy hats, then by all means, wear a cowboy hat. Women love the cowboy look. If you're going to a cigar bar where everybody is wearing newspaper-boy (Fred Sanford) type hats, then a hat would be appropriate. Going to a baseball game? Ok, you can wear a ball cap. If you're going to a crowded club, leave your damn hat at home. First, a club can get hot if there's a ton of people in there or if you stay out on the dance floor. A hat is just going to make your head sweat like a fat guy in summer. If it's crowded, the hat is going to get knocked around which will make you look and feel like a fool. Also, chicks can't get a good look at your face if you're wearing a hat in a dark club. Many girls have told me that if they see a guy wearing a hat, they automatically assume he's bald. Therefore, they rule the guy out and err on the side of caution, preemptively. Unless you are bald (whereby a head covering may be justified), that cool hat you think is a necessity to your wardrobe is not doing you any justice.

Moving on down to your choice of shirts. If you're planning on a nice, quiet evening at an upscale bar, you should wear a long sleeve button up. You don't want to roll into a business atmosphere looking like a hobo. Some casual slacks and maybe a sport jacket is in order for this type of outing. If you're headed to the club and plan on drinking, dancing, and getting crazy, stick to a t-shirt and a pair of jeans. A black, Jack Daniel's t-shirt exhibits one of the best looks I can think of for a club. The black gives you that bad-boy effect while the white writing pops out under the neon and black lights. You don't have to tuck it in if you don't want to. It's a matter of preference. If you're slim and trim, tuck it in and show off your flat stomach. If you're sporting a few extra pounds, don't even think about it. Now, if you know you're absolutely not going to hit the dance floor, wear the long sleeve button up with your jeans. Might as well look a bit more GQ while your shy ass is sitting on the sidelines.

The one thing that a king never wears on a date is a *fucking* tank top or a wife-beater. All you muscle-bound guys out there, listen to me. Nobody, male or female, wants to see your sweaty *fucking* armpits while they're in a social environment. Keep your tank tops where they belong–in the gym. If you're buff, go on and wear a tight t-shirt and show off your muscles. That's the appropriate attire and not your Tap Out gear.

Any type of footwear is ok for the club except for white tennis shoes, flip flops, or open-toed shoes. Why? Ever had your toe stepped on by a big American bitch wearing high heels? Make sure you're wearing some sturdy shoes for the club environment. If you're going to be scuffing the hardwood floor of a country bar, make sure you wear shoes or boots with a leather sole. You can't slide your feet on the hardwood with rubber-soled shoes. They stick and you'll look like an idiot trying to dance. Why do I suggest you not wear tennis shoes on a date or to the club? I don't know, but I think it just makes you look sloppy. For some reason, many of the methamphetamine dealers I used to arrest always wore brand new, white tennis shoes to the club. They looked like idiots out there on the dance floor. Their legs looked like two Q-Tips sword fighting. I can't recommend that for your attire while ho-hunting.

There, how simple was that? It's either jeans and a t-shirt or a long sleeve shirt and a sport jacket. Too easy. Baggy jeans, clothes that are too big, too small, or are multi-colored, have never worked out for me. There's no need for excessive jewelry, either. Big gold necklaces? They only look good on body-builder types. They probably do not look good on you. Keep the bling down to a minimum unless you're at a rapper's convention trying to score.

On special occasions, I do rock it with the white Miami Vice / Don Johnson suit with a black, silk shirt. I even add a few accessories to the look such as my sunglasses and maybe a gold ring. There will come a time when you need to stand out in the crowd. It's up to you to decide when that is. Weddings, New Year's Eve, and concerts are appropriate events to step up the game with your attire.

Learn to Dance

Lesson number four is that you have to learn to dance. *Relax, you don't have to be John Fucking Travolta to fill this requirement.* There are three dances you need to know to enhance your club appeal. The first dance you need to learn is the Two-Step. This little dance is responsible for getting me laid on more occasions than I can count. It's simple to learn and just as easy to teach to a clueless chick. It's such a versatile dance that you can kick it to almost any song no matter the tempo. While it's traditionally seen in country bars, I've personally Two-Stepped with girls in damn near every club I've been to. Ninety-nine percent of the women I ask to dance tell me they don't know how. I respond by saying, *Cool! No problem. You're in luck because I'm a dance instructor.* After a brief laugh, I'll drag them out to the very middle of the dance floor in front of everyone and act as if we're in our own little world. I'll even point out to them that all eyes are on us. In front of the whole bar / club, I'll give them sixty seconds of dance lessons. Within a minute or two of them stepping on my feet, they get into sync and soon we're the life of the party. It's really that damn easy.

The second dance you need to master is the slow dance. This is idiot proof. All you have to do is hold onto a chick and sway back and forth. *How fucking hard is that?* If you try to tell me you can't slow dance, I'm going to consider you to be an absolute moron and that you can't tie your own shoes. There's no help for you if this is the case. You might as well go hang out with Albert.

Last, but not least, you've got to learn how to get down, kick it freestyle, and cut a rug. Maybe you have absolutely no rhythm. That's ok. You just need to add Jack Daniel's. It will help loosen you up a bit and allow you to feel the beat. The majority of men in the bars and clubs are what I call bench warmers or spectators. They sit on the sidelines and watch everyone else have a good time. They watch me and the Hoy Dog break bitches down on the dance floor like they were shotguns. They are basically wasting their time because women want to be entertained. If you can entertain them long enough for them to feel comfortable with you, then you're probably getting laid. The reality of it is that you don't have to be a great dancer. You don't even have to be a good dancer. You just have to drop your inhibitions and get out there. Presence is really the only requirement. Most dance floors are so packed that it's standing room only, anyway. A lot of times there's no room to even think about getting creative. You just end up swaying back and forth with the mass of bodies moving about. Whether you look good or look like shit, you have to get out there. If you look like a dancing chicken, you'll at least make the girl laugh. Laughter leads to comfort and familiarity. Comfort and familiarity lead to sex.

Know your Quarry

(Yeah, let me first give credit to an old-school player who some of you insiders may know. I stole that line from him, even though he uses it in a more professional context.) Lesson number five is that you have to know your quarry. You have to understand the basic non-verbal cues given off by a bitch which are indicators of her personality and intentions. When you first spot a girl, don't just look at the size of her tits and decide you're going to focus in on her. Look deeper into the situation and observe the fine details. They tell a tale.

One of the first things I look for is a woman sitting by herself. If she is alone, to me, that is a good sign. You can interpret a myriad of theories as to why she's not with anyone but they really don't matter. The fact is, she's sitting by herself which makes her vulnerable. She's looking for someone to talk with to break the awkwardness of being alone in a social environment. The other good thing is that there's no one to interrupt you while you're charming her with your wit. Take advantage of the situation and move in quickly before the next man scoops her up.

Now that you've focused on a girl, take a gander at what she's drinking. Take note of this and look even deeper. If she has a beer sitting in front of her, is it full? Is it half full? Is it almost empty? In addition to this, look at the condensation on the bottle. If the bottle is full but has no condensation, it means the beer has gotten to room temperature. Why? Because she isn't really drinking it. It's just a prop. She's not the least bit tipsy and doesn't have any intentions of getting that way. A stone-cold-sober chick is much harder to get into bed than a chick who has been drinking. That's not rocket science. Now, if the beer bottle is still sweating and it's almost empty, that tells me the girl drank it in a hurry. She's on a mission to get a buzz. That's obviously a good sign and you may have a chance with her. Is this starting to make sense?

*...**More philosophy on drinking as it pertains to women.** If a girl is drinking beer out of a bottle, it can mean several things. However, if a chick has a draft beer in front of her, it tells me she understands the economics of getting drunk. Draft beer is usually cheaper and you get more of it. All of*

us hard drinkers know this. Therefore, if given the chance, I will hone in on the girl with the draft beer before the one drinking out of a bottle. Here's another related tip from experience: If an upscale girl with class rolls to your house, crack open a bottle of wine. Why? Because if you serve beer or mixed drinks to an intelligent chick, she will count how many drinks she's had and cut herself off at two or three. In her mind, she does not want to tarnish her good reputation by allowing you to get her drunk on Natural Light—cheap and dirty tactics. However, if you pour her a glass of wine, it is a constant refill process—sexy and elegant. Neither one of you will be able to count or quantify how many full glasses you drank. Plus, it's acceptable and romantic for a girl to admit that the two of you "shared" a bottle of wine together and then made passionate love. It's not glamorous for her to report to her friends that she single-handedly killed a six-pack of Bud Ice and then got railed out from behind for an hour. Listen, if you're cheap like me, you probably buy wine that comes in a box. No problem. Go out and buy one expensive bottle of wine to keep on hand. Once it's empty, just refill it with the cheap shit from the box. No girl is going to know the difference. It's charming to pour wine from a bottle. Refilling a wine glass while your halfway in the damn refrigerator trying to get the valve on the box to work? Not cool.

The next indicator I look for is whether or not she's a smoker. In my experience, if a chick smokes, there's a ninety-nine percent chance she's coming home with me. If she's smoking menthols, that's the smell of a one hundred percent certainty she's giving up that ass. My theory on women smoking in bars is not based on anything scientific. But, I believe it is a reflection of their overall persona. A chain-smoker has an addictive personality and has a tendency to act on impulse. To me, chain-smoking also indicates nervousness and low self-esteem. You can address the self-esteem issue in your approach and fill that void for her. A few compliments carefully crafted will put a chain-smoker at ease. Therefore, the more cigarettes a woman smokes at the bar, the better your chances of getting into her panties. If you smell menthol, you're golden. I'm not exactly sure what it is about bitches who smoke menthols, to tell you the truth. Maybe it's just that those chicks are extra trashy to begin with. Either way, I'm looking for a smoker, specifically with menthols, chain-smoking like it was going out of style. Whenever I smell a menthol cigarette nowadays, it brings back so many memories I'm temporarily overwhelmed with nostalgia. Menthol smells just like *pussy* to me.

Take a look at how she's dressed. This isn't always foolproof but I evaluate their wardrobe as well. I look for girls who are wearing plain old blue jeans. The type of blouse isn't too important to me but the shoes are. If a chick is wearing a pair of tennis shoes, in my experience that's a plus. I can't tell you exactly why. Some guys love high heels. To me, high heels are unpredictable. They scream gaudy. They scream, *I'm a princess so you have to kiss my ass.* A pair of tennis shoes means that she would rather be comfortable. They scream, *Let's go back to my place. I'm tired from working all day but I'm getting drunk and I want to get fucked.*

The lone chick is probably the easiest to prey on because there's no external pressure on her. There are no witnesses to tell of her actions with the stranger she just met. She doesn't have to drop off any of her friends or feel compelled to ride home with them. If she's got kids, they're probably sleeping soundly at her mother's house. Since she only gets one night to herself per week, she's going to go all-out and make it count. She's the captain of her own destiny for that one night and is looking for some action. The stars are aligned in your favor in this situation. It's up to you to seal the deal.

• • •

What about the scenario where chicks are rolling as a pair? Two girls sitting together at the bar. This is the second best situation because they're probably good friends. Good friends trust one another to keep secrets. Start by using the basic tips I just described and see which one you want to focus on. Don't get stupid and immediately go for the good-looking one. Use your observation skills for a minute and try to pick the best horse. If they're both giving off similar cues, move in and strike up a conversation. To make sure you don't get stuck focusing on the wrong girl initially, roll up in the middle of them. Divide and conquer. If you're in the middle, they both naturally have to focus on you and cannot exclude you from the conversation. This gives you their undivided attention for those first few moments which are critical to either being in with the ho's or getting rejected. Introduce yourself and sound confident. It's ok to use my world-famous pickup line. *Hey, how you doing? My name's Mark.* That's all it takes to break the ice and begin the dialogue. The first thing I focus on is finding out who has obligations later that night. Inevitably, one (or both) of them will have to pick up their kids or get some sleep because they've got to get up early for work. Once I detect a deal-breaker, I can naturally focus my energy on someone else. Why sit there and talk to a chick for hours when you already know she cannot kick it with you due to logistical issues with children? Move on to the next girl.

After determining who has a flexible schedule, you are free to work your magic. Anything is possible at that point. She could tell you to go get fucked or that she wants to fuck you, or anything in between. The best case scenario when dealing with the duo is that her friend proactively departs to pick up her kids and thereby removes herself from the equation. I may have already mentioned that simplicity is the key. The more obstacles and people you can take away from the equation, the better your chances are of getting laid. Remember, the girl wants to hook up with you most of the time. She just can't allow you to know that up front and she damn sure doesn't want anyone else, which sometimes includes her friend, to know. A chick's girlfriend is obviously going to interject her advice which could lead to a cock block.

● ● ●

Let's talk about the situation where there's a table full of women. You have to sit back for a minute and figure out what the occasion is. If it's blatantly obvious it's *Girls' Night Out* then you're probably not going to get into anyone's panties. They've rolled as a unit and will make sure everyone makes it home safe as a unit. Can't say that I blame them. But, not all group gatherings are *Girls' Night Out*. It could just be a get-together after a hard day at the office—a loose gathering of hens for drinks after work. This is a good scenario because everyone drove themselves to the bar. There was no pact made prior to arrival. It's every bitch for herself. Personally, I've done very well with these types of situations.

How do you approach a table with a dozen women sitting at it? *Confidently*. This is where you've got to throw back a couple shots of Jack, grab a set of balls, and just say, *Fuck it*. Roll in strong on them bitches and introduce yourself. Yep, *Hey, how ya'll doing? My name's Mark,* is exactly what you need to say. When you do that, you interrupt the mundane chatter and discussion of boring office politics and effectively hijack the conversation. You become the charming entertainer. Half of the women in this situation will be old married hags who haven't had any romance in decades. They'll immediately fall in love with you because you had the stones to do what you just did. They'll let you know real quick who is available, who just broke up with her boyfriend, and who needs to find a good man. I've had this happen time after time. The old bitties did the hard work for me. No need to pick up on the cues. They told me who to focus on and even gave me plenty of background information to run with. Some have even said, *This girl right here needs to get laid,* while pointing at one of their crew. Was it because I was the best-looking guy in the bar? Hell no. It was because I was the only guy in the bar who had the nerve to approach them.

> ***...Hey, I know that not everyone has the confidence*** *to walk up to a table full of strange women and spit game. They say the number-one fear in all people is public speaking. People would rather face a snake in the grass than get up in front of an audience and have to speak. I'm well aware of that. Why do I have the ability to do this? It's not courage, my friends. It's because I really don't care if I get shot down. It doesn't bother me if I do. I'm not afraid of rejection. I've been rejected hundreds of times and will certainly get shot down hundreds more before I die. So what? Do I really give a shit that a group of hens, who I'll probably never see again, didn't invite me to sit down? Please. I'm not losing any sleep over that and neither should you. I've said many times that I'm going to give every woman the opportunity to turn me down. If they're cordial while shooting me down, I thank them politely and move on. If they're nasty with their response, I always tell them, Don't be so damn picky, bitch. I wasn't being picky or else I wouldn't have come over here to talk to your fat ass. No matter the outcome, you have nothing to lose and everything to gain by taking action. Scared of looking like a loser in front of the other guys in the club? They're sitting on the sidelines! They're the spectators! You're the man in the arena! Worried about your reputation? First of all, you just made it through a divorce. You have no reputation. Second, are you really worried about your reputation in a nightclub? Quit worrying over what other people think about you and live your life. Take some risks.*

Spend your time talking to the entire group and play it cool. Don't be overeager or zero in on anyone. Eventually, as the night wears on, the married chicks will have to begin to excuse themselves. If you're on point, the chick who's available will be the last woman standing. That obviously means you're in. She feels comfortable because the whole group got to know you and thinks you're a nice guy. They're all gone so there are no witnesses to interfere with her decision to roll home with you.

In a nutshell, if it's *Girls' Night Out*, be subtle. If it's girls having drinks after work, be cocky. There's a huge difference. If you roll in strong on *Girls' Night Out* it will be like jumping into a lion's den with steaks tied around your neck. Those bitches will make it a sport to ban your ass from the table. You will look like a jackass. But again, who really cares? If you're not sure of the situation, introduce yourself and see where it goes. Drop your inhibitions and get into the game.

Win Them Over With Words

Lesson number six is that you have to win them over with words. You can be the best-looking guy in the world but a girl isn't just going to roll home with you because you're physically attractive. Well, maybe if you're Tom Cruise or Brad Pitt, but not if you're Mark Blackard or Joe Blow. Your appearance is immediate but very shallow. It is less than twenty-five percent of the reason a chick decides to go home with you. When she looks at you and likes what she sees, she's saying, *I could fuck this guy*. She's not saying, *I am going to fuck this guy*. Only on rare occasions do you pull a girl based solely upon your looks.

It did happen to me one time in particular when the Hoy Dog and I were at a place called Club 64. We had been in there for hours trying to hook up but things just weren't going our way. We decided to call it a night and headed toward the door. Hoy was in the lead and walked by a thick, black chick sitting on a bar stool. She was from Somalia and had a nice, big, round ass. She grabbed him and had a brief conversation which I couldn't hear. According to Hoy, it basically went something like this:

"I want to go home with your friend tonight," she said.

"Ok, I think we can arrange that," Hoy advised.

By the time I walked up, Hoy broke the news that the chick wanted to go home with me. All I said was, *Let's go*. We were checked into a hotel room in less than thirty minutes. It turned out to be one of the best nights I'd had in a long time. We rocked it out and were still going at it when the sun came up. I never even caught her name. All I remember is that she was a nurse.

Sometimes, it will be that easy. But the majority of the time you're engaged in a battle of wit with a girl. If you win, you get laid. If you lose, you go home alone. So, what should you talk about? It all depends. You will obviously start out with the basics of where she's from, what type of business she's in, her family, etc. Let that play out in the beginning to get acquainted and get the background info out of the way. Afterward, you've got to take over the conversation to where it's only about you and her. Stop making any reference to her work or family. Neither of those subjects will get a woman horny. Go forward and talk about what you want to do with her. I'm not saying to tell her you want to stick your cock in her mouth. Don't be an asshole. Get romantic but keep it real. If you use generalizations like, *I want to take you for a long walk on the beach*, you're going to sound like a tool. Talk specifics. Be descriptive. Let her imagination run wild with what you're telling her. For example, I used to start out by asking girls if they liked going to the beach. The answer was always yes. As they'd been asked that a million times before, I'm sure they thought they were about to be bored out of their mind with the standard rhetoric. What they got was personalization. I would start talking about how I used to live in Miami and about specific beaches I'd been to. I'd talk about how clear the water was in the Keys and how I loved to hit South Beach. Then, I would tell them about my boat. I made sure to tell them she was an old boat and how little I'd paid for her. I wasn't trying to impress the girls with the boat because of the perception that it cost a lot of money. What I was doing was making them fall in love with the nostalgia of the story. I was painting them a picture of me, on an old, beat-up boat, listening to Jimmy Buffett and Bob Marley, drinking frozen margaritas, while kicking it around the Bahamas. I would talk about how lonely I used to get out on the open ocean because I usually didn't have a girl with me. By the time I got through telling a chick about the *1 Muff Diver* and our voyages together, she would be hooked. I was no longer Mark Blackard, a stranger trying to get into her panties. I was Jimmy Buffett and Ernest Hemingway rolled up into one person, entertaining her with tales of adventure on the high seas.

After informing a chick that the *1 Muff Diver* was sitting on a trailer at my cabin and that I could show her the old girl, that's all it took. They wanted to be a part of the action because most girls live safe, boring lives. They were suddenly and unexpectedly intrigued. Their guard was lowered and I was in. I would take them straight to my house, pour a couple of drinks, kick on the batteries to the boat, and turn on its interior lights. We'd climb aboard and sit under the stars while sipping rum and Coke and listening to Jimmy Buffett. The girls were always curious and intrigued by the small sign that read, *Warning: Boat or Captain Subject to go Down at any Moment*. I would raise the flag the *1 Muff Diver* flew under which would seal the deal. It was a pirate flag with a Jolly Roger and the words, *Surrender the Booty*. Since the *1 Muff Diver* had a small cabin on the front, we would end up going at it down below. I can't tell you how many chicks I shagged aboard the old girl while she sat on a trailer in my driveway. It was five times the amount of chicks I shagged on her while out to sea. Can you see how that works?

● ● ●

Maybe you don't have an old boat or stories as intriguing. That's ok. The point is that you have to break down the formality between you and the girl you just met. You have to take it from formal to informal and you've only got a matter of hours to accomplish the task. If at the end of the night she still feels like she has to be proper and formal around you, be rest assured you're not getting into her panties. She has to be able to relate to you in some way and that some way has to spark her interest. Figure out a way to mesmerize her and take her mind off the fact you're trying to screw her and you've won the game.

I shouldn't call it a game, but in a way it is. As a friend of mine named Tim put it, *The problem with Western bitches is that they want to play too many fucking games. They want to get laid but they make you play games with them first.* I second what he has said. I've often asked chicks over breakfast the next morning about why they made it so damn difficult for me to get them in the sack. *Why did you make me work so damn hard to be able to make you feel good?* The answer was pretty universal that they wanted to sleep with me all along but they just didn't want me to think they were easy and therefore, a whore. I would always ask them what the difference was. We were eating breakfast together after screwing for hours. The outcome was the same. The games just meant that we got to my house at 4:00 a.m. and were now both sleepy as hell. We could have left out the damn games and made it to my house by midnight. We'd have drunk less, saved money, had a better night of sex, gotten some sleep, and felt much better the day after. All that extra work playing games was for what? They all had a good time and most would return for round two and three or more. The follow-up rounds were always much more enjoyable because the bullshit games had already been played and were out of the way. We could then enjoy each other's company and knock boots without first having to put a puzzle together.

Play the Numbers

Lesson number seven is that you have to play the numbers. Quantity over quality. If you go to a club and only talk to two or three girls, don't start to wonder about why you didn't get laid. If you do pull the first girl you speak to, then congratulations. But chances are you won't. You need to use a shotgun approach. Talk to as many girls as you can until you zero in on that one solid prospect. If you don't, your odds will be drastically lower than mine. Why? Because I'll keep introducing myself until I get one to bite. If I leave a club at the end of the night without a woman in tow, I can assure you of one fact: There isn't one lady in there who does not know my name. If I strike out it's because I went down swinging. I struck out only after talking to each and every chick available. I gave all of them an opportunity to turn me down. I didn't go home alone because I gave up after speaking with two or three. You have to play the numbers. Increase your odds by increasing the quantity of chicks you talk to.

An easy way to do this is to pick a spot near the ladies room as a vantage point. In the world of tactics, this is what's called a fatal funnel. There's nothing perverted about it—you're just letting them come to you instead of you going to them. Every woman who comes to the club will at some point have to frequent the ladies room. If you are posted near there off to the side of the flow of traffic, you will get to take a look at each and every girl in the club in a short period of time. You can use this method to scope out any prospects you didn't see previously. If there's one I really want to talk to, I just say hello as they're headed to pee. Once they come back past me, I engage them with my pickup line and see where it goes. Work smarter, not harder.

The 1 Percent Rule

Another aspect of playing the odds starts by just being out there. You have to get your ass out of the house and beat the streets. Women are everywhere. They're at the grocery store, Walmart, clubs, bars, restaurants, concerts, walking downtown, at the park, etc. If you sit at home feeling sorry for yourself, there is a zero percent chance that you're going to get laid. No bitch is going to come to your house, ring your doorbell, introduce herself, and then take off her clothes. It's not going to happen unless you're in the middle of a good dream. However, if you get out of the house and roll to the bar, there is at least a one percent chance you're going to get into a girl's panties. Now, I'm no statistician, but to me that's a one hundred percent increase in probability that you're going to score. I call this simple element of philosophy *The 1 Percent Rule*.

● ● ●

Let me tell you about an incident that happened to prove my point on this. It was around ten years ago when this occurred. I was on a business trip to New York and was booked into the Crown Plaza Hotel. I was traveling with a co-worker who was also somewhat of a player. We had discussed the fact that as soon as we got checked-in we were going to hit the hotel bar. When we entered the hotel lobby we could hear a lot of people carrying on in the lounge, which was around the corner and out of sight. *Hell, yeah,* we both thought. We agreed to drop our bags in the rooms and meet as quickly as possible. After washing my face and taking a piss, I met back up with my buddy. We were both excited as hell when we turned the corner and walked into the bar.

Our excitement turned into quiet laughter when we took a gander at the crowd. There were about thirty guys in there with one ugly, fat chick. We both looked at each another in disbelief. We discussed going somewhere else but we really didn't have time. We had an early morning appointment we had to make. We sat down at the bar and ordered some food. We talked about our bad luck and how the bar looked like a dude ranch. I made the comment that as long as we were in the bar, there was at least a one percent chance one of us would get laid. If we went back and holed up in our rooms, there was a zero percent chance for either of us. He laughed and agreed with that assessment.

Less than two minutes later, a good-looking blond walked into the lounge. She was wearing a long dress with flowery patterns on it. It appeared to me as if she was on her way to church instead of the bar. She had some nice titties, was slender, and was around forty years of age. She sat down at a table, turned her body toward me, and just stared. We locked eyes for at least five seconds before she turned back around toward her table. Could it be that my one percent theory was about to be proven?

My buddy asked, "Did you see that shit?"

"Yeah, sure did," I replied, in a cocky and confident tone.

"What the hell are you going to do about it?" he inquired.

"I can tell you one thing. I damn sure ain't going to sit here with your ass all night," I said calmly.

With that, I dropped my buddy cold and walked straight to the girl's table. After quick introductions, we found ourselves having a great time. My buddy finally got disgusted due to my new-found luck and called it a night. The chick turned out to be a saleswoman for a school textbook company. She was married with a couple of kids. I think she was from Virginia, but I'm not sure. She was on a two-day business trip to New York City.

After a few drinks, we decided to venture out. But first, she wanted me to go up to her room so we could smoke a joint. I told her it wasn't my cup of tea and to just handle that little task herself. I'd wait in the bar. She disappeared around the corner and I figured it was the end of my night. However, about fifteen minutes later she returned, reeking of the chronic and in an even better mood. *Cool!*

We hailed a cab and the chick told the driver, who was from Nigeria, to take us to a club. There was apparently a language barrier because the guy drove us straight to a strip-joint. The old girl got pissed at the driver and cussed him up and down. We got out and walked until we found a small bar that was still open. They had a band, which I ended up singing in for a few songs. It was a great time and we eventually made it back to the hotel and ended up in her room.

We rocked it out until her alarm went off at around five. She immediately got up and started working on her laptop. She asked me to help her with an Excel spreadsheet because she didn't understand how to enter the correct formulas. *What? Fuck that,* I thought. *I'm outta here.* I had my own business to handle, I was tired, and had no real motivation about looking at a spreadsheet while still half-drunk. She gave me her number and we ended up keeping in touch for a few months afterward.

The moral of the story? That slim, one percent chance can quickly become a one hundred percent certainty. Get your ass out there and advertise yourself. They say that a funny thing happens when you don't advertise—nothing. Remember that. I merely put myself on display and ended up tagging an 8.0 with nice tits.

The Early Bird Gets Laid

Lesson number eight is that the early bird gets the *pussy*. The worst thing to have to endure is when you've scoured the crowd, picked out a target, profiled her actions, and decided that she's prime for the picking, only to watch another man beat you to her by five seconds. You have to strike quickly my friends or you'll be left out in the cold. A huge key to my success with pulling bitches was because I had the balls to initiate a conversation and the fact that I did it quicker than the guy standing next to me. Know that the numbers are stacked against you before you even step foot into the club. There will inevitably be three dudes per every girl in the joint. Competition is fierce if you're merely looking at the 3:1 ratio by itself. How to you circumvent the shitty ratio and take yourself out of the competition altogether? Just be the first *motherfucker* to strike. It's that easy. Most guys roll into a club and have to get settled in, have a few drinks, get comfortable, etc. I drink prior to and while en route. As I walk through the door, I'm sucking down the last drop of beer from the last can in the six-pack. When I take my first steps into the establishment, I'm already on my A-game and ready to do battle. There's very little downtime with my strategy.

Increase your odds by getting to the club early. If I'm kicking it out, I want to be in the club by 9:00 p.m. Sure, that's early and I'm usually the first person in there. That's quite alright. If the club closes at 3:00 a.m., that gives me six solid hours of hunting women. If I can't pull a chick after six hours of work, it just wasn't meant to be that night. Now, contrast that to a lot of other dudes who roll in at 11:00 p.m. or midnight. That only gives them either four or three hours, respectively, in which to take care of business. If a guy gets there at midnight, I already have a one hundred percent advantage over him based on time alone. I've had three more hours in which to work my magic. That's huge! Plus, I can scope out the chicks as they roll in and get first dibs on who I want to talk to. Some men go with the philosophy that the later they arrive, the drunker the bitches will be. Therefore, they won't have to buy so many drinks. You can go with that theory but basically you're looking at all of the girls who either aren't trying to hook up or they're my leftovers. Players like me have already scoped out those chicks and scratched them off the list. Show up late and you're already behind the curve.

● ● ●

A few years back, my buddy Dirty and I used the *Early Bird* tactic on a couple of bitches. Don't worry about why we call him Dirty. It's not pertinent to the story. One night, Dirty and I decided to kick it out and ended up at a pool hall. It was a Monday night so most of the clubs were closed. Regardless, we strolled in and it was eerily similar to the dude ranch I had encountered at the Crown Plaza in New York. The only difference being there wasn't even a fat chick in sight. There were nothing but men in the place and now there were two more. We decided to shoot some pool and not worry about the fact there were no ho's available for us to pursue. I briefly explained my one percent theory to Dirty. We laughed about it and carried on.

About thirty minutes later, the front door opened. Two trashy bitches walked in and stopped to get their bearing.

Dirty said, "Grab em' dog! Quick, before someone else does."

Those were words of wisdom but I was already headed toward the door. I walked up and introduced myself.

"Hey, how ya'll doing? My name's Mark. Come on, me and my buddy got a table right over here."

That was literally all it took to get the two ladies in tow. While I did this, around thirty hard-dicks were watching and kicking themselves because they weren't quicker on their feet. They couldn't believe I rolled in strong, less than five seconds after the girls' arrival. They learned an important lesson that day and I didn't even have to explain it to them.

We ended up playing pool with the girls, drank maybe two more beers a piece, and then suggested we kick it back to their house. They accepted and the four of us rolled out. The time from first contact to departure for their home? Less than one hour. Since I was drinking, I let the short chick drive my bright-yellow Suzuki Aereo rental car while I rode shotgun. Dirty rode with the tall, dark-haired bitch in her vehicle. We made one stop at a convenience store. Dirty and I sat in the car while the two bitches went inside. They both emerged with a case each of Bud Ice. That was the moment when we both realized we were about to get laid. Rednecks know that Bud Ice has a greater alcohol content than Bud or Bud Light. These girls were making preparations to party and get railed out by Dirty and me.

On the way to their townhouse, the bitch driving my rental car ended up side-swiping a brick mailbox which fucked up the whole right side of the car. Thank goodness I had purchased the additional walk-away insurance. It was my fault for letting her ass drive after having a few, but better her than me if we had gotten stopped by the police. We finally made it to their townhouse and got settled in. We all started drinking and talking while chilling in the living room.

Less than thirty minutes later, my man Dirty politely asked the two ladies if he could use their restroom. They pointed the way and he disappeared from the scene. I continued the conversation which, at that point, was still semi-formal. A few minutes passed and I heard the sound of the bathroom door open behind me. No one paid any attention to it. Suddenly, Dirty emerged from behind the couch and stood in the middle of the room.

The short, thick bitch suddenly said, "Oh. My. God..."

The tall girl and I turned to see Dirty standing in front of us. He was buck naked. Everyone's jaws dropped.

Dirty clapped his hands together, looked at me and said, "Alright dog, let's get this party started."

With that, he dropped down to his knees in between the tall girl's legs. He spread them wide open, pulled down her shirt and her bra, and went to sucking on her right tit. The short chick in the chair was speechless. She just sat there observing the carnage with her mouth wide open. Sensing she may be the party-pooper, I said, *Fuck it*. I joined Dirty in the breast feeding and started sucking on the left tit. Old girl just lay back even further and let out a sigh of satisfaction. She was loving it. She was into it and was soaking up all of the sexual attention she could get from the two players. We tag-teamed the tall chick for several minutes until the short one started getting jealous and feeling left out. Dirty disengaged from the right tit and grabbed up shorty. He carried her into the kitchen while I began to shag the tall chick on the couch. I was having a great time with old girl and she was enjoying the action.

About twenty minutes later, Dirty emerged from the kitchen after apparently busting a nut on Ms. Shorty's face. He sat down in the recliner and watched as me and old girl went at it.

"Yo dog, hurry up," Dirty said. "I've got a dentist appointment tomorrow. I need to get back to the house."

What the hell did he just say? His statements made both me and the tall girl pause and stare at his silly ass.

"Yo man, fuck your dentist appointment. My dick ain't on a fucking timer," I said, and went back to the task at hand.

Dirty's girl walked into the living room and began to watch the action as well.

"Hey girl, go over there and help my boy hurry up. I got a dentist appointment tomorrow," Dirty told Ms. Shorty.

With that, the girl came over to the couch and started rubbing my balls while I railed out her friend. It felt good and I wasn't really paying much attention to her because I was fucked up on Bud Ice. After a few minutes, I felt something tickling my balls. I looked down and realized that Dirty was licking Ms. Shorty's snatch and had his head right up in the mix. My balls were raking the top of his head and his hair was tickling the shit out of me.

"Yo dog, move your fucking head. Your hair's tickling my balls!" I yelled to Dirty.

He got repositioned and the sexual pile continued. Eventually, the carnage came to an end and we rolled out of there. It had been a damn good time with those two pool-hall bitches.

● ● ●

What's the moral to the story? The early bird gets the *pussy*. Strike quickly or be left out in the cold. As a side note, we told that story to several co-workers later on during a discussion about chasing women. The majority of them looked at us as if we were gay. Rumors began to fly. Listen, just because your balls scrape the top of your buddy's head while engaged in a drunken foursome does not make you gay. I fail to see the correlation. Consequently, all of those who criticized our actions were the most boring, *pussy-whipped*, bible-thumping stiffs you could ever imagine. They'll die and be buried with absolutely no stories to tell. Their lives will amount to thirty years of being slaves to the machine and their fat-ass wives. Exciting? Not to me. Hey, live your life the way you want to live it but don't impose your boring ass on me or my crew. Don't like the adventure Dirty and I undertook with the pool-hall girls? No problem. Everyone's entitled to their opinion. However, I'll bet you one damn thing—people who have heard that story remember it clearly. I don't remember any of the stories told by the stiffs.

● ● ●

Let me clarify something for my gay friends out there who don't know me. I'm not using the term gay in a derogatory sense. I am not homophobic so don't start hammering me (no pun intended) when you don't know anything about me. If you do, I'll line up a few of my gay friends and some lady-boys to square you away. Regardless, I'm straight. The Hoy Dog and Pablo Escobar are straight. We are not narrow-minded, though. You're all welcome to come to dinner, hang out at my crib, or kick it to the club with us anytime. That doesn't change the fact that we like women. Clarifying my stance is not meant to say anything negative about anyone. It just pisses me off when holier than thou conformists run their flappers and pass judgment on others. The haters in question were being judgmental toward Dirty and me, while simultaneously expressing their prejudice toward homosexuals and the gay community.

Online Pimping

Way back before online dating was commonplace, I was already in the game. I remember that when I told a friend of mine I was going on a date with a girl who I had met on the Internet, he got concerned. He strongly suggested I not do it because it could be a setup. He thought I was either going to get raped, robbed, or ripped off in some way. I told him to relax and not to worry. She seemed like a nice girl and I'd even talked to her on the phone a couple of times. I rolled out and ended up meeting the young lady in the parking lot of a grocery store. She turned out to be a good-looking girl. We decided to grab something to eat and ended up at a local restaurant. As we walked in, out of nowhere, my stomach suddenly started to churn. I almost shit my pants before I made it to the men's room. I'm not sure why I had a sudden onset of the runs but I ended up spending most of my time in the crapper while the girl ate. Dinner was pretty awkward but I was eventually able to get the date back on track. We decided to grab a movie and spend some more time together. We hopped in my truck and headed for the theater. As I was pulling into the parking lot, shit pains hit me again right in the gut. I was able to hold it together long enough to buy the tickets and get through the front door. I handed her a twenty-dollar bill and told her to grab some popcorn—I'd meet her inside the theater. I sprinted to the can and blew it out for a good forty-five minutes. Every time I tried to get up off the toilet, my ass would explode again. My stomach finally calmed down and I found myself inside the darkened theater trying to locate the poor girl. Since she had already watched over half of the movie by herself, the conversation was nil. We left the theater in silence and I dropped her off at her car. That's the last I saw or heard from her.

The next day I reported to my friend that the girl I had met on the Internet ended up being hot and that the date was a huge success! Well, not exactly that particular outing but the fact I had successfully pulled a real chick via digital means. It changed everything. I would end up hunting girls on various websites such as American Singles and Yahoo Personals. I kept up my game in the bars and clubs as usual. However, whenever I had some downtime, I was spitting out digital game to all the honeys online. Think about it for a minute. You can chat with chicks without having to leave the house or get dressed up. Most of the time, I was sitting on the throne when I was browsing. What a better time to have to play the typical mind games with American chicks than when you're taking a dump? Don't they call that multi-tasking?

It took me a while to perfect the process. In the beginning, I would always invite the girl to dinner. That ended up breaking my damn wallet. I was going broke just trying to feed all of the bitches. The bad thing was that half the time, I really didn't click with the girl. Since I figured that aspect out over dinner, I still got clipped for thirty bucks even though it was a dead end. Due to the number of chicks I was pulling down, I had to amend my game plan to save money. It all came to me one day while I was in Barnes and Noble at the Mall of Georgia. I loved browsing there and having a cup of hot chocolate in the coffee shop upstairs. I was sitting there alone, looking out over the parking lot when I had an epiphany.

Within five minutes, I had formulated the perfect game plan to use for screening the Internet vixens. I should have applied for a patent and licensed the procedure.

You see, one of the first problems you face when you meet a girl online is that she has inevitably posted an old picture of herself. Sometimes the picture was taken ten years before. Sometimes the pictures bear absolutely no resemblance to the real person. I used to get so damn pissed when a woman purposely misrepresented herself and her appearance. I never did that. I posted a recent picture of myself and listed my correct height and weight. What you saw on my profile was what you got—no surprises. I got deceived on so many occasions it was time to turn the table on the fraudulent bitches. The layout of that particular Barnes and Noble store was perfect for my new strategy. Here's what I would do...

First, I would suggest to the girl we meet up during the day over a cup of coffee instead of going to dinner. That way, it would be less formal and we both could feel at ease and get to know one another in a quiet, comfortable atmosphere. I would act stupid as to where to go but would then suddenly *remember* that Barnes and Noble had a coffee shop upstairs. They would always love that suggestion because there was no stress to it. It was just a quick meeting over a cup of coffee and not a real date—low key. I would tell the chick to meet me there around 1:00 p.m., but I'd get there thirty minutes early. I would stake out a table by the window so I could see the parking lot. I would tell the girl to give me a ring when she arrived and that I would meet her at the front door. In reality, I was upstairs scoping her out from my perch. When the girl would call, I could get an initial look from a distance. If the chick lied about her weight and turned out to be a beast, I'd make some excuse as to why I had to call off the date. End of story and money saved.

If the chick looked ok from a distance, I would tell her to meet me in the coffee shop upstairs. As she was coming up the escalator, I would be going down and take a gander up close. It's kind of comical that none of them recognized me during their ascent. If the bitch had been deceitful with her profile, I would keep right on rolling, walk out the front door, get in my car, and bounce. I wouldn't even answer any more of her calls. End of story. Think that's mean? That's not mean at all. It's called karma—what goes around comes around. If you have to lie about what you really look like, I've got no sympathy for you. Don't you think that if you lie about your appearance it's going to be blatantly obvious the first time we meet? How fucking stupid can you be?

...Ladies, if you're a 6.0, don't try to tell me you're a perfect 10. I won't sleep with you just because of the principle of the matter. If you're straight-up about things, I really don't care if you're a 2.0 with a club foot. I'll still rock you out like a champ.

If the chick was truthful and I liked what I saw, I would ride the escalator to the bottom, cut an immediate u-turn, and head back up. I would entertain her over a cup of hot chocolate and see where it went. If we weren't studying one another, I would thank the girl, tell her it was a pleasure meeting her, and we'd part ways. There was no harm and no foul. I was only out a few bucks. She was only out her time. A few of these girls I actually kept in touch with to compare notes on our online exploits. If the girl and I ended up hitting it off, the sky was the limit. Since we were at the mall we could catch a movie and then go to dinner afterward. My success rate after buying a girl dinner went from around ten percent to one hundred percent just because of the Barnes and Noble approach. The interview over the cup of hot chocolate would tell me right then and there whether or not things were going to swing my way later on that night. It was pure genius.

● ● ●

The highest caliber of women whom I've had the pleasure of sleeping with were pulled from online dating sites. Typically, they were businesswomen, nurses, teachers, etc. Most had a bachelor's degree or better. They came from stable families who were often affluent. They were quality chicks who had marriage potential. They weren't like the trash I usually pulled from the clubs. You may ask yourself about why, if they were such good girls, did they engage in online dating in the first place? The answer is simple. It's because they didn't have time to be hanging out in the club. They had school or their career which took up the majority of their time. Most of them didn't drink at all. Therefore, a bar was the last place they wanted to go. Online dating for them was convenient. Don't get me wrong—those chicks were just as freaky in the sack as a coked-up stripper. They just couldn't advertise it. They had to be productive, reputable members of their company, business, or organization. If they had been seen getting ground down to a pulp on the dance floor of some club, it could have affected their professional reputation. However, if they were getting pounded out like a porn star aboard the *1 Muff Diver* while secluded on my five acres in the woods, they were down with it.

Working bitches online is like farming. You can't expect things to mature overnight. You've got to plant a seed and allow it to grow. The good thing is that there's a year-round growing season. You have to continually plant seeds to keep a steady flow of ho's in the pipeline. If you keep at it religiously, you'll find yourself meeting bitches at the Barnes and Noble every couple of days. It's like shooting fish in a barrel. Too easy.

Summary

These tips are obviously not meant to be an all-encompassing playbook on how to pick up women. There are volumes of texts which have been authored and are dedicated to the cause. This chapter was just a snapshot of tactics and techniques that have worked for me. Try adopting some of my principles and see where they get you. Maybe they will get you slapped and shot down on every occasion. Maybe they will get you laid. Whatever you do, just don't go out and try to impress women by spending money on them. Sure, they'll take the gifts and ride the benefits but they'll look at you as the *jackass* who pays for it all. Meanwhile, tigers like myself, Pablo Escobar, and the Hoy Dog are railing them out as soon as they can shake you for an afternoon.

CHAPTER 12

LOVE FOR THE LADIES

This book would not be complete without me showing some love for all of the decent women in America. I know you're out there—somewhere. There's not many of you but I've heard that you do exist. We've looked for you in bars, nightclubs, Walmart, grocery stores, online, the mall, and even in many churches. We have come to the conclusion that a good American woman is just as elusive of a creature as *Bigfoot* and on the verge of extinction like some whales (no pun intended).

What some of you may find perplexing is that a lot of women are down with the *Kingdom Rule* concept. They like the comfort and security the principles bring to their lives. It takes the uncertainty out of many areas which causes them to worry. The principles shift most of the burden of success or failure to the husband who will in turn be forced to act like a man. Let me share a story with you about a nice British woman who unexpectedly found herself being educated and seduced by the king.

● ● ●

A few years back, I was on a flight to Bangkok. It originated in Rome with a ten-hour layover in Dubai. After boarding the plane in Dubai, I received a nice surprise when I discovered who my seat mate was going to be. She was a tall, blond-headed chick with very nice, fake titties. She knew they looked good and had those puppies out for public display. Everyone on the plane was straining their necks to get a closer look at her tig-old-bitties. We were sitting in the very last row of the plane which inadvertently provided for a bit of seclusion. I was by the window and she had the aisle seat. Once she sat down, I breathed a sigh of relief that I wasn't stuck next to a fat, sweaty, white guy or an Arab brother who hadn't bathed in two months. Hell no, the chick smelled GOOD. *It should be a pleasant flight for me*, I thought. I had my ear plugs in, my business section of the paper at the ready, and really didn't want to be bothered. However, in less than two minutes after the girl sat down, she started running that flapper. *Here we go.* Just another Western bitch with a bad attitude and a sense of entitlement who wants me to think she's important.

● ● ●

Let me back up a minute. I had just spent ten hours in the Marhaba (*welcome* in Arabic) Lounge drinking unlimited Budweiser and Jack Daniel's and Coke. Do you know how dangerous it is to put a poor redneck like me in a lounge with free beer and Jack Daniel's? For ten hours? With no supervision? Allow me to make my own drinks? *Are they fucking crazy?* Have they never heard of the American redneck? If they were remotely interested in actually making money, they would either not serve free beer or refuse to serve rednecks. Their choice. Either way, I broke their wallets during that ten-hour stay at my table right next to the beverage station. Needless to say, they were very happy to see me go. I vaguely remember talking with the Hoy Dog at some point who strongly advised me to slow my roll or else they probably wouldn't let me board the plane. Good advice, but it wasn't adhered to. Since it was free, I felt a sense of duty (which is ingrained in all rednecks) to drink as much as I physically could. I did make it on the plane without getting ejected so everything worked out ok.

● ● ●

Now, there are definitely worse things that can happen to you, but I really wasn't in the mood to chat with the chick. I just wanted to relax and go to sleep once the business section bored me to death. Within a matter of ten minutes I had been involuntarily enlightened by her life's story. After listening to her, I felt like an asshole for initially not wanting to be sociable. The poor lady had lost her husband about a month prior due to a sudden illness. They had been married for twenty-three years and had one daughter. It was a sad story and you could tell she really needed to vent to someone. Unfortunately for me, that someone was the king. I was a bit tipsy and feeling just fine. A hard-luck tear-jerking story was not in my plans. Turns out, she was on her way to Thailand to deal with the vacation house they owned there. That's the setting for the conversation which followed. For some reason, which I suspect to be the effects of two additional mini-bottles of wine I drank while listening to her, I began to explain how the king lives his life. I shared some of the concepts and gave her the down and dirty. She expressed very quickly that she was not into the *Kingdom Rule* concept and thought I was crazy. As with a lot of extremely attractive women, she acted as if she had the upper hand and was somehow in control of the conversation. I let her think that and kept right on preaching.

● ● ●

Initially, as with most women, she went through the phase of, *There is no woman in the world who would put up with you and you would be a terrible boyfriend or husband.* I told the girl she was entitled to her opinion and should always be the captain of her own destiny. However, she would not make it around me with her current attitude and would definitely be shown the door in rapid fashion. I explained to her about the magical portal to freedom. I wasn't trying to get into her pants and I certainly wasn't trying to impress her. She wasn't what I was looking for in any form. If she were, I would not have been on a plane to Bangkok. I would have been in the U.S. or England looking for girls. She was merely a nuisance who was keeping me awake. Since she had interrupted my tranquility and opened up the conversation with her life's story, she was fair game for some ground truth about me and my philosophy.

I broke it down for her about the way it is in my life. She pointed out the fact that most women would not tolerate me for very long. After reiterating to her that I was downright comfortable with being the only member of my kingdom, she finally caught on. The novelty for her was that for some unknown reason, she didn't have the power over me like she has with every other man she meets. *What the hell was going on?* I'm sure the thought crossed her mind that I must be gay. Why else would I not be kissing her ass? She was tall, slender, blond-headed, had a tight body and a firm ass, and had big, fake tits. Why wasn't her charm working on me? I will concede that she looked good, especially with the boob job. But who gives a shit? For $5,000 dollars you can put tits on anything. The entire conversation just killed her and I was loving it. From her perspective, here was an average-looking guy, way too short for her, too cocky, dressed like a bum, apparently not rich, and with no particular claim to fame, shooting her ass down like she was a Skud missile.

After several hours of me preaching the principles of *Kingdom Rule* and dutifully informing her that her place was in the kitchen with her mouth shut, she was just itching for me to ask for her number. She was waiting to regain some type of control over the conversation. She was patiently waiting for the opportunity to dish out some rejection and regain her self-esteem. *Nope. Sorry, girl. You've got nothing for me.* As we were landing, she apparently couldn't take it anymore. The entire incident had not worked out like she envisioned and she wasn't about to leave things unsettled.

She asked me if I wanted her e-mail address. I said, *Sure, go ahead and give it to me.* I had no intentions of ever contacting her. I just wanted her to squirm a little bit more over the fact that she opened the door and I never called. She gave me her e-mail address and cell phone number. I told her I would hook up with her on the weekend to see if she had any cooking skills. Again, false hope. As we deplaned, she gave me a big hug and pushed those huge titties up against me. For a split second, she had my attention. They were nice, and for a short moment I contemplated playing her damn games so I could tag that ass a few times. *Nah.* It just wasn't worth the effort. I dropped her number on the floor of the jet way and never looked back. Maybe one of the airline employees found it and gave her a ring.

● ● ●

What's the moral of this short story? Believe it or not, women dig the *Kingdom Rule* concept. I was never mean to the girl during the entire conversation. I just told her exactly how I felt about women and shared with her my expectations of them. I described to her how she would have to act if she wanted to reside in my castle. So, why was the girl trying to hook up with me? Some people may argue that women are attracted to men who are assholes. While we've all seen this to be the case at times, I don't believe that's really why they're attracted to these types of guys. A woman doesn't want a man to be a jerk to her. She doesn't want to be around a dick-head who's mean or belittling. What she wants is someone who will take charge and make her feel secure.

Women are only attracted to assholes because they fill this void as a side effect of their meanness. Women endure the negatives of the situation because that's how bad they need men to be assertive. Why do nice guys always finish last? Because a nice guy acts too much like a damn woman, is too passive, and therefore, a woman doesn't feel secure around him. He's just too much of a *pussy*—a limp dick. A straight woman wants a real man to take care of her.

●●●

Since I've only been concerned with the men of the world up to this point, let me turn the spotlight on the ladies and ask them if they are happy with their lives. Are you satisfied with your marriage or are you just staying with your husband for the sake of conformity? If you're not happy and are just doing what everyone else expects, you're not doing yourself nor your husband any justice. I want you to realize as well that you're not going to live forever and that life is short. If your home life or your sex life is shitty, then maybe you should think about making a change. It is highly possible that your husband is so afraid of you he'd rather be miserable than begin to cross you. If this is the case, you need to be the one to take some action for the good of the both of you. *Woman-up* and explain to the poor bastard that it's time for a change. Just don't be surprised when he's more than willing to go along with your suggestion.

●●●

If any of you ladies do decide to initiate a divorce, make sure you and your husband re-read *The Art of Divorce* chapter. Consider what I've said. My specific advice to you (the woman) is to not be a greedy bitch! Listen, I've just told your husband to give you everything in the house. I've advocated that he concede and give you the high end of the scale when it comes to child support. I'm basically giving him instructions and advice which will make your life better, much quicker. But, if you act like a typical American bitch and drag on a divorce unnecessarily, run up an outrageous attorney's bill like Pablo's *ex-cunt*, and try to deny a father ample time with his children, I've got nothing else to offer you. You will be relegated to the category of the typical nasty, greedy, American woman with her sense of entitlement. Your actions will classify you as a welfare recipient who receives LBS (*Lazy Bitch Support*). Does your dignity as a woman mean anything to you? Or, would you just rather live a nasty existence like the rest and steal as much money as you can through LBS? Yeah, I know. Most of you just want the money.

My ex-wife robbed me for ten years. Now, her days of being a thief are over. I'm no longer being robbed. However, she will carry the burden of being a lazy sloth who refused to work, all the way to her grave. That's the extent of her legacy. How do you want to be remembered by your family and children? If you would be civil about things, you could be considered a classy woman and still get most of what you want.

● ● ●

Did your man cheat on you? If that's why you're headed toward divorce, get over it. *It fucking happened.* What's done is done. No one cares about the reason except for you, honey. The judge and the attorneys don't care about why he screwed that waitress. At this point, it's only about the numbers. If you would leave the feelings of revenge and your scorn out of the business end of divorce, you both would be able to put a lot more money in your pockets. Most uneducated women want their day in court so they can tell the whole world what a shitty husband their man was to them. Is that really worth tens of thousands of dollars? How about this option instead. Just go on Facebook and Twitter and type out every nasty thing you want to say about your soon-to-be ex-husband and hit *Post*. There, the whole world knows what a cheater he is. Now you two can sit down at the Waffle House and sketch out a settlement agreement. A lawyer can type the thing up and file it for less than a grand. You can then get on with your pursuit of happiness.

● ● ●

Let's go back to Pablo's situation for a minute and talk money. Because his wife was a *cunt*, they both lost a ton of money, unnecessarily. Because of her unwillingness to negotiate and act civil, she ran up a $20,000 dollar debt to her attorney. The judge, inevitably and in his infinite wisdom, ordered Pablo to pay this. First of all, Pablo didn't have $20,000 dollars. However, had he not paid it, the attorney would have gotten an order to garnish Pablo's wages, possibly filed a lien on his house, and gone after him any way she could. Pablo unwillingly had to take the advice of the judge and borrow the money from his retirement fund. How could this have been handled differently so that both parties actually benefitted? Consider my thoughts.

Most people, including me, do not have $20,000 dollars they can disperse without having to borrow the funds. Neither did Pablo. An amount that is within our reach is around $5,000 dollars. I could scrape up that much if I absolutely had to and so could he. If his wife would have been civil, Pablo could have said, *Look, if we can agree on everything* *and keep the lawyers out of this, I'll give you $4,000 dollars in cash.* This would have saved Pablo $15,000 dollars. It would have put some cold hard cash in the bitch's pocket. The lawyer would have made $1,000 dollars to merely file the paperwork. Pablo and his wife could have walked away divorced, happy, and with their dignity in check. The only unhappy party would have been the lawyer because she just got robbed of $19,000 dollars-worth of her *services*. But, the way that it broke down in reality, the only winner was the lawyer. She got paid twenty grand. Pablo's in debt. His soon-to-be ex-wife lost out on four grand. They're still not divorced. It was an absolute waste of cash.

● ● ●

Ladies, put your pride and scorn aside when it comes time to part ways. In America, the only people who really benefit from an uncivilized divorce are the lawyers. It does not have to be that way. Here's how I recommend you go about circumventing these buzzards. I know that your emotions will be running wild during this period of time. You don't want to be around the asshole. That's understandable. What you need to do is identify one or two people from your side who can mediate the negotiations. Don't pick your redneck friend who suggests you immediately *Pearl Harbor* the guy and fuck up his boat. Pick someone who's a bit older, passive, and level-headed. You need someone to help keep you in check. You don't need someone who's going to get you riled up. Don't choose someone who's involved emotionally, such as your father. It's natural that your father wants to kill your soon-to-be ex-husband. That's a given. I recommend maybe your aunt or uncle who is not your mother / father's brother or sister. The aunt or uncle who married into your family. They're on your team but they can still be objective. I recommend that your husband do the same.

There is a ground rule that I feel should be adhered to. If you insist on bringing your best friend for moral support, she must remain silent throughout the proceedings. Your best friend is just that. She will go to hell and back with you. She knows your secrets. She may have been party to the carnage and deceit. She knows too much. Her mere presence can inflame the situation and fuck up the talks. If she opens her mouth and runs that flapper, negotiations are certainly over. If she is truly your friend, she will understand this rule and adhere to it. The girl can roll for moral support only! Instruct her to *shut the fuck up* during the proceedings. It's merely a business meeting. It's only about the numbers and the kids.

● ● ●

Speaking of the kids, let's address the issue of *visitation*. First of all, I hate that *fucking* word. The asshole who associated that term with a father spending time with his children should immediately be put to death. If the bastard is already dead I'm going to go take a big-ass shit right on his grave. *Fuck him.* I say him, but it very well could have been a her. Terminology like this and the associated laws, rules, and precedents that go with it is why America is unraveling. It's exactly why the young people of America are out of control. It's the reason our teenagers are walking into schools and movie theaters and opening fire. The liberalistic laws of our civil justice system have effectively removed the father and prevent him from being able to discipline his children. As Pablo recently put it, *The system has failed us as fathers. We do everything we can as men to take care of our children but the system just tears us down. It doesn't allow us to be dads.* Pablo was right on the money when he said that.

● ● ●

Who came up with the bright idea that it was a good thing for a child's welfare and future to suddenly remove the father from the equation? The man is divorcing the woman—not his children. Children go from having a dad to having a man they barely know pick them up every other weekend. How in the hell did America come to this? Children need both their mother and their father to be in their lives. It makes me sick to think about how my beloved country, the United States of America, has become so *fucked up*. After a mass shooting, every politician in the country wants to start an anti-violence task force and save the day. *It's too late, motherfuckers.* Your screwed up laws have taken dad out of the equation. Dad is the person who can be on duty twenty-four hours a day, seven days a week, three hundred sixty-five days a year to police his kids. Your anti-violence task force doesn't accomplish anything tangible and is about as useful as the hair on my nuts. A major cause of the violence in America is that our laws have removed dads from their children's lives.

For the ladies, ask yourself why I just harped on this subject. It is because if you act like the typical, nasty, American bitch and use the law to withhold your kids from their father, you will pay the price. The price you'll pay is that your kids will eventually get out of control. They will run all over you. They will not respect you. You can tell them to do something and they'll tell you to go get fucked. Your life will get more difficult as the kids get older. You will fail if you try to raise those badass kids alone in order to punish your ex-husband. If they disobey you, there is no one to back you up. However, it doesn't have to be that way. You don't have to try and raise the knuckleheads by yourself.

※ ※ ※

Take a breath, clear your mind, and forget everything you know about the culture of divorce in America. Take the word *visitation* out of your vocabulary. Your new way of thinking should be that nothing changes when it comes to the kids. If dad wants to see the kids every day, encourage him to show up and be heard. If dad wants to pick up the kids from school every day, encourage him to do so. It will save you gas money. Tell dad that if the kids get out of control, you need and expect him to bring his ass over to the house and deal with the problem. Even though your marriage failed, let dad know that he's not off the hook when it comes to helping raise the kids. Even though things have become nasty between the two of you, if you take that position, dad has no choice but to *man the fuck up* and help. Money alone will not make your life easier, I promise you. Imagine having the ability to summon dad and his belt at any time of the day or night to deal with disciplinary issues which may escalate outside of your control. If your children know that you and dad are unified when it comes to their welfare, they're going to act right. In a typical divorce situation, once the kids realize that you and dad aren't on speaking terms, they discover they can suddenly get away with anything. Don't believe me? Just go ahead and be a typical American bitch and use the word *visitation*. Don't say I didn't warn you when your kids end up hooked on meth and are doing a stretch for breaking into cars. It's up to you.

If you elect to take my advice and use this approach, the pressure shifts to the man. The responsibility for the success or failure of your children shifts back to the king. If your kids end up in prison, it's not your fault. It's the king's fault. You allowed him free reign to continue being a dad. Therefore, the king must govern himself accordingly. Even though I am here representing my fellow man, I'm not giving him a free ride or advocating he shuck any of his duties as a father. If you open up the door, he better be engaged with the children. If he doesn't, then he truly is an asshole. If he has the ability and opportunity to spend time with his offspring, but doesn't, I'll personally revoke his man-card. He will be forever banned from *The Players Club*.

The majority of men in America have had the role of being a father taken away from them by some fool judge and a nasty ex-wife. If any of you classy women voluntarily take my advice and act like true ladies, your ex-husbands had better represent the oppressed fathers of America in a gentlemanly fashion. If they fuck up, the real kings of the world will publicly shame them until the end of time. Just e-mail me their names and some photographs.

● ● ●

Listen, I'm recommending that the man give you everything without a fight. I'm telling him to bust his ass and help you with the everyday routine of raising the kids. I'm insisting that he act like a king. If you act like a lady, your life and the lives of your children will be better for it. If you're nasty about things, you alone will have to bear many burdens, unnecessarily. Govern yourself accordingly. You're the captain of your own destiny.

● ● ●

As I was doing a little bit of market research for this book, I discovered a few things I really had not thought about. I reviewed the subject of divorce for men on Amazon.com and took a gander at the books for sale. Their rankings were terrible and most of them only had one or two reviews from male readers. I quickly realized that apparently my fellow man does not read books on divorce! *Who knew?* As I sat at my computer and thought about it for a minute, it really should have been obvious why. Every time I break up with a girl I truly care about, reading a damn book is the last thing that comes to mind. My brain cannot even begin to focus on reading an entire book while all of the drama is going on. Between working extra hours, drinking, and chasing new women, there is no time to read.

When looking at the books on divorce written for women, I discovered that they ranked well and most had dozens of long-winded reviews by female readers. Women going through a breakup apparently read every divorce book they can get their hands on. That should have been obvious as well. If you're an unemployed housewife, you have plenty of time on your hands to begin with. If your man has left the home, you have even more time to kill. Reading fills that void. Reading books about divorce comfort and empower you. It all makes perfect sense.

I suddenly realized that from a business standpoint, my primary audience may be the women of America whom I have written about. The ladies of America, whom I will probably piss off, may be the only demographic who actually reads this work of art. Damn what a predicament I have found myself in. Ladies, it's only logical that you will love this book because the stories will give you plenty to gossip about—and you know you love to gossip. Women love to read romance novels with steamy, graphic details of forbidden love and sex. Well, this book has all of that except it's not as graphic. Women of America love to read self-help books, too. *The King's Chronicles* has given you ladies all of the answers on how to keep your man from going astray and even what to do if he does. This could be the best book Oprah Winfrey probably won't recommend you read.

Therefore, I have to show some love for my ladies. You will probably end up being the king's biggest fans and supporters. Whether you are single, married, divorced, or separated, there are lessons here for all of you. And, I do know what many of you are wondering. Yes, technically I am single and available. Unfortunately, I typically do not date American girls. However, I could possibly make an exception or two in a rare instance. Just send me an e-mail and a couple pictures of yourself in a bikini for my review. Oh, and make sure you're not the jealous type who is afraid to share. There's enough of me to go around.

CHAPTER 13

I BELIEVE IN BOOTY

Sometime around 1994, my dad and I were eating dinner at a Japanese Hibachi grill in Marietta, Georgia. We had spent the day at a drop zone north of Atlanta. Back then, I would have spent every dime I had on skydiving. Anyone can tell you that there's nothing better than jumping out of an airplane except maybe safely walking off the DZ.

Now, my old man has always been in the game. He's an old-school player from way back and has four marriages under his belt. They say that the apple doesn't fall very far from the tree. In my case, that is an absolutely true assessment. He and I have been more like friends my entire life and have chased women together for decades. So, as we were being seated at the restaurant, we positioned ourselves right in the middle of a table full of ladies. We immediately started working some game and found ourselves entertaining the rather upscale group. About halfway through dinner, everyone at the table was drunk on sake (Japanese rice wine) and whatever else we were drinking. We were all laughing and having a good time watching the cook work his magic. For some reason, we started talking about skydiving.

"Do you jump, too?" a beautiful lady asked my dad.

"Hell yeah, I do," my dad replied.

"How high do you jump from?" asked another chick.

"I usually jump from ten thousand square feet," was the reply.

He added the *square* in there because he was in construction at the time. I was the only one who picked up on the comedy. From skydiving, the conversation turned to religion. The ladies went around the table asking each other about what religion they practiced. When they got to my dad, he happened to be sipping on some sake. Without looking up and in the most serious of tones he responded to the question.

"I'm a Buddhist," he said.

The ladies were all intrigued by this and the quiet manner in which he had said it. They obviously hadn't realized they were sitting next to a serious religious man of a different faith.

The next question posed was, "Why did you become a Buddhist?"

The reply given, while in between two sips of sake was simply, "Because I believe in booty."

There was a pause of silence. A few seconds later, everyone was laughing their asses off. He had made such a funny joke without really even thinking about it. However, I've pondered that statement often since that comical dinner experience. But, what I've thought about has nothing to do with religion. I basically came to the conclusion that whatever brings me happiness is what I will subscribe to. I'm not going to use the word worship because I don't worship anything.

What do I believe in? *I believe in booty.* To further expand on this, let me say that I believe in chasing women. I believe in getting drunk. I believe in hanging out with my buddies. I believe in dancing the night away. I believe in spending time around beautiful girls who love to party. I believe in living life like a king. Why? Because all of these activities make me happy. Religion does nothing to make me happy. It just reminds me of how much I hate being told what to do for a useless purpose.

From most people's perspective this makes me a sinner and they'll swear I'm going to hell. Maybe so, if you choose to believe the nonsense. That's your choice. However, don't try to force your beliefs on me or think that you're any better than I am. If there is in fact freedom of religion in America, put me down as being the Pope of the church that focuses on women's asses and drinks Jack Daniel's during communion. There, that's my religion if you're confused—*Jack Daniel's and pussy.*

● ● ●

Why am I harping on religion right now? It's because you probably grew up the same way I did. You grew up in the church, studied the bible, were taught not to drink, were told to settle down and get married, have kids, etc. That programming is so ingrained in you that you will feel dirty, guilty, and ashamed, if you even think about leaving your wife or making any type of change against the biblical norm. I understand where you're coming from. It took a lot of courage for me to question American societal expectations. You just have to ignore pretty much everything you are told you *have* to do and start doing things that you *want* to do. Focus on the things that make you, the man, happy. I'm in no way advocating that you do anything illegal, take drugs, rob banks, etc. That's self-destructive behavior and you'll be the king of a fucking jail cell. I'm referring to the fact that you have the right to pursue happiness. It is not illegal to divorce your wife. It is not immoral to find a new woman. Why? Because the word immoral is a subjective term. That means it's only an opinion. To bible-thumpers, going to a strip club is immoral. In my world, it's immoral to arrive at the strip club after happy hour ends. To bible-thumpers, it's immoral to drink alcohol or get drunk. In my world, it's immoral to forget the limes while you're at the liquor store. You see how that works? Morals are your personal feelings toward things. Weak-minded people often base their morals on the ethics of institutions such as the church. Ethics are the beliefs and principles of an organization. People without a strong will want and need others to lead them. Morals ingrained in the minds of the weak are nothing more than the result of programming by the religious assertive, based on no factual evidence. Grab a set of balls and adapt your morals to suit your own standard of happiness and not what the Baptists or the Catholics have dictated.

• • •

How did a guy like me, who grew up in the deep South and went to a Baptist church, and who came from a religious family, end up with this mentality? I'll tell you how. It's because for some reason, I've always had the drive to get to the bottom of things. It's ok to pull the wool over my eyes initially but at some point I'm going to figure out your scam. Sometimes, it takes a while to truly evaluate a situation and get to the ground truth. For many years, I was duped into believing in God and whatever else the church pressured me to accept. You are easily influenced by your environment and what adults preach to you when you're a child. It's not very easy to go against the majority, let me tell you. I just experienced this with the release of my first book.

I'm not sure why more people don't raise the bullshit flag on religion and start living their lives the way they want to. Shouldn't it be apparent from the start that if a preacher truly believes in what he's telling you, he would have no reason to accept that fat paycheck the church pays him? My preachers out there, if ya'll truly believe there is an after-life, then your religious asses ought to be working for free, shouldn't ya'll? You're telling me that I'm going to be judged and am going to hell for my deviant lifestyle, but what about you? You're taking money from people in your congregation who can barely pay their bills. Practice what you preach. No minister, pastor, cleric, imam, priest, rabbi, or preacher should get a paycheck nor need one if they really believe what they're saying.

● ● ●

Enough of the discussion on hypocrisy. I recommend that you never forget what's fresh in my mind all the time. You are going to die. Life is short. Adopt that mindset and break out of the box your wife and your church have locked you into. Personally, I would rather live as a king in a shit-hole of an apartment and die a year later, than live like a religious conformist in a mansion for fifty years. I guarantee I would have a better life in the apartment eating Ramen noodles everyday and chasing women. Damn, thinking about Ramen noodles just made me hungry. Think I'll go get some from my favorite street vendor in a few minutes.

● ● ●

Someone asked me if I thought this should be called a self-help book. I never really thought about it until then. I'm not very good at the business end of writing books, nor how to market the damn things. I just like being creative and typing while drunk on rum. For some reason, the words simply pop out onto the screen after a few drinks. Anyway, what started out as a concept to set the record straight with the greedy bitches of America evolved into a textbook of sorts. Maybe, after reading this, you do not share the same sentiment or see the educational value. However, I have tried to provide learning lessons and invoke thought by sharing theory, conducting case studies of historical events, and by interjecting opinions that many share but are afraid to voice.

The first book I wrote was a contribution to my country. I had to call out the rich assholes in Congress and the defense industry who are bankrupting my beloved nation and dropping bombs on innocent children around the world. Fuck all of you monsters, by the way. If I'm wrong and there is in fact a hell, I'll see ya'll down there. I'll get my ticket for chasing *pussy*, drunkenness, and bad behavior. You'll all be there for murdering babies for profit and stealing from American citizens.

This book is my contribution to the American male. I believe there are valuable learning points contained in these pages, just like a textbook. As far as being self-help? It's up to the reader to decide. Why? Because most men in America can read but only a few have the courage to act.

Personally, I think this is more of a map than a book. A map leads you somewhere you want to go or takes you out of a place you don't want to be. Use the book as such—a map to freedom. Think about how you physically use a map and compare the similarities. First, you have to know where you're standing. If you don't know where you're at, it's difficult to plan where to go without taking additional steps. So, ask yourself right now, *Where am I with my life? Am I happy? Do I really want to live the way I'm living? Am I in a hurry to go home at night or do I hate going home? Can I even remember the last time I got laid? Am I only staying with this woman because I'm afraid to pay child support or because of the kids? Do I have to ask my wife for permission to go drink a couple of beers after work?*

Orient some of the concepts in this book to your situation to further assist you with an objective evaluation. Afterward, you need to decide *if* you want to get to a better place. If so, I've given you the map that will take you out of your unhappiness. At this point, you need to determine *where* you want to go and *which path* you're going to take to get there. It may not be the same course of action I would choose, but there's always more than one way to skin a cat. Pick the route that's best for you.

※ ※ ※

As we near the end, let me speak briefly to all the girls in America who gave me the clap. Not trying to exclude any of the other vixens, but that's where the lion's share of the culprits are from. I'll try to be subtle...

Really? Are you fucking kidding me? What the hell was that all about? You mean to tell me that you screwed a man so damn nasty that he either didn't know or didn't care about the fact razor blades and fire was shooting from his dick? You want to call me low-rent? *Screw you.* I knew within a few days that I had the clap and took steps to correct the problem—every time. Therefore, it's a little bit hypocritical of you to say anything bad about me for what I've said here or my principles of *Kingdom Rule*. I don't go around knowingly giving girls the clap. That's downright cruel and I could never be a party to that. I inadvertently gave three girls the clap in my entire history of sleeping with women. As soon as I knew, I let them know so they could get treated. I still feel bad about that to this day, even though I did it unwittingly after sleeping with one of you trolls the night before. I guess I have to concede that you all were hooking up with just as many men as I was women, and gave it to me unknowingly as well. Probably, but it could be the fact that you're just a bunch of lazy bitches who don't take care of your personal hygiene nor your health. Maybe that explains why you initially wanted to use a condom. You knew you were really about to put it on me (pun intended).

While I did rack my brain in an attempt to call you out by name, you must not have left any hint of an impression on me. I can't remember any of you. I do remember some of your professions, though. Catching the clap from a social worker, a registered nurse, an E-4 in the U.S. Army, multiple girls who possess master's degrees, a PhD candidate, and several government employees was not expected. Oh, and the married flight attendant. Didn't see that one coming, either. I would and do expect that consequence from some girl who I've pulled from a backwoods country bar or a downtown dive. You know, a girl who is unemployed, smokes menthols, and has a name like *Patience* or *Cherry*. But, you bitches in the demographic I've just described have one important element in common to combat this—*You all have good health insurance!*

What is mind-boggling to me is that you ladies had to have slept with a nasty, unclean, lazy individual before me. I possess none of these traits. The hypocrisy of the way you portrayed yourselves as being pure, clean, and not really believing in pre-marital sex, was comical. If you want to get mad at anyone after reading this book, get mad at the asshole who gave you the clap because he obviously isn't a gentleman and doesn't follow my principles of *Kingdom Rule*. The king didn't give you the clap. Don't be upset with me.

If any of you vixens out there want to discuss the situation or maybe even apologize to me for the unnecessary heinousness on your part, I'm available to chat. If you really want to clear your conscience, you can fork over some money and reimburse me for my medical expenses as well. It's the right thing to do.

I'm sorry to have to say this, but a prostitute has more class than any of you in this group. Why? A prostitute is respectable because she is straight-up about things. She's honest with herself, about herself. You American girls are the biggest hypocrites I've ever dealt with when it comes to getting into your panties. You portray yourself to be so perfect, so delicate, so above getting bent over and pounded. Yet, you're just as promiscuous as a street prostitute, only displayed in a different wrapper. You lack the class to be called that, due to your deceit and dishonesty with yourself. The men of America should file a class-action lawsuit against all of you for false advertising. Maybe even stage a boycott and refuse to sleep with any of you for a few months. See if that doesn't change your attitude real quick. Probably not, but still a good idea.

∙ ● ●

I want to make the argument that prostitution should be entirely, perfectly, and respectably lawful. First of all, how in the hell did we take the world's oldest profession as they say, and at some point make it illegal? I'm not even going to research the when, or the who, or the how this came about. When you talk about prostitution in America today, the societal norm is to think bad thoughts. It's such a terrible thing to talk about. Let me break down the hypocrisy in calling prostitution a crime.

First, let's talk legality and establish who has jurisdiction over a vagina. Exactly who does a *pussy* belong to? Does it belong to the United States government? The church? The bible-thumpers? The socially dysfunctional who oppose having sex? Or, could it possibly belong to the woman that it's attached to? For this point in my argument, I think that even the abortion rights groups will side with me on this one. That's kind of funny because they're mostly feminists. Regardless, I think they will agree that a woman's body is a woman's body. It should be her decision as to what the hell she wants to do with it. In the abortion debate, I understand how the right to life groups argue their point of view. It is because to them, there is a victim involved in the form of an unborn child. Their position is that the fetus is a person and that it should have the same rights as you and me. Now, I'm not here to choose a side on this because it would take an entire manuscript to properly explain my position on abortion. However, when a woman merely commits the act of prostitution, no one is being victimized. If she voluntarily has sex with a man, tell me who the hell the victim would be?

∙ ● ●

I believe that the woman who carries the vagina around in her panties is the sole person who should have jurisdiction over it. Control of her *pussy* should not lie with the idiots who compose the United States government, state government, county government, or the city in which she lives. However, all of these entities have laws which dictate what a woman can and can't do with her own damn body.

Listen, before you get too pissed off, let me say that I'm not condoning or justifying the tactics used by pimps, drug use, or the other underground activities associated with prostitution in America. Those are separate issues, which are actually perpetuated by the fact prostitution is illegal in the first place. What I'm talking about is the fact that religious conservatives have exerted their beliefs and values just a wee bit too far in my book. I've got no problem with anyone worshipping anyone or anything in the privacy of their own home or in their church. The problem I have is when their beliefs affect others, especially when they succeed in getting them codified into law. *Mind your own fucking business and stay the hell out of everyone else's.*

A woman has the right to decide exactly what she wants to do with her life and her body. Therefore, it is crazy for there to be any laws against using your own body to make money. It is ludicrous that the idiots who steal from the people (politicians) to make their living think they can govern a woman's vagina. To expand even further on these laws, I think it may be illegal in some areas of the U.S. to masturbate. If that's the case, I'd be on death row if I were to be convicted of all my crimes against society. Personally, I strongly believe that my dick belongs to me. If I want to stick it in an ugly woman, masturbate, or paint it green and swear to you it's a cucumber, that's my right. Don't tell me what to do with *my* penis and don't tell a woman what to do with *her* vagina.

●●●

Now that we've established who really owns your body parts, we will move to the second point in my argument. More legality, but let's ask about what exactly constitutes payment for services rendered? Yep, more hypocrisy. If a man directly pays a woman to suck his dick, both he and she are now criminals. *Bonnie and fucking Clyde.* Clear cut, right? Now, let's evaluate a typical date in America. I'll even describe a respectable date as if you're picking up a nice Christian girl at her parent's home.

So, the first thing you do is go out and buy some flowers. Why? Because that's a respectable thing to do in American culture. Show up with a bouquet of flowers so she'll know how much of a gentleman you are. Price? Say, $20 dollars. You're out of your favorite cologne so you stop by the mall and drop $60 dollars. Gotta smell good. *No spray, no lay,* as the vendor in the bathroom of the club always says. You pick up the girl in your car and drive to the restaurant. Price of gas these days? Just say $3 dollars a gallon. Therefore, you're out another $15 dollars on transportation costs. You arrive at the restaurant and enjoy a nice meal. Between drinks and dinner, you're out around $80 dollars. Now you've got to take the bitch to the movies. That's easily another $50 dollars because you know an American girl has got to have popcorn, a big-ass Coke, and a damn grande-sized chocolate bar. After the movie is over, you drive her home. Add another $15 dollars on transportation costs. At the end of the first date, you've spent $240 dollars. Now, I said she was a good Christian girl so I'm trying to give her the benefit of the doubt that she didn't give up the ass on the first date.

Let's move to date number two. This time, you take her out to a sports bar for wings and drinks. No more *Mr. Nice Guy*. Tonight, it's all about getting the chick drunk and trying to get some action. Drink after drink you pay for, in an attempt to get the girl drunk enough to at least suck your dick in the parking lot. By the time you roll out of there, you're out a cool $50 dollars on wings and beer. You get into your car with the girl and somewhere between the Jägerbombs and the white Zinfandel, she has decided to give you head. The second that her lips touch the head of your dick, you both have technically just engaged in prostitution. *What?* Yep, you're now considered a John and your Christian girl is a fucking hooker. *Shit! What happened?* Well, you paid around $290 dollars for a blow job. Shame on you two. The church isn't going to be happy when they find out about this shit.

● ● ●

Explain to me how there is any difference between giving a woman payment with cash (illegal) versus giving her payment in the form of food and drink (perfectly legal). Either way, the girl is giving up the *pussy* in exchange for financial gain. She is benefitting monetarily from the transaction. Oh yeah, that thing called love makes it different, right? Ok bitches, you may have me on that one. But wait, what constitutes love? You can't measure that. I've fallen in love with every woman I've stuck my dick in—that includes the so-called prostitutes. I fall in love quick! Am I still a criminal for being a romantic or do I get a free pass? Make a decision! It's the amount you say? Is it ok for a bitch to accept free meals worth $200 dollars, but not ok for her to directly accept $200 dollars in cash to give up a piece of ass? I smell hypocrisy all over this situation.

If your wife doesn't work, you are obviously paying her rent, buying her food, and paying her car payment. That could add up into the thousands every month. But, just because you have a piece of paper from the government called a marriage license, it's ok for you to spend big money on her. If she does happen to give you some *pussy*, is that because she loves you? Do this experiment to see if it's love or if you are actually *paying* for her *pussy*. Stop paying any of her bills and stop buying her food. If she still gives you some ass after three months of this, then I'll believe that she's having sex with you for love and not the money. *Damn, I'm on a roll here.* I shouldn't be celebrating because it's such an idiotic subject to pick apart. All men, in some form or fashion, pay for *pussy*. That's the way it is. To demonize those who simply pay for sex with cash is hypocrisy at its finest.

● ● ●

Men, in order to accurately determine how much you personally pay for sex, I want you to use a simple formula to figure it out. This will determine your CPF, or *cost per fuck*. Don't laugh because it isn't a joke. You need to know this information in order to properly evaluate your personal situation. We're going to use numbers to paint a picture of how you live your life which will help put things in perspective. Take it seriously.

First, add up all of your monthly bills. Include everything. If it is just you and your wife, divide the number by two. This will provide you with your monthly cost for having a bitch in the first place. Then, add up all of the times you've had sex with your wife for the past year and divide by twelve to get a good monthly average. Take her share of the monthly bills and divide it by the average number of times you get laid on a monthly basis. That will tell you exactly how much you're paying your wife every time she lets you fuck her. It may be a mind-boggling amount for some of you men out there. Some of you may come to realize that your fat, nasty, ugly wife is the highest paid prostitute of all times and qualifies for the Guinness Book of World Records.

Here's a sample worksheet for you to follow along with:

monthly bills = $3,000
wife's share = $1,500
number of times you have sex in 1 month = 3
CPF (*cost per fuck*) = $500

If these numbers are anywhere near what's going on in your household, realize that you are paying $500 dollars every time your wife has sex with you. Is she really worth it? Not in my book. Now, if you are getting laid every day and your CPF is $50 dollars or less, that's bearable. Your life may not be all that bad. If you have a CPF over $100 dollars you need to seriously consider making a change. No woman's *pussy* is worth that much money per session. You are basically paying her to be your keeper. Is that really how you want to spend your money? Is that really how you want to live out the rest of your days? If you're ok and content with that type of lifestyle, then by all means, knock yourself out. This guy could never live like that.

CHAPTER 14

PLAYER SECURITY

I need to discuss some security issues to make you think before you roll out and start slaying ho's. Chasing bitches, drinking, traveling the world, and wrecking havoc is not without its share of risks. As a matter of fact, it's an inherently risky activity to engage in. If you hit the trail long enough and hard enough, you will endure certain ramifications. I'm going to share some of my experiences which pertain to player security so that you may learn from my mistakes. Do not consider this chapter as the exclusive source of everything you need to know in the realm of player safety. No such text even exists. Your travels and pitfalls will not mirror mine nor the next man's. Here we go...

Carry Only the Essentials
When you decide to gear up and hunt down some strange ass for the night, plan for the worst case scenario to happen. That could mean you either get robbed, have to run from the police, or escape from a jealous husband. The unfavorable possibilities are endless when you're out getting rip-roaring drunk and fucking with women you just met.

The first thing you need to do is sanitize and minimize the contents of your wallet. As a matter of fact, don't even carry a wallet when you're partying. Leave your wallet at home. You don't need it and it could cause you a ton of problems if you lose the thing during a drunken adventure. The only items that should be in your pocket are your driver's license or I.D. card and an ample amount of cash. That's it. Do not even think about bringing your ATM card with you during a night of partying. You will inevitably end up at the strip club and get persuaded to make a huge withdrawal by some coke-headed whore named *Luscious*. Don't do it. I speak from experience. Don't even bring a credit card. That can cause just as many problems as an ATM card. If you are one of those who insists on having your plastic with you, let me offer some suggestions. Have your bank set your daily withdrawal limit on your ATM card to somewhere around $200 dollars. That way, if you get drunk and pull two hundred bucks before midnight and another two hundred after, you know ahead of time you're not going bankrupt. Do the same with your credit card. Have the credit card company put a daily limit on it as a security precaution. In addition to this, I used to have a sticker on the back of my credit card that read, *Do not accept this card if the cardholder is drunk. If I've left this card at a bar, please call me at XXX-XXX-XXXX so I know where to pick it up.* You may laugh, but I've had to retrieve my credit card from many bars the next day after a night of partying. Putting some type of contact number on the back makes it easy for the bartender to get in touch with you so you can pick it up and sign the receipt.

By only carrying cash and your identification card, you minimize the negative impact of either losing your shit or getting robbed as you come out of a seedy establishment. Getting your cash stolen will piss you off, but it's temporary. Getting your plastic stolen can cause you all kinds of problems and headaches.

Avoid Conflict

Do not carry weapons of any type when hunting for bitches. This includes guns, knives, brass knuckles, etc. You don't need them. If the police show up for whatever reason and pat down everyone in the club, you're going to jail if you've got any of these items on you. If a fight breaks out, don't get involved. It serves you no purpose. Your immediate course of action is E&E (escape and evasion). The objective is to escape the fighting and avoid potential injury, while evading the cops who are already on their way. Your mission is to hunt down ho's. Fighting with other men has nothing to do with that mission and is senseless. It always amazes me when a couple of assholes bow up and fight in the middle of an establishment filled with beautiful women. They erroneously believe they are impressing someone but in reality they just look like two dumb-ass dick-heads exhibiting severe self-esteem issues. If something breaks out, grab your wing man and get the hell off the scene. You can roll to another club and continue your hunt. If someone bows up on you, take a diplomatic approach and attempt to diffuse the situation. What do you care if some dude thinks you're a *pussy* by backing down? It doesn't bother me a bit. I'm not there to impress the gentlemen with my fighting skills.

I'm there to meet girls. If someone wants to fight with you, avoid it at all costs. Men who pick fights in bars are usually those who aren't going to be successful in pulling a woman anyway. They're trying to entertain themselves because they know subliminally that they're utter failures with the ladies and have no hope of getting laid. Bouncers get paid to deal with assholes and drunks who want to fight. Let them take out the trash if someone is giving you problems.

What? It's not in your nature to back down from a fight? *Good.* That means you and the loser you're fighting with will get ejected from the club. That's less competition for me because two hard-dicks are removed from the game. I appreciate you guys doing that for me. I'll think of you two when I'm knocking boots with one of the girls ya'll *were* talking to.

Use Hotels

By far, the best policy when engaging in a one-night stand with some strange chick is to get a room at a hotel. This is so damn obvious that I'm ashamed to have to bring it up. With that said, I hardly ever followed my own advice and took most bitches back to my crib. By investing fifty dollars on a cheap hotel room you are capitalizing on the anonymity of the situation. She won't know where you live nor have the opportunity to steal any shit while you're taking a shower. The best scenario is to have her sign for the room and put it on her credit card. Give her cash money for your share or even give her the whole amount. If she signs for the room, you're free to leave at any time with no strings attached. The hotel won't have your personal information on file by doing things in this manner. If the chick doesn't have a credit card, go to a cheap, locally owned establishment. They'll usually let you rent a room without a credit card, unlike the major chains. Be sure that either you both drive to the hotel or take a cab. You don't want to get stuck having to give the girl a ride somewhere the next morning. You need to be free to bounce out of there at the moment of your choosing.

Have an Escape Plan

If for some reason you find yourself going with a girl back to her place, this is the most important lesson you could ever learn. If you end up in unfamiliar territory, a simple escape plan can possibly save your life. Let me talk you through how I roll in situations like this. First of all, assume that everything a girl tells you from the minute you meet her is a fucking lie. If she tells you she's single with no kids, that means her husband is out of town on a business trip. If she says she's divorced, assume she has a restraining order against some crazy bastard. If she says she lives alone, assume that her boyfriend gets off work in a few hours and will soon be on his way home. Gentlemen, if you haven't figured it out by now, women lie! They are devious creatures. American women love to play games with men even if it means that someone could get physically injured by doing so.

If you ever make the decision to go back to her place, it has to be a *hit and run*. You cannot, under any circumstances, fall asleep in her bed and cuddle. You might as well play Russian roulette while you're at it. You are going into harm's way. Look at it as such until you prove otherwise.

You may inevitably find yourself following her back to her crib. When you arrive, under no circumstances do you park your car in her driveway. Park on the street. If possible, park several houses down as well. Don't worry about what she thinks. Just tell her your car leaks oil and you don't want to mess up her driveway. Let me back up a minute. Prior to rolling out for the night you should pack an entire change of clothes including underwear, socks, and shoes, and leave them on the back seat. In addition, you should put an extra key in a magnetic case under the bumper of your vehicle. A single car key should be on a breakaway chain that you can hang around your neck.

Secure all of your cash, credit cards, I.D. cards, etc., in your vehicle. Leave your cell phone as well. When you walk into that chick's house, you should only be carrying one car key which is hanging around your neck like a charm. Your pockets should be empty. You should be carrying nothing. The reason for this is that if her boyfriend comes home early from work, you need to have the ability to break contact and flee the scene of the crime. As long as that car key is hanging around your neck, you can run buck naked if need be. If you lose the key hanging from your neck during the madness, you already know you've got the spare in the magnetic box. Jump out a window or run out the back door. Do whatever you've got to do to get back to your ride. Leave your clothes behind because they are expendable at this point. If you have followed my advice, there should be nothing of value left behind for her boyfriend to search. Get to your vehicle and drive your naked ass out of there. When you're safely far enough away, pull over, grab your clothes off the back seat, and get dressed. Once you calm down, you can drive home and thank your lucky stars you didn't get killed.

How do you think I formulated this strategy? It was developed through trial and error after being misled by unscrupulous bitches. Sometimes a woman will do shit like that on purpose to make her old man jealous. Sometimes they're just plain crazy. You have to always be on guard and have your escape plan wired tight.

Where There's a Will, There is a Way Out

Let me tell you a story about escape and evasion and how being mentally prepared possibly saved my life. It's kind of funny now, but I assure you it wasn't at the time. Several years back, I had the opportunity to go hang out with the Hoy Dog up in Myrtle Beach. I was living by myself at the time and didn't have a girl in tow. I met up with the Hoy Dog and his old lady at their friend's beach house. The friend had been gracious enough to lend them the house for the weekend. It was decided that his old lady and the kids would hang out with us during the day and roll home at night. This would allow the Hoy Dog and me to relax during the evenings. That was the deal. His old lady gave him a stern warning that we'd better not be trying to sneak out and party. There would be hell to pay. *No problem*, she was told. We were just going to hang out, smoke cigars, drink, and talk business. Unfortunately for her, as they say, *There's no business like ho-business.*

At around six, his old lady packed up her car and headed back home. Their house at the time was about thirty minutes away from the beach. As soon as it was confirmed that the coast was clear, the music started thumping. Jack Daniel's and Coke was served over ice. We kicked back on the deck overlooking the water and began to scheme. After a few drinks, we decided that it was worth the risk to head out for a few hours. *Fuck that bitch and her orders.* After getting dressed, we fired up Hoy's little pickup truck and headed toward the club. While Hoy had some worry in the back of his mind about getting busted out, I was a man on a mission. Yep, you know what kind of mission I'm referring to.

We hit the club and started working our magic. Within an hour I was hammered out of my mind. At some point, I pulled a black chick and a white chick and was grinding them both down on the dance floor. Hoy had quit drinking and was continually putting in bullshit phone calls to his old lady while standing out in the parking lot. He wasn't having a good time at all because of worrying about her ass. Meanwhile, I had sealed the deal with the two bitches that they were coming with us. Hoy had other plans.

When we got ready to leave, I told the girls to just follow us back to the beach house. Hoy coaxed me into the truck with him and off we went. For some reason, Hoy started driving like a madman on crack. He was cutting hard lefts, then a hard right, he ran two stop signs, and ducked into a parking area with a boat ramp. He stopped the truck and killed the headlights.

"Hey, bro. I think we may have lost the girls," I said with worry in my voice while looking around.

"Yeah, uh, I think you're right," Hoy replied.

At the time, I was too damn drunk to realize what had just occurred. Hoy knew that if he had tried to openly veto the ho's from coming back to the beach house I'd never have gotten into the truck. Instead, he went along with what I was plotting just long enough for me to buckle my seat belt so he could hit the gas. *Sneaky motherfucker!* That was definitely playing dirty pool with me but he was right and was the sober voice of reason. There was no way in hell those bitches were coming back to the beach house. It was suicide to even contemplate it. I'm not mad at Hoy for purposely losing the ho's and playing it safe. He did what he had to do. Unfortunately for the Hoy Dog, luck was in my favor that night.

● ● ●

We stepped out of the truck to take a piss when headlights suddenly shined into the darkened parking area. The car paused and then pulled right up alongside Hoy's truck and honked the horn. Low and behold, it was my girls. They had somehow stumbled onto us in our hiding spot. Hoy had a look of amazement as they jumped out and we started talking. He didn't know what to say. However, he did know one thing for certain. That one thing was that King Marcos wasn't falling for his trap a second time. There was no way in hell he was going to get me back in his truck. Before the Hoy Dog had another opportunity to interfere with my mission, I jumped in their car and the three of us bounced. I know Hoy was worried about getting busted out but the real reason he wasn't into the operation was because the white chick was too big for him. She wasn't fat by no means. But, as you already know, the Hoy Dog is too damn picky and can't get motivated about a thick girl.

We made it to their townhouse a few minutes later and continued the drinking. The white chick turned on the stereo and cranked the volume. The bass was thumping, we were dancing, and a good time was had by all. It was a wonder the neighbors didn't call the police because we were making so much noise. The rest of the night was pretty much a blur until around nine the next morning. For some reason, I felt like someone was watching me. It was a strong enough feeling that it woke me up from a drunken slumber. As I came to, I realized that I was on the couch with the black chick. We were spooning and I had my right hand in her panties. My left arm was wrapped around her and I had a nice grip on her left tit. Once I oriented myself to the couch and the girl, I looked up and realized there was a white guy standing behind the couch looking down at me. He was wearing a bath robe and looked just like a short version of Jesus. He had a cordless phone in one hand and was covering the microphone with the other. Our eyes locked and he just smiled. For a few moments, I thought I was still dreaming. *Where the hell did this white guy come from? He wasn't here last night during the partying. And why does he look just like Jesus? What's going on?*

"How you doing man?" he asked.

"Good, bro. What's going on?" I replied.

"Awe, nothing. I'm Jennifer's husband. I was upstairs when you guys rolled in last night. I was too tired to party and stayed in the bed. Sorry to be rude but it sounded like you guys had a good time."

Damn, this guy was cool. Jennifer never said anything about having a husband nor mentioned the fact he was upstairs asleep. I was grinding and groping on the bitch for hours without that tidbit of knowledge. I suddenly felt a bit guilty because her husband was being such a nice person. We had a quiet, brief exchange which set my mind at ease. He wasn't the jealous type who was about to crack me over the head with the phone because I'd partied with his old lady. I let out a small sigh once I realized I wasn't about to have to do battle. However, that sigh was immediately followed by a gasp.

The white guy nudged my girl and said, "Tay, wake up. Big Will's on the phone. He says he's on his way over here to kick your ass because you didn't come home last night."

What did he just say?

Old girl cracked open her eyes and turned slightly toward the sound of his voice. The white guy repeated what he'd just said. Tay finally spoke.

"Tell that *nigga* to quit all that nonsense. I ain't got time for his stupid ass," she said.

"He wants to talk to you," said the white guy as he handed the phone to her. She put it to her ear and started in on Big Will.

"What you want?" she asked, while pouring on a twang of Ebonics.

I couldn't hear exactly what Big Will said but it sounded like he was doing some yelling. Tay responded with some directives.

"Bring yo' ass over here if you're so bad. I ain't got time for yo' shit," she said. "Go ahead... *Come on, nigga*. Walk yo' black ass on over here."

She handed the phone back to the white guy who then calmly walked upstairs, seemingly unconcerned about the pending drama.

"Who the hell was that?" I asked franticly.

"Oh, that's my boyfriend. Don't worry about him," she replied.

"Why do they call him Big Will?"

"Because he big."

"How big?"

"Oh, he big," was the reply.

For some reason at that particular moment, a scene from the movie *Porky's* popped into my head. You know, the one where the big black guy comes crashing through the door with an axe.

"Does Big Will know where you're at?" I asked.

"Oh yeah, this is my best friend's house. But don't worry about him because he ain't going to walk all the way over here."

"How far does he have to walk?" I inquired.

"Oh, it's about a good mile. He ain't going to walk that far," she said confidently, while settling back in against me.

● ● ●

I began to consider and evaluate what the white guy had said. The white guy had said that Big Will was *on his way*. That meant Big Will had already departed his present location and was en route with vengeance in his heart. Now, the white guy was fresh from a good night's sleep. Tay and I were both still drunk. I deduced that the white guy was the most accurate source of information due to the circumstances. I immediately went into survival mode and jumped up off the couch. It was time to escape and evade because Big Will was *on his way*. It was impossible to determine how far along that one-mile stretch he'd already come. He could be walking up the driveway. He could be about to ring the doorbell or even kick down the door. *Move man, move! You're running out of time!* I grabbed my jeans and pulled them up over my naked ass. I grabbed for my front pocket and detected the two items that were sensitive—my driver's license and cell phone. I knew that those two items were the only things worth worrying over. I slipped on my shoes (no socks), grabbed my shirt, and hauled ass out the front door. I didn't even take the time to close it behind me. I ran through the front yard and hung a right onto the street. I was at a full sprint. At the next stop sign, I took another right onto a two-lane road. I realized that I was in the middle of the hood. People stared as I rolled by them at light speed. They probably hadn't seen too many white guys running through the middle of their neighborhood with no shirt on. Looking back, I bet they thought I was running from the police for some reason. Hell no, I was running from Big Will.

The sun was beginning to beat down on me like a convection oven. I ran for damn near three miles until I finally got calmed down and realized Big Will wasn't going to catch up to me. As I approached a major intersection, there was a pharmacy on the corner. On the side of the pharmacy, I spotted some nice, shady bushes. I made a beeline for them and crawled inside. The moist soil and the shade was just what the doctor ordered. I leaned up against the cool brick on the building, took a breather, and tried to recover from the unexpected 5K fun run.

A few minutes later, I pulled out my cell phone. For some reason, I had turned it off the night before. When I powered it on there were dozens of voice mails waiting for me. The majority were from a frantic Hoy Dog trying to get me back in pocket before his wife made it to the beach house. While I was listening to the messages, my buddy Dave beeped in on the other line.

"Hello?"

"Dog, are you ok?" Dave asked.

"Yeah, I'm in some bushes," I said.

"You're where?"

"I'm in these bushes outside a CVS Pharmacy. They're cool to the touch. Like nature's air conditioner," I said, with my raspy morning-after-the-club voice.

"Everybody's been worried sick about your stupid ass. Where the hell have you been?" Dave demanded.

"Running from Big Will," I said.

"Who the fuck's Big Will?" Dave asked.

"Tay's boyfriend."

"Who the fuck is Tay?" asked Dave.

● ● ●

Allow me to let you in on a little secret about my friend Dave. He was the *King of Gossip*. Dave knew everything about everyone. That made him a good person to know if you needed something done, needed a favor, or were in some kind of trouble. That made him a bad person to know if you weren't in good with him. Knowledge is power and Dave usually had dirt on everyone. As part of his intelligence-gathering techniques however, he would often trade a secret for a secret or be the first one to break a developing story. Hey, that's the nature of the beast. He often entertained others with tales of my exploits which probably shouldn't have been made public. I really didn't care because I enjoyed the fact that many people lived vicariously through me. I was happy to be able to entertain them.

● ● ●

What I didn't know at the time was that Dave had put me on speaker phone in front of a room full of people. He apparently found the conversation to be quite comical and decided to share the love. Hey, what are friends for?

"You know…Tay. The fine little sister I pulled from the club last night. She's a hood rat but I love that bitch," I said.

"Were you at her house? Did her boyfriend catch ya'll together?"

"Naw. We were at some white chick's house. A white dude said Big Will called and was on the way to kick the shit out of Tay."

"Why did he want to kick the shit out of her?" asked Dave.

"Because that bitch didn't go home last night. She spent the night with me on the couch," I said. "I woke up this morning with my hand in her panties. That girl's got a big-ass bush, dog. Felt like a Brillo pad. I don't know why Big Will don't make her shave that shit down a bit. He must be one rough *motherfucker*," I said.

"Is he still after you?"

"Naw, dog. I pulled a Forrest Gump and hauled ass out of there. I was at a full sprint for at least twenty minutes. Almost passed out from the heat," I said.

"Dude, where exactly are you? The Hoy Dog's old lady is on her way to the beach house. He's freaking out. Tell me where you're at and I'll call him so he can pick you up."

"Bro, I'm in the bushes at a CVS," I said.

"No shit. Now give me a street name, dumb-ass," Dave replied.

I peeked out of the bushes and read the street sign for the main road. While I was doing this, a car pulled up and parked right in front of me. An old man around seventy years old got out and stepped up onto the curb. As he walked by, he paused and looked into the bushes. He had apparently heard me talking and decided to investigate further. Once he caught sight of me, kicked back with my shirt off, it startled him. He scurried toward the entrance.

"Damn it. Some old fucker saw me. He's probably telling the manager right now. I bet the cops are on the way. Tell the Hoy Dog to step it up a bit," I advised.

"Ok Skippy. Hang in there. He'll be there in a few."

With that, Dave called the Hoy Dog and gave him my location. He promptly arrived and scooped me up. We made it back to the beach house in just the nick of time. I was getting in the shower when his old lady arrived. We had avoided a near disaster. Later on in the afternoon the Hoy Dog counseled me on my behavior and the predicament I had put him in with his wife. I apologized to him and assured him that, if I had it to do over, *I'd do the same damn thing*. He agreed with that assessment and we both laughed. Hey, life is short, my friends.

● ● ●

What's the moral of this story? *Where there's a Will, there's a way out.* Have an escape plan. Be ready to go from a deep sleep to running a 5K in a matter of seconds. Hey, pimping and chasing ho's is a risky business. If you're not prepared to deal with unexpected drama at a moment's notice, keep your timid ass at home. It's a dog eat dog world out here. Stay in the game long enough and you'll have a Big Will to deal with as well.

Wear a Condom

Ok, those of you who know me can stop laughing right about now. I will admit that it's very hypocritical of me to advocate the practice of safe sex. It is extremely hypocritical. The truth is, I've only worn a condom on a handful of occasions. I've purchased condoms a hundred times. The boxes never got opened and I ended up giving them away. So, why am I advising others to make sure they wear a rubber? Because it's the right thing to do. Don't think so? Keep reading. This paragraph is going to get a bit graphic, so prepare yourself. Why? Because young men have to be damn near shocked before they believe or remember certain lessons in life. I feel that the educational value of this topic warrants the nastiness.

During my adventures in chasing women, I've caught the clap, or Chlamydia, so many times that I've lost count. (Yes, I know some people argue the clap is a nickname for Gonorrhea, but who cares. In my world, the clap means Chlamydia.) The number of times is somewhere in the dozens. The reason? Predominately because I didn't wear a condom. Ok, you think you're safe because you always wear a rubber? Guess what gents? You can also catch the clap from oral sex as well. If you're about to get a blow job, do you tell the chick to hold on while you put on a condom? I think not. A lot of the time, a blow job precedes the normal progression to getting laid. If you allow the girl to suck your dick prior to donning a condom, you've already been exposed. It is estimated that approximately four percent of the female population has Chlamydia. Most girls don't even know they have it because they do not exhibit any symptoms.

As a man, I can pretty much assure you that you're going to exhibit some symptoms. Within a few days of getting the gift that keeps on giving, you will begin to experience slight paranoia—at least I always do. Subliminally, my body is telling my mind that I've got it. You'll start to feel a slight tingle in the tip of your pee hole. When you take a piss, that initial tingling will start to itch. Another day or so and that itch will turn to a burn. If you milk your penis, an off-white or yellowish puss will emerge. This will eventually start to freely ooze out on its own. Just the act of taking a piss will turn into a nightmare. It will be the equivalent of having three hundred razor blades slide out of the end of your cock while someone holds a flame from a cigarette lighter underneath. If you stay in denial for that long, it's going to hurt you. Trust me. The first time I caught the clap I was in denial. I didn't know what to do. I didn't want to accept reality. I thought that sexually transmitted "diseases" were something that only heroin junkies contracted. I refused to go to the doctor until late in the game. It got to the point that I wouldn't drink anything. If I did, I knew I'd eventually have to pee. That would mean pain. I finally gave in and drove myself to the clinic.

● ● ●

Most visits to the doctor result in the patient experiencing some type of pain in some way due to some type of procedure. Whether it is just a pin prick on your finger to check your blood sugar or a quick immunization, there's usually pain involved. If you show up and tell them you think you have the clap, you're in for a type of pain that would make waterboarding feel like an oil massage. The first thing the doctor is going to do is pull out a sterile swab that looks just like a Q-tip, only longer. Yep, that Q-tip is going straight into your inflamed pee hole. The doc will typically have you stand up, drop your pants, and put your hands on your head. He, or she, is going to grab your cock, insert the Q-tip, and give that *motherfucker* a couple of quick taps to get it to the proper depth. These two taps are the equivalent of taking two shotgun blasts. The pain has to be on the same level. It will hurt you so damn bad that it temporarily sends you into the black. You inhale half a breath. You can't speak. You can't move. You can't think. You are effectively paralyzed due to the amount of pain that just shot through your nervous system. You realize that you're up on your tip-toes but don't remember how you got there. It is sensory overload at its best. When the doctor pulls that Q-Tip out, it is the equivalent of him ripping a three-foot long strand of barbed wire out of your cock in a split second. You immediately collapse onto the exam table and curl up in the fetal position. For the next ten minutes, you try to recover and come to terms with what just happened.

● ● ●

Waterboarding? That's a waste of time and requires too much equipment. Want to torture someone and violate their basic human rights in an even more heinous way? Just issue every dumb-ass CIA agent a fucking sterile Q-tip. They can carry that shit around in their pocket. One tap on the old Q-tip while in the pee hole of the victim is worse than ten sessions of waterboarding.

If you do end up catching the clap, don't go out and kill yourself. The clap is easily treated with antibiotics. You're usually feeling better in a day or so and it's totally cleared up in about a week. You will live through the ordeal but it fucks with your head and prevents you from getting laid for a while. Therefore, try to minimize your exposure by wearing a damn condom. I'm not going to talk at length about HIV, AIDS, Syphilis, Gonorrhea, or any of the others. They're out there as well and are all good reasons to wear a condom. But, Chlamydia is the most commonly contracted STD in the States.

According to the Centers for Disease Control (CDC), there were approximately 2.86 million new cases of Chlamydia in 2012 in the U.S. alone. For those of you who have teenagers or if you're in the following age group, you need to be aware of this statistic: One out of every fifteen sexually active females aged fourteen to nineteen years of age has Chlamydia. I read another study which found that almost ten percent of all U.S. Army female recruits tested positive for Chlamydia.

The point here is that if you end up shagging enough girls, the odds are you're going to catch something. Minimize this risk by always having condoms on hand. You are rolling the dice every time you sleep with a strange woman. Enjoy the action, but be smart about it. This section was a bit graphic but most men don't casually browse the CDC's website and are most often ill-informed. Now you're educated a bit.

● ● ●

Perhaps the single-most important reason I can cite for wearing a condom is the number 18. Eighteen years is the least amount of time you'll be paying an American bitch child support if you're stupid enough to get her pregnant. Your life will be absolutely miserable for eighteen long years, my friends. Fuck Chlamydia and Gonorrhea. That shit is only temporary. Fuck AIDS. That shit can only kill you. You're going to die anyway. *Eighteen Years* is the scariest disease known to American men. It will fuck with your head, your heart, your everyday life, your wallet, and your sanity. It's a cruel *fucking* disease that kills you slowly. In certain states, it can run even a few years longer. It's a painful death. I wouldn't wish it upon my worst enemy. Listen, I'm not saying anything bad about babies or children themselves. It's not about them. It's about the power their mother suddenly has over you, the man.

I've come up with a great idea that could possibly sweep America. Maybe someone else has already thought of this and deserves the credit instead of me. I don't know. However, this concept could eventually bankrupt many divorce attorneys and make child support enforcement agencies obsolete. The idea is that if you're a player in America, you should have "18 YEARS MOTHERFUCKER!" tattooed on the top side of your dick. That way, if you're about to stick your cock in a woman it will be a subtle reminder to wear a condom. It's probably the most innovative idea I've ever thought about. I realize that some of us will have to use abbreviations due to the lack of space but it should work just as good. If you are stupid enough to screw an American chick without a condom, you're beyond hope. I got lucky. I'm extremely fortunate I'm not paying child support in thirty states. Don't do as I did. Do as I say and wear a rubber. While I would never do this, the safest route is to get a vasectomy before getting into the game. I would love to eliminate this particular risk but I just can't fathom someone cutting on my nuts. They work just fine like they are and I'm quite satisfied with their performance.

This might be taking things into the realm of paranoia but let me throw something else out there. If you do wear a condom and bust a nut in it, make sure you take the damn thing with you. If you make good money, a trailer-park bitch would love for you to breed her ass so she can get that 18-year free ride. If you leave a rubber full of semen behind, what's stopping her from inserting said semen into her snatch when you're not looking? Don't trust these *cunts* with your jizz. They look at it the same as cash. In reality, it does equate to cash in America. Sperm can live outside the body for a short period of time in the right conditions. Keep that in mind.

Don't Shit Where You Eat

Stay away from women in your workplace. This is another area where I've occasionally violated my own principles for the sake of a quick piece of ass. Hypocrisy aside, I'm telling you to not even think about it. Listen, there are millions of ho's out there for you to choose from. There is no need to take the risk of causing conflict, awkwardness, or stress at your place of employment. Every man you work with is trying to shag the same woman you may be eyeing. Several people within the company have already screwed the girl and have video evidence to prove it. Because of all the attention, the girl will have an even nastier attitude because she believes she's a princess. Do yourself a favor and stay out of that rat race. There are few to no secrets in the workplace. Office politics can affect your chances of promotion and even alter your career path. If you end up hitting on just one crazy bitch who complains to human resources, you are done. You'll be known as the guy who was involved with an incident of sexual harassment. I see no valid reason for you to chase women at your work. If that's your game then proceed with the utmost of caution. Don't say I didn't warn you when things go south.

One incident in particular solidifies my opinion on this matter. I'm not going to describe it in detail because it was an awkward situation that ended up causing me problems. Basically, I was shagging a chick I worked with and we'd kept it a tight secret. The owner of the company took a liking to the girl and started trying to romance her, publicly. Suddenly, the secrecy of our affair became paramount to both of our jobs. I mean, when a rich cat is openly trying to true-love the chick you're railing out on a daily basis, what can you do? She wasn't studying the guy but he wouldn't give up. We were on constant pins and needles when we were out in public together. It was stressful but we kept up our routine until disaster happened. We were together one night and were rocking it out with a marathon session after getting tanked up on margaritas at the Mexican restaurant. I set the alarm for 5:00 a.m. because we both had to be at work the next morning. I woke up at around 9:30 a.m. to take a piss and casually looked at the alarm clock. It was blinking 12:00 which obviously meant the power had been off sometime during the night. I grabbed my watch and shrieked when I realized we had overslept. We scurried to get ready but it was too late. When we both hadn't shown up or called, it didn't take a rocket scientist to figure out we were somehow in cahoots. To make matters worse, the supervisor called my wife and asked her about why I wasn't at work. She told him I had been working at my second job the night before and should have gotten off in time for my shift. During the conversation, the supervisor took it upon himself to ask my wife if she knew my girlfriend because she didn't show up for work either. We were stone-cold busted at work and with my wife at home. That incident was the prelude to my first divorce.

What's the moral of this story? Yeah, I know. Set two alarms. Get an alarm that's battery powered. Set the alarm on your cell phone, etc. I'm tracking on all that. Setting only one alarm when you're out creeping is a rookie mistake. No, the real moral to the story is that you do not shit where you eat. Separate your professional life from your personal life and don't chase bitches at work.

Invest in a Taxi Ride

Strange women are capable of strange things. The police will show you no mercy if you're caught drinking and driving. If contraband (weed, cocaine, meth, etc.) is found inside your car, you're getting charged for it. Cleaning puke out of your car is a pain in the ass, as well.

These are just a few good reasons for you to take a taxi while partying and chasing bitches. Sure, it will cost you a few dollars but it will be the best investment you ever make. If you drive your car to the club, I don't care what your initial game plan is. Maybe you just plan on having one, staying sober, and calling it a night. That idea will go right out the window if you meet a hot chick who wants to party. Even if you realize you shouldn't be driving, you're still going to be reluctant about leaving your car in the parking lot overnight. You're going to be tempted to try and make it home. How do you avoid this? It's simple. Don't bring your ride into the equation to begin with. Get a friend to drop you off at the club or take a taxi there in the first place. Then, you know with a near one hundred percent certainty that you're not going to drive home drunk. That is of course, unless you pull a chick and are stupid enough to get behind the wheel of her car. Don't laugh, it happens all the time.

If you leave with a girl that you just met, how in the hell do you know she doesn't have an ounce of cocaine, a gun, and a pound of marijuana in her purse? You don't. Therefore, do you really want her riding in your vehicle? I damn sure don't. If you get stopped by the police, her natural reaction will be to get rid of the contraband and stuff it under the seat. Once the cops bring out *Rin Tin Tin* and he proceeds to scratch the shit out of the passenger door, they're going to search your vehicle. When they find her stash, she's going to claim no knowledge of it and tell them she just met you. You're going to claim the same. At that point, you both are probably going to jail. You, the driver, are certainly taking a ride.

What if you decide to ride with her? How do you know there's not three dead bodies in the trunk of her car? You don't. See the problems that can arise from just getting her back to a hotel room? The safe way all around is to take a cab. Don't be cheap about this principle. If you end up getting charged with *Driving Under the Influence of Alcohol* it's going to cost you at least $10,000 dollars. A cab would have cost you $20 dollars.

Smoke and Mirrors

I've already said that you should never try to impress any woman with money or even the perception that you have money. It's not necessary and it attracts the nastiest of American women—the gold diggers. Be yourself. You are who you are. However, you don't have to give a strange woman your entire biography to accomplish a one-night stand. Trust me when I say that ninety percent of what she's telling you is a lie so don't feel bad about doing what I'm about to describe.

You need to come up with a basic cover story. It doesn't have to be anything elaborate. You don't have to portray that you're some big tycoon or a CEO of a major company. Just don't tell the girl what you really do for a living. It's irrelevant to the fact you're both wanting to get laid. My cover story that I used on hundreds of occasions was that I was a garbage man. The chick would typically laugh when I told her that because she thought I was joking. I would say, *No really, I've been working there since I was eighteen and have great benefits. I've got my weekends off and it pays the bills. There's no shame in my game. I have a good time with the guys I work with.* End of story on the questions about my profession. The chick appreciated my *honesty* and realized that it didn't fucking matter what I did for a living anyway.

● ● ●

Never give a girl from a one-night stand your real name. Why? Because once again, it's irrelevant. There are many women whom I've slept with that only know me as Marcos. If I did give them a last name it was something I'd thought up while looking at the label on my beer. Why do they need to know your last name? Think about it for a minute. If they've got a crazy boyfriend like Big Will, do you really want to give them the capability to find you on Facebook? I would shit my pants if that incident happened to me today in the current age of social media. Imagine me sitting down and logging into Facebook to see a friend request from Big Will. That will never happen because Tay only knows me as Marcos. Good luck to Big Will if he can pick me out of the millions of guys named Marcos. The only evidence Big Will has to identify me is a pair of socks and my underwear that I left behind during the hasty departure. Damn, come to think about it, I hope Big Will doesn't get a hold of a copy of this book. He's probably the type who holds a grudge.

Summary

This section is not meant to be an all-inclusive handbook on player safety. As a matter of fact, I've only scratched the surface of this topic. I could write volumes of case studies on shit that has happened to me during twenty-five years of ho-chasing. Some of the shit is so surreal that I'm not even sure if there are any learning points which can be derived from the stories. The only lesson which can always be cited is that women do crazy shit. Never let your guard down for one minute or you'll get clipped in some form or fashion. This is especially true when playing the dating game with American girls.

CHAPTER 15

CHOK DEE KOP!

In the Thai language, *Chok Dee Kop* basically means *Good Luck*. I want to wish everyone who has taken the time to read this text the best of luck in making improvements to your life. Whether some of the discussions have motivated you to act or merely invoked thought, I hope you've learned a thing or two in between the pages. Maybe you thought the book was a total waste of time and pure nonsense. That's the chance a writer takes every time he / she decides to publish material for public scrutiny. Regardless, I want to say thank you for taking the time to read something I've written. You've bestowed an honor upon me by doing so. Whether or not you agree with anything I've said, I do hope you were at least entertained and possibly even laughed a bit. Maybe you read this purely for the entertainment value and have no plans on making any changes in your life. I respect that more than anyone. You're the captain of your own destiny. As long as you're happy, that's what is important. If your life is absolutely miserable, just remember that life is short.

● ● ●

It is still very hard for me to believe I actually put a book together. It's even harder to believe that I've now finished a second book. I'm not sure why I can sit down and crank out page after page when I can't seem to focus on even the simplest of tasks these days. I have to give credit to my favorite brand of rum here in Thailand. It's called Uncle Tom and has what looks like an old fishing-boat captain for the logo / branding. It's one of the cheapest bottles of rum you can buy over here. On the label, it doesn't say rum, it only says *R*. They produce vodka as well. On the vodka bottle it only says *V*. On their bottles of gin, it has a *G*. For some strange reason when I start drinking the *R*, I get so focused in on the task at hand I can't stop. Words flow onto the screen without me even having to think about them. That's one for the shrinks to weigh-in on but if it weren't for rum, I would never have finished either one of my manuscripts. They would still be disorganized Word documents buried on my laptop.

Writing a book is mentally exhausting. When I pick up a book these days, my heart goes out to the author because I know how much work went into producing a 256-page document. It doesn't matter if it's a best seller or the worst seller. It takes a lot of effort to get the thing into print. That's especially true with independent authors and self-publishers like myself. We end up doing all of the editing, type-setting, design, etc., without the help of a large production team. I like it because I maintain total control over what gets printed. I own all the rights. However, by doing everything on your own, it takes a lot out of you as well. I wouldn't have it any other way.

● ● ●

What is the next adventure? Well, I've already got another book inside my head that's just waiting to make it onto paper. I'm going to delve into the realm of historical fiction and have a little bit of fun at the expense of the U.S. government's poor reputation. The plot and the characters have already been created and the chapters have already been outlined. With that said, I think I'm going to take a break and delay its start a bit.

Ever think about writing a book? If you have, what's stopping you from doing so? Take the advice given to me by my friend, Abe—*Just start writing.* If you need some help putting your project together, send me an e-mail and I'll share with you what I know and how my books made it to print. Again, thanks for giving me the opportunity to entertain you through words.

Consult with the King

As we begin to close, allow me to offer one last helping hand. If you are going through a divorce and need advice, give me a call. If you just need someone to mediate a situation and broker peace, I can handle that as well. I offer this service to men and women alike. Professional consulting firms and mediators are going to charge thousands of dollars for what will seem like the most formal experience you've ever had to go through. You will both feel like you are in the principal's office getting lectured. Add the opinions of two attorneys and their fees into the equation and you will end up in debt with no divorce. Now, I'm not going to work for free but I'm definitely the cheaper route.

If you are merely having issues and want to save your marriage, I can assist with that as well. Man or woman, I will objectively and blatantly tell you what I think is wrong and recommend options to improve the situation. We'll get together in an informal setting instead of at a cold and dreary office. For the first session, we'll meet at Hooters for beer, wings, and some down and dirty conversation. For the second session, we'll have a nice dinner at a fine restaurant with a view of the city. *Tit for tat*. What's good for the goose is good for the gander. A couple will get more out of two sessions with King Marcos than a year's-worth of therapy with Pablo's counselor, Dr. Nut-Nut the man-hater.

Ladies, you say you won't hire me as a *marriage counselor?* Oh really? Hmmm... Let us evaluate this for a minute. How many of you have successfully gotten your husbands to go to marriage counseling? Not many of you girls have even been able to get your man to submit to the injustice, much less actively participate. I've already told him he's a *pussy* and a moron if he goes. However, this isn't the traditional counseling session I was referring to. Just suggest to him that the two of you go hang out with the king for a night at Hooters and see what his response is. He will probably be interested and actually look forward to the experience. I will make sure he pays attention and participates. See how that works? Now ask him if he wants to go talk to Dr. Phil or Dr. Nut-Nut about your problems. Let me know how that one works out for you. I'm available ladies, but with a tight schedule.

● ● ●

Why do I offer this service? Well, while writing this book I came across perhaps one of the most heinous websites I've ever browsed. It was a divorce consultation service strictly for women. I'm not going to name the site because I refuse to give the asshole the publicity. However, his service is geared toward helping the woman and her attorney with a financial strategy to get as much money, property, and benefits as possible. *An advisor to the attorney? You mean a blood-sucking vampire needs advice on how to suck blood?* It was so sickening to read that a male is the one who founded the service. I won't call him a man because he does not deserve the title. His service basically encourages women to split with their husbands by showing them the profit in it—purely for money without the need for cause. Services like his encourage women to be useless and to neglect their man because it pays for them to seek divorce. I must say to this individual and his company, *Fuck you*. You and your service factor in to why American families are becoming extinct. You are the reason why American men are treated so poorly in the first place. You are the reason that American women have an ingrained sense of entitlement and think they should be paid for nothing. You're advertising the profitability of divorce to uneducated, unemployed, lazy-ass women who are only qualified to be housewives in the first place. I would hate to be you, my friend. I think you'll make it to heaven, only long enough for St. Peter to personally kick your ass before sending you south.

It is people, organizations, and services like this which are causing America's children to be reared without fathers. It's a trickle-down effect. The U.S. government taxes dad to the point that he can't stay home and manage his household. They rob dad of time and the opportunity of merely being present in the house because he has to work two jobs to make ends meet. Assholes like the aforementioned and the attorneys take away the rest of the power of the father and render him useless when he actually is available. They encourage women to be terrible wives. It's how they make money. Now you know why you can't go see a movie in America or send your child to school without some dysfunctional teen shooting up the place—taxes and assholes are responsible.

What's the difference between them and my philosophy? *Kingdom Rule* is designed so that everyone is happy, well taken care of, and to ensure the family is living within its means. I don't advocate divorce itself without cause. I merely advocate taking action immediately when a situation such as divorce is inevitable in the end. If either the man or the woman is unhappy, the relationship will usually end at some point. That's obvious. Therefore, make some changes and see if things get better. When the family can't pay its bills, divorce usually follows. By locking down the finances, a potential divorce due to the stress of foreclosure and bankruptcy is derailed. If the woman is unhappy after the man locks down the finances, divorce was inevitable anyway. Why delay the process? Make tough decisions in a timely manner and get on with enjoying the little time you have on this earth.

● ● ●

One more thing. I have to admit that the sub-title of this book is actually somewhat of a misnomer. I'm not here discriminating against any woman on the basis of age, race, religious preference, or where they come from. Maybe some of you have already figured that out and know the true point of the text. Congratulations on being independent thinkers. For others, you may be trying to figure out how to label me as a racist. Good luck on that one. You're having a tough time with it because I'm a white guy complaining mostly about white women while loving the dark-skinned sisters. Just stick with calling me a pig. You can maintain your credibility that way.

Think I'm a misogynist? That's funny as well. The word *misogyny* means: a hatred of women, according to Merriam-Webster. I love all women. All of you ladies out there have a chance to be with the king. I won't turn you down if the right parameters are met which have already been described. I spend most of my time with women and very rarely hang out with other men. Makes so sense at all to accuse me of hating the female gender.

What I'm truly against is the outrageously impractical sense of entitlement ingrained in some women. This sense of entitlement leads to laziness and greed. It just so happens that it is very prevalent in America. What I dislike is a lazy bitch. The only thing I discriminate against is a shitty attitude. But, I don't think that a *bitch* or a *shitty attitude* is listed or covered under the Civil Rights Act so I'm entitled to have this opinion.

An associate of mine said I should have used the words *Western women* in the sub-title. He's from Australia and has the same perception of the women there. A British pal agreed in regards to the ladies of the United Kingdom. Maybe I should have listened to them and changed it. I wouldn't want the bitches in the UK or Australia to feel left out.

I will never concede to the social pressures of the West and agree that I owe a woman money and property merely because she lived in my castle, ran up my electric bill, and ate my food. It should be the woman who pays the man during a divorce for giving her a free ride for all those years. That procedure would actually make sense. It would put a halt to most divorces and force couples to work through their problems, as both parties would be motivated about staying together. As it stands today, only the man is truly motivated about working out marital problems because he knows he's going to get robbed in the courtroom.

The Keys to the Kingdom

In closing, let me simplify this manuscript. As a man, if you're unhappy, then change your mindset. Implement *Kingdom Rule* and adhere to the *Declarations of Independence*. If it doesn't fix things at your home, get a divorce. Apply for a passport and go international in your search for a keeper. Head for a country where English is not the primary language.

For my ladies, let me simplify what you can do to keep your husband interested and faithful to you. Pardon the brashness of the simplicity. This is what a man needs to stay happy:

1. A lot of sex
2. A lot of blow jobs
3. Good food
4. A clean house
5. Daily massages
6. For you to *shut the fuck up*

Any questions? Pretty self-explanatory if you ask me.

I asked one of my girlfriends about the top six things a man needs. She is well aware of the above list but left out number two during her answer. I was somewhat puzzled at her response.

"Jamaica, did you forget something?" I asked.

"No, I left one out on purpose," she said while giggling.

"Why?" I inquired.

"Because I don't really like to do that," she replied, and we both burst out into laughter.

You had to have been there but it was funny as hell. She was being a comedian but it brought up a good point that needs to be addressed. Many women will only want to do one or two things on the list. However, that's like working at a restaurant and refusing to wash dishes, take out the trash, or wait on customers. Imagine telling your boss that you only want to pour drinks and refill the napkin dispenser. Hey, it's your job. If you don't like your chosen career, find something else to do. In the case of marriage, if a woman doesn't do her duty, the man will find some part-time help if you know what I mean.

Thanks for Reading!

Care to Comment?
Please Visit My Website at:

www.markblackard.com

Also by Mark Blackard:

Killing Sheep:
The Righteous Insurgent

The true story of a former narcotics agent sent to Afghanistan to catch Taliban bomb makers, terrorists, and drug smugglers.

ISBN: 978-1-936956-00-5
www.markblackard.com

The author and his rag-tag team of Afghan police officers waged a private war against the Taliban in order to enforce the law and protect the citizens of Nangarhar Province. Their efforts were often suppressed by U.S. military commanders, even though the U.S. military was the entity that funded the program. Their methods and appearance would earn them the name of "The Dirty Dozen." While operating solely under the constraints of Afghan law, they were able to accomplish what coalition military forces could not: catch bad guys without killing innocent civilians and without infuriating the locals. The author questions why conventional military mentality is still being applied to counter-insurgency operations. Between Vietnam, Iraq, and Afghanistan, the lesson should by now be learned that one cannot make friends in a predominately poor, uneducated culture, while being governed by U.S. military formality, rules, and regulations.

www.ingramcontent.com/pod-product-compliance
Lightning Source LLC
Chambersburg PA
CBHW070638050426
42451CB00008B/208